Saladdin Bahozde

Fascism or Whatever You Want to Call It

De Gruyter Contemporary Social Sciences

Volume 56

Saladdin Bahozde

Fascism or Whatever You Want to Call It

—

Confronting the Beast Locally and Globally

DE GRUYTER

ISBN (Paperback) 978-3-11-160892-1
ISBN (Hardcover) 978-3-11-160920-1
e-ISBN (PDF) 978-3-11-160904-1
e-ISBN (EPUB) 978-3-11-160907-2
ISSN 2747-5689
e-ISSN 2747-5697

Library of Congress Control Number: 2025930223

Bibliographic information published by the Deutsche Nationalbibliothek
The Deutsche Nationalbibliothek lists this publication in the Deutsche Nationalbibliografie;
detailed bibliographic data are available on the internet at http://dnb.dnb.de.

© 2025 Walter de Gruyter GmbH, Berlin/Boston, Genthiner Straße 13, 10785 Berlin
Cover image: © Fernando Zóbel Estate
Typesetting: Integra Software Services Pvt. Ltd.

www.degruyter.com
Questions about General Product Safety Regulation:
productsafety@degruyterbrill.com

To the foreign to domination,

those who are foreign at home and wherever fascists might feel at home,

those who do not take permission from anyone to claim the world as home, and no amount of expulsions and exiling would make them grow an inner little fascist,

and the lovers in/of the Jin, Jiyan, Azadî movement who have defied the sacred borders and the borders of the sacred.

Preface and Acknowledgments

This, like my other books, was written out of a sense of necessity, that is, because I felt somebody had to do it. While the problem of fascism continues to be widely neglected, more books and articles on the topic have been published over the last ten years or so. Some of these publications are insightful and useful in different ways and on various levels whereas others, in my view anyway, are not. What seems to be missing in the relevant publications I am aware of is a critical theory capable of reconceptualizing fascism. It should go without saying that fascist forces, movements, and discursive formulas have changed in different ways in different places. However, the field of fascism studies is, for the most part, stuck in the same circle that has been produced and reproduced by conventional historians despite the considerable efforts of a number of critical historians, such as Enzo Traverso, Domenico Losurdo, and the late Eric Hobsbawm, to emancipate the field and/or the discipline.

The monopoly of fascism studies by the orthodox discipline of history has contributed to the universalization of the false assumption that fascism belongs to the past. Even when the signs of the rise of fascism become too strongly present and alarming to ignore, the standard reaction involves repetitions of the same old procedure, namely, comparing and contrasting the present actors and events with those from the historical period of about two to three decades in the first half of the twentieth century in Europe, especially Italy and Germany. Even some of the scholars who argue for less orthodox definitions of and approaches to fascism have barely quit the habit of deploying the same method of comparing and contrasting the contemporary potential cases with what is assumed to be the original and therefore authentic models.

Another severe shortcoming of the field of fascism studies is its narrow geographic scope. Reducing fascism merely to one of the problems of the white man is itself a symptom of internalized racism. This particular racism is a worldview that perceives the human world based on the ontologized category of whiteness. To this dominant mentality, all those who do not fall under the category of whiteness are perceived negatively, i.e., as non-whites. While philosophy, politics, sociology, psychology, personhood, individual creativity, and arts are almost exclusively attributed to whiteness, the non-white is imagined through a myth called culture, which is an ambarella pseudoconcept that is used vaguely to refer to anything from traditional attire, dance, and food to spiritual rituals and religion. Often the elites of or from societies in the global south commit the culturalization of the perceived non-white more fanatically than any other culturalist.

The negatively perceived subject is assumed to be a cultural rather than a political and philosophical creature. Fascism requires a degree of political and ideolog-

https://doi.org/10.1515/9783111609041-202

ical sophistication, and, more importantly, a sense of racial and civilizational superiority. The dominant mentality cannot even entertain the idea that a non-white subject could have a problem/sense of superiority. It is for these reasons that the geographic framework of fascism is usually restricted to the European and Europeanized zones (an exception was made for Japan mostly because of the alliance between Imperial Japan and Nazi Germany). There is an urgent need to address the rise of fascism in different parts of the world, including not only Europe and North America but also other regions including West Asia, North Africa, and the Indian Subcontinent.

As this book shows, extreme rightists in Europe and the Middle East have a lot in common. Certainly, they share a similar mode of perception and adopt the same *ideological form. Ideology form* is what this book suggests as a new conception of fascism. Like racism or sexism, fascism does not designate a particular ideological configuration or a single universal worldview; rather, it signifies the *form* many otherwise extremely different and even opposing ideologies take. As fascism, or whatever you want to call it, has been on the rise since the end of the 1980s, critical theories capable of reproblematizing and reconceptualizing it are long overdue.

The critical theory of fascism I have been advancing goes against the institutionalized perception and conventional authority, so I did not anticipate the recognition, let alone acceptance, of my theory by the establishment. Precisely because of this, I am deeply grateful to everyone who has helped in the publication of this and my previous works on fascism. Without their support, this book would, at best, have been just another dead manuscript buried in a digital folder somewhere known to nobody other than myself.

Writing this book involved many complex stages over the years. I wrote and published a number of thicker and more philosophical books while different chapters of this book were shaping and reshaping. Some parts of the book are based on previously published articles and commentaries. I want to start by sending my special thanks to those who played a role in publishing any of those articles and commentaries, thereby helping defy the establishment and the conventional perspective at large. Below I will list the names of the journals and platforms where what became parts of this book had appeared first. I sincerely thank the respective editors, reviewers, publishers, and all the members of the teams who assisted in any way.

Chapter 3 is mainly based on "Fascism as an Ideological Form: A Critical Theory." This article was published by *Critical Sociology*, which is one of the journals of Sage Publications. The article appeared on the OnlineFirst section of the journal's website on July 15, 2022, and then in 2023, volume 49, issue 4-5. The article was also redrafted to become Chapter 2 of my book *Critical Theory from the Margins*, which was published in 2022 (paperback edition in 2023) by the State University of New York (SUNY) Press.

The foundational idea of Chapter 5 goes back to an invited article titled "Fascism is Alive and Well," a Turkish translation of which was published in issue 21 of the journal *Demokratik Modernite* in 2017. The chapter is more closely based on an article titled, "Exclusionary Politics (or Fascism) in the Middle East." This was published by *New Political Science* in June 2023, issue 45, number 3. The journal is a Taylor & Francis publication. Chapter 3 of my book *Fascism in the Middle East: Nationalism, Islamism, and Imagining Other Futures* was based on the same article. This means that Chapter 5 in this book is also largely similar to Chapter 3 of *Fascism in the Middle East*, which was also published by Taylor & Francis Group in January 2025 as part of Routledge Focus on Modern Subjects, a Routledge book series edited by the internationally renowned critical historian and anthropologist Saurabh Dube.

Parts of chapters 7 and 8 are based on two articles. The first one, "Russian Nationalism, NATO, and the Threat of Nuclear Annihilation," was published on October 8 2022 by LINKS, the International Journal for Socialist Renewal. The second article was published by *Marxism and Sciences* in 2022, volume 1, issue 2, under the title, "The Cost of Freedom in the Neoliberal World of Blood and Oil."

Some of the discussion about Rojava and culturalism originates from a 2019 article titled, "The Left's Culturalism and Rojava." It came out in issue 9 of *Contours Journal*, an online journal published by the Institute for the Humanities at Simon Fraser University under the direction of the esteemed and committed critical theorist Samir Gandesha.

Moving to those who directly helped in the creation of this book, I would like to start by acknowledging my sincere thanks to the unanimous reviewers for their encouraging comments and constructive suggestions. Their collegial reviews were key in making this book possible.

Several people among those whose efforts were essential in the creation of this book had worked tirelessly in the making of another book of mine, *The Death of Home*, as well. The list starts with the acquisition editor Andre Borges, who once more placed his confidence in my work, securing a punctual and enriching review process and then advocating for the simultaneous publication of the hardcover and paperback editions of the book by De Gruyter. It has been a true privilege to work with Andre on three projects, including an upcoming one, *Exile and Spatiality*.

Once the contract was signed, I was extremely fortunate to have the pleasure of working with Michaela Göbels, De Gruyter's Content Editor, again. Michaela oversaw all the stages of the process and was as usual remarkably patient and understanding, making herself available from the beginning of the first stage to the end of the last. As soon as I mentioned that ideally I would prefer a picture of one of Fernando Zóbel's paintings for the cover, she worked determinedly trying multiple avenues to materialize my wish. Sure enough, one evening in mid-January

2025, as I was typing these lines at the Mehsa Amini Campus of the Asian University for Women in Chattogram (previously Chittagong,) Michaela emailed me the news that permission for the use of the ideal cover image had been obtained. Speaking of the cover, I also send warm thanks to the design team in appreciation for all their patience and work.

I am greatly thankful to Jonathan Hoare who did an impressive job diligently copy-editing the manuscript with an extraordinary sensibility for editorial issues. His contribution helped improve the consistency of the spelling of the names, the accuracy of the references and sources, and the overall quality of the manuscript. Then, Kalpana Sagayanathan oversaw the production stages through the final proof. I am grateful to Kalpana for ensuring clear planning and prompt communication during the process that led to the final stage of the production process.

Last but not least, my sincere gratitude and deep appreciation go to everyone who labored behind the scenes to turn my writing into an actual book with a life of its own. I am indefinitely indebted to them and impressed by their invaluable contribution to the book creation. Being out there in the world, this book owes its existence to the labor of those who took part in the pre-production and production procedures, including the editors, copyeditors, typesetters, designers, cataloguers, paper manufacturers, printers, and all the other workers and team members. Thank you all for your solidarity and participation in the struggle against fascism. Together, we shall prove that the violent reality that produces endless false truths is not in any way the best possible world. In the margins, postnihilists and antifascists are actively challenging the undreamability of an egalitarian world, already making a better world possible.

Contents

Chapter 1
Fascism Today

At no point in history have so many people lived under the rule or threat of fascist forces or whatever those exclusionary tribalist forces may be called. Currently, in mid-2024, more than two billion people, about four times the population of Europe including the USSR in 1939, live in countries that are affected by violence and oppression. Political oppression is the norm in Pakistan, Myanmar, most of the countries in Central and West Asia, the Caucasus, Belarus, Turkey, and most of the countries in North, East, and Central Africa. The extreme right is already ruling in India, Poland, Hungary, Italy, Finland, Slovakia, the Czech Republic, and Croatia. In Holland, Sweden, Germany, France, Britain, the United States, and Argentina the extreme right seems to be on the rise. Contrary to the predictions of the prophets of neoliberalism, such as Francis Fukuyama (1992), who cheerfully announced that with the fall of the USSR, the world had entered the end of history crowned by the ultimate triumph of liberal democracy, never have so many people been so ruthlessly dehumanized, exploited, and oppressed. Nor have power and privilege ever been so concentrated in capital, which is, in turn, concentrated in the hands of few individuals. We are living in the age of the decline of the bourgeois liberal state, not in favor of something more democratic but something that is openly tribalist, sectarian, extremist, militaristic, and exclusionary, something that is and should be called fascist.

The Republican Party and Donald J. Trump have made their intention clear that they want to designate Antifa as a terrorist organization. Wherever anti-fascism is criminalized, it should be obvious that fascism is ruling. When we are not allowed to call a system totalitarian, then the system is certainly totalitarian. I make these claims as an expert, but they actually should be common sense. Fascism, however, first takes over the so-called common sense and eventually ends up with a totalitarian regime if it is not resisted in time. Gradually but steadily fascism transforms what is considered normal. Within a decade, the citizenry could lose all its political power.

Fascism is now more powerful than ever as it continues to rise in various parts of the world, from the Indian Subcontinent to the United States. Yet, with a few relatively insignificant exceptions, fascists tend not to own the label. This is mainly because after World War II (WWII) the term "fascism" lost most of its popular appeal and the term "fascist" increasingly became viewed as a derogatory word intended to discredit opponents. Moreover, given fascism's endless variations, mutations, adaptations, and discursive strategies of camouflaging, we need to reconceptualize fascism to enhance our theoretical tools of critical diagnosis and analysis. Critical research of fascism and anti-fascist education and mobilization

https://doi.org/10.1515/9783111609041-001

are urgently needed wherever a combination of some or all of the following phenomena emerge: homogenization of society, proliferation of ultranationalist rhetoric, religious antagonism against out-groups, exclusionism aimed to other, minoritize, or marginalize people, political appeal to irrational frames of reference such as blood or theology, political glorification or unlimited exercise of power, anti-individualism, and racist, nationalist, or religious expansionism.

While for the last decade or so there has been a surge in academic publications on fascism, there is desperate need for a critical, unitary, and inclusive theory of fascism capable of capturing the historical and geographical scope of the phenomenon. That is what my work on fascism, including this book, tries to accomplish. It establishes a critical theory of fascism, creating a new conceptual and analytic system capable of assessing, diagnosing, and exposing fascist ideologies and movements in whatever historical and geographic circumstances and disguises they may emerge. In the meantime, this book conducts in-depth analyses of the current rise of fascism especially, but not only, in two extremely sensitive global loci: the United States and the Middle East.

This volume is motivated by a sense of urgency to re-educate, mobilize, and confront fascist forces locally and globally. As the children of this historical era, we have an intellectual obligation to confront its ideological diseases critically and uncompromisingly, which is what this project aims to do by confronting fascism in a concise but not reductionist, and effective but not simplistic manner. The project's main merit is the balance between the width of its scope and the depth of its analysis. It is meant to contribute to the production of knowledge by enriching the intellectual public sphere both directly and academically. It is beneficial for scholars and opinion makers but also and even more importantly accessible to the broader public.

Google Books Ngram, which is a special search engine for indicating the frequency of the uses of any term in English books up until five years before the time of the search, shows that the use of the word "fascism" has reached its highest point since the end of the 1940s. Only for the period between 1934 and 1949 does the word come up more frequently. Even more interestingly, the use of the term "anti-fascism" reached a record high in 2019, ten to twelve times more than at any other point in the years during, before, or after WWII until the mid-1970s. Since the mid-1970s, the use of the word "fascism" has been going up almost constantly.[1] This is an interesting indication especially considering the fact that the academy

---

1 As of the time of writing these lines, in mid-2024, the Google Books Ngram data is not available beyond 2019.
Fascism:
https://books.google.com/ngrams/graph?content=fascism&year_start=1915&year_end=2019&corpus=en-2019&smoothing=3

generally has been extremely conservative in terms of potential deployments of the term. The conservative conviction in the academic establishment may be apparent to any observer who is capable of recognizing the disciplinary semi-monopoly of fascism studies.

More to the point, the fact that fascism as a field of study has been mostly assigned to history is telling. Even as such, with some exceptions—e.g., Eric Hobsbawm, Enzo Traverso, Domenico Losurdo, Robert Paxton, and Sarah Churchwell—most of the historians remain conservative if not outright anti-Marxist. Outside history departments, some philosophers, including Antonio Gramsci, Leon Trotsky, Max Horkheimer, Theodor Adorno, Terry Eagleton, and Slavoj Žižek, offered crucial observations about fascism, but their works are rarely cited in fascism studies almost certainly because of the prevalent anti-Marxist prejudices in English academia. The conservative and anti-Marxist politics of the production of knowledge are of course relevant, albeit ironically, to the subject matter of the rise of fascism.

Another irony here is that some of the surge in the use of the term fascism certainly has to do with the works of the conventional scholars who seem to be more troubled by the frequent uses of the term than the rise of fascist forces or whatever those forces may be called. For conventional scholars, whether advocates of historical or generic definitions of fascism, the surge in the use of the term must be good news insofar as it keeps them in business as experts. Be that as it may, in addition to the substantial increase in the use of relevant terminology, there are too many other indicators of the rise of fascism to justify the typical denialism that dominates much of the academy, which is certainly part of the problem.

In the name of the best possible world, the advocates of neoliberalism have been indoctrinating their respective followers in every corner of the world that the only universal is capital. At the same time, they have popularized a metaphysical formula of inclusion-through-exclusion thereby self-fulfilling their identitarian prophecy of totalitarian tribalism. Parallel to this idealist hegemony, what has been constructed socially and naturalized metaphysically is contemporary casteism. Within the same process of delegitimizing and fictionalizing socialism, class talk came under vicious attack and was eventually pushed out of both political and scholarly realms.

Antifascism:
https://books.google.com/ngrams/graph?content=antifascism&year_start=1915&year_end=2019&corpus=en-2019&smoothing=3
Interestingly, the term "capitalism" too has reached its highest point of all time:
https://books.google.com/ngrams/graph?content=capitalism&year_start=1915&year_end=2019&corpus=en-2019&smoothing=3.

As the analytic canon of class struggle was swapped by fictive and mystifying identity categories such as nation, culture, and religion, an identitarian industry of ideology was established that in turn rendered all objective factors, such as the material conditions of life and ecology, apolitical, insignificant, or irrelevant. In the dominant frame of reference, myriads of identities are produced precisely in order to sustain the politics of oppressive illusions and suppress every potential politics of social emancipation. It is no wonder that with the global rise of neoliberal hegemony and the demise of Marxist language, idealist doctrines such as the clash of civilizations and culturalism became prevalent. A more bluntly fascistic ethos such as race-war or make-it-great-again occasionally surfaces but the phenomenon is the same. What varies is the *discursive strategies of camouflaging*. Fascism is the most accurate term to designate the core ideological form and its embodiments in social movements, whether they emerge in the Indian Subcontinent, West Asia, the Caucuses, the Mediterranean, Europe, or the Americas.

The American military has 800 bases spread over thirty-eight countries. The polluting gas emissions from this single establishment amount to a devastating war on the environment. For nearly five decades, conservatives, whether the secular, evangelical, Islamist, or Hindutva strains, have been alleging that socialism is dysfunctional. It is as if capitalism had not already proved itself to be not only the most dysfunctional but also ecologically catastrophic and therefore biologically suicidal system, to say nothing of its biopolitics of governmentality and sociology of power, which together systemize the maximization of exploitation qualitatively and quantitatively.

In a book titled *The Death of Home*, published by De Gruyter in 2024, I show how through the meticulous commodification of shelter and production of homelessness, the capitalist order predetermines that the vast majority of members of human society will be nothing more than sources for generating capital, which makes a larger portion of the miserable majority dispensable as it makes the dominant more powerful (Bahozde 2024). Increasingly, every human need, including shelter, food, water, and air, every activity and inactivity, and every movement and rest, is primarily turned into a means of exploitation. This regime of biopower is so encompassing and totalitarian that it even prevents thought from conceptualizing the miserable conditions precisely because there is no longer any distance separating the miserable from their misery. It prevents language from articulating the lived reality because there is no longer a frame of signification other than what has been imposed by capitalism, which has transcended and surpassed monotheistic absolutism. Under capitalism, the cost of life is death, and death is not an option. Death imposes more enslavement on those who may prefer it over such a miserable life. After all, the miserable have to prostitute themselves as laborers in order to make enough money to buy their graves.

Authoritarianism and even more so populism have been gaining currency as alternative terms to what I believe can best be designated as fascism. Obviously not all regimes that are labeled authoritarian are fascist, but all fascist regimes can easily, though misleadingly, be called authoritarian. During the Cold War era, the term authoritarianism was used frequently to water down the damning implications of Western states' association with certain totalitarian and fascist regimes. Otherwise, the Western bloc habitually employed the term totalitarian to label states that did not meet the standards of liberal democracy, such as free elections and a free market economy. For instance, Augusto Pinochet's Chile, we were told, was authoritarian, but Cuba was totalitarian. Despite many recent attempts to market populism in academia, it is even more misleading and hollow as a presumed concept. Attempts to deploy the term populism as a pseudo-concept often can be considered as a mere continuation of the prologue prejudices and ongoing campaigns to blame the ignorant public, "the rabble," "the masses," for the rise of a right-wing elite. The problem is that the charge itself is rooted in right-wing elitism. More importantly, to describe what is taking place in the world today as populism is to underestimate the actual threat.

1 The Argument, Objective, and Structure

There is a common assumption that any assessment or potential diagnosis of fascism must be determined comparatively vis-à-vis Mussolini's Fascism and/or Hitler's Nazism, which I refute as a problematic procedure because it dismisses the fact that fascism has changed drastically over the last century, just as democracy has changed immensely since the time of its Ancient Athenian model or even since the 1920s. There is also a habit of limiting the scope of fascism to the West, and, contrary to appearances, often this is done not despite but due to the endurance of Eurocentrism in the research area. The unspoken, and perhaps unconscious, Eurocentric premise is that Middle Easterners, for instance, cannot even be fascists, for they are usually imagined as mere victims of Western colonialism/imperialism or as societies whose sense of politics is determined merely by religion and culture. In both cases, the non-European other is falsely homogenized. The truth is that all societies have right and left political movements, so neither fascism nor progressive movements should be conceived as exclusively Western or Eastern phenomena.

This book has three main objectives:
1. provide a new theory capable of capturing all historical and geographical variations of fascism;
2. critically assess the implications of the global rise of fascism; and
3. discuss the desperate need for an international movement against fascism.

The outcome is a critical theory of fascism. My main proposition is that fascism is an *ideological form* as opposed to an ideology or an ideological system. Fascism should be understood on the basis of its mystifying, exclusionary, reactionary, and violent form as opposed to its non-existent "philosophy." It is a trait of certain ideologies and movements rather than a particular universal ideology.

The book's structure thematically follows its main objectives. Chapter 2 offers a critical theory of fascism, adding conceptual flexibility to the term "fascism," and thereby saving it from encyclopedic rigidity and orthodox scholasticism (Ahmed 2023b). Chapter 3 points to the global danger of fascism by showing that fascism has never been so powerful if we consider the size of the populations that are ruled by fascist regimes, including India, Pakistan, Iran, Turkey, Hungary, and possibly the United States following the 2024 presidential elections. In Chapter 4, I analyze Trumpism and the alt-right movement as the continuation of the American fascist movement. Chapter 5 focuses on the problem of fascism in West Asia and North Africa especially in terms of the rise of nationalist and fundamentalist movements in the region. Fascism has not been sufficiently challenged or problematized based on the inclusive and democratic premises of, and in the public sphere in the area that is known as, the Middle East, making a discussion of the problem in the Arab world, Iran, and Turkey particularly critical. Chapters 6, 7, and 8 broaden the scope of the discussion while using some of the concepts that will have been developed in the first five chapters. Chapters 6 and 7 focus on the conflict between NATO and the Russian Federation and its international implications. Chapter 8 continues to use a broad viewpoint in terms of international relations and global politics in the prevalent order. Finally, Chapter 9 brings the various components of the inquiry together to provide a final analysis of the problem of fascism in today's world and the potential way forward toward a non-fascist, non-exclusionary, and non-violent world for all. Parts of the analysis rely on the Frankfurt School's Critical Theory and my earlier works, such as *Revolutionary Hope After Nihilism* published by Blooms-bury in 2022 (Ahmed 2022a), and *Critical Theory from the Margins*, published by SUNY Press in 2023 (Ahmed 2023a; paperback edition in 2024).

Constructing a new theory for problematizing fascism, this book is meant to break free of the cycles of historical and so-called generic definitions that have framed much of fascism studies since the early 1950s.[2] Given the fact that every fascist movement entails its own chauvinism, we need to realize that no two fascist ideologies would share the same perspective. That is to say, because the identity

---

2 While "fascist studies" is used commonly, for semantic reasons, I prefer "fascism studies." By the same token, it can be said that this book contributes to fascism studies—that is, the area that researches fascism, as opposed to research that is rightly or wrongly dubbed fascist.

of the in-group versus out-group necessarily differs from one fascist movement to another, it is pointless to search for a universal program or philosophy of fascism.

Moreover, fighting a fascist movement does not necessarily amount to being anti-fascist. Comprehending this point will help clarify a major confusion especially among Western leftists and liberals, some of whom are habitually deceived by the alleged anti-colonialist and anti-imperialist agenda of Third World exclusionary (read as *fascist*) movements. In the absence of a popular left, fascist states could very well produce fascist opposition. Therefore, building sympathy for a political force or movement merely on the basis of its opposition to a fascist state runs the risk of unknowingly supporting fascism. It is more common for fascist movements to conflict with each other, so in a world such as ours, adopting the pragmatic principle of (forming an alliance with) "the enemy of one's enemy" often translates into partaking in a fascist pact. By the same token, the only possible anti-fascist front is a universal, post-nationalist, secular, inclusionary, egalitarian, and progressive one. That is to say, there can be no such thing as anti-fascism unless all forms of fascism are fought on multiple local, regional, and global levels. To be anti-fascist is to reject fascism everywhere. If one's sympathies and enmities are based on the identity of the excluded and the included, then, whether knowingly or unknowingly, one is actively supportive of fascism.

In addition to pointing to the devastating implications of the rise of fascism in various parts of the world, I make a case about our, the educated public's, passive role in empowering fascism. Namely, I argue that our inability to be shocked can only further embolden fascist movements and weaken potential democratic tools of maintaining a peaceful and dignifying space for all. Fascist movements gain popularity gradually, and when they have enough followers, taking over the state institutions can happen very rapidly. Therefore, part of my critique is aimed at the liberal optimism and compliance with fascist movements especially when liberal governments criminalize anti-fascist movements. The book also presents in-depth analyses of fascism in the United States and the Middle East and North Africa (MENA) region, but it also focuses on the fascist ideology in post-Soviet Russia and the implications of NATO's policies.

Why is the focus on the United States and the Middle East? The short answer is that the United States has an overwhelming influence on global politics while at the same time global politics considerably affect and are affected by the political climate in the MENA region. The United States is a dominant player on the international stage, and MENA is a decisive center of the international stage. American hegemony has international dimensions, ramifications, manifestations, etc. while, at the same time, MENA is the place where a great deal of international hegemony is tested, challenged, reshaped, etc. In the meantime, the ongoing war between the Russian and the Ukrainian armies, and the increasing involvement of NATO calls for a discussion of the racist and fascist implications of that conflict as well.

2 Why the United States?

Every drastic shift in American politics most probably has a global impact, so the rise of fascism in the United States is especially alarming. Given the hegemony of the American canon, what becomes legitimate in the United States will become legitimate in many parts of the world. Nothing serves the spread of fascism in the world better than the spread of fascism in the United States. Be that as it may, there are three more nuanced points to make concerning the link between fascism and the United States.

First, considering the social and political history of the United States, the growth and continuation of American fascism should be historically anticipated. The foundation of the United States was utterly racist, imperialist, and genocidal. After the War of Independence, which freed the colonial rulers from the leash of the British monarchy, the racist regime of slavery and the colonial exploitation of the land not only continued but in fact multiplied. In 1776, the birth year of the American Declaration of Independence, you had to be a white, male landowner to enjoy the right to vote. All women, all racialized (that is, non-white) men, and all landless men were deprived of the right to vote. It would be another 144 years before some women, namely white women, would be allowed to vote.[3] Until 1952 Asian Americans were denied citizenship and the right to vote. As of the late 1950s, there were places in the United States where native Americans were not allowed to vote. Finally, to put things in perspective, twenty years after the fall of the Third Reich, thanks to the Civil Rights Movement led by African Americans, racial restrictions on the right to vote were lifted through a federal legislation act known as the Voting Rights Act of 1965.

The United States has always justified its foreign policies and global politics in the name of liberalism and democratic rights, but it has been the largest colonial empire of racial hierarchy. By the admission of its elites, including President Biden, racism is systemized in the United States. American foreign policies and global politics brought the world to the verge of nuclear catastrophe on multiple occasions. Indeed, the United States has been the only country to use atomic bombs, killing hundreds of thousands of civilians. Yet, while Stalinist crimes are commonly associated with communism, somehow, nobody seems to associate racist and genocidal acts with liberalism. This brings us to the second point regarding the dismissed links between American capitalist hegemony and fascism.

---

3 Interestingly, a year before that date, in 1919, Afghan women from all backgrounds, gained the right to vote.

Second, except for the duration of WWII, the US as a state has never shaped its global politics on an anti-fascist basis, and, in fact, it stands out globally for its support for fascist regimes and movements. Examples of such regimes are the Apartheid regime of South Africa, the Shah regime in Iran until its fall in 1979, the Franco regime in Spain until Franco died in 1975, the Kemalist (and later Islamist) regime in Turkey to this day, and the Saddam Hussein regime in Iraq until 1990. As for fascist movements supported by the US, examples include Baathism in Iraq (until 1990), and Islamism in Indonesia, Pakistan, Bangladesh, Afghanistan, Saudi Arabia, and Qatar. Today's Sunni Islamism is a direct descendant of the Mujahideen movement of the 1980s, which was proudly and openly supported by the United States, Pakistan, and the influential Wahabi regimes in the oil-rich Arab monarchies at the time, especially Saudi Arabia and Qatar. Today, the Qatari, Turkish, and Iranian support for Islamist movements around the world is not surprising given the fact that those three regimes are at the heart of religious fascism. But why does the prime representative of liberal democracy in the world end up supporting fascist regimes and movements over and over again? The third point about the subject of fascism and the United States is concerned with this particular question.

Third, we tend to conflate democratic procedures within a state and supposed democratic policies by that state. There is nothing in any democratic system within a state that could inherently rule out advancing undemocratic (read as fascist) policies by that state. The realm of international politics is vastly detached from the realm of internal national politics. In the United States, especially, rarely are state officials elected in light of their agenda for or views on international relations, global politics, or foreign policies. For the last one hundred years, elected American presidents, acting on behalf of the United States, have committed some of the most racist, totalitarian, imperialist, and exclusionary acts in the international arena. Donald Trump may be a fascist leader supported by a fascist base, but the state does not need a fascist leader to behave as a fascist state on the international stage. Trump's second term in the White House will have unique global significance mainly but not only because of the symbolic and ideological ramifications in terms of emboldening fascist movements across the world and rendering fascist mockeries of democracy more widespread in countries that are already ruled by despotic and fascist regimes.

The privileged are often fearful of losing their privileges, so the persecution complex is not uncommon, especially during times of economic uncertainty. Fascist ideologues play an essential role in intensifying and politicizing the persecution complex among the lower middle class and the poor within the majority in order to further racialize all class problems. There is nothing more characteristic of the rise of fascism than the racialization of class politics, which transforms every potentiality for a socialist revolution into a race war, which is of course led by fascists. It is no wonder that even the liberals in the capitalist class always prefer fascists over communists. During severe crises, capitalist elites allow fascists to assume positions of political leadership; without fascist politics, the social unrest will most likely take the shape of a class revolution. Fascists, in turn, feed into the persecution complex and try everything to spread the belief that the world is fundamentally and eternally structured on the basis of nations and that great nations could become miserable in the absence of a wise, fearless, and honest patriotic leadership.

The revival of tribal anxieties, such as the sense of being threatened by the outside world and betrayed by state politicians and elites, gave rise to a desperate search for a new savior, a father figure who does not hold back from saying it as it is, a leader who does not shy away from standing for family values and national/racial interests, etc. The fascist leader presents himself as the ultimate guardian who protects the great nation that is about to lose its greatness forever because of the alleged threats of elimination from without and decay from within.

The nationalist father figure is mandated with a semi-sacred task: to make it great again, and the rest of the story is fascism unfolding. The following fascist pattern is universal from the beginning to the last stages. First, during the first years of the savior's reign, a degree of growth in the national economy may be achieved. In this stage, there is also a substantial increase in the exhibition of national strength, often through deploying forms of bullying and intimidation, directly reflecting the leader's own personality, against the most disempowered both within the country and regionally. These perceived victories result in the second stage: more popularity for the leader, who in turn gains more confidence in his own wisdom and way of governance. Within a few years, the father figure becomes adamant that his historical role is a metaphysically determined mission. In the third stage, the absolutism reaches its ultimate peak, whereby the leader becomes the nation, and the nation becomes the leader. He treats his hallucinations as pure visions freshly revealed to him by a divine power, and the fascist ingratiators who surround him act as if that is the case. If the leader has a bad dream due to, say, overindulging, the following day the visionary dream could be converted into an executive order of some sort.

Once the nationalist mission that is executed under the leadership of the savior becomes a divine plan, no amount of failure will deter him from going ahead with his plan and seeing it through to the end to make the nation great again. In the fourth and last stage, the destruction has already begun and will not stop until the savior is physically removed from the scene. Every single time, the one who is mandated to make it great again will only succeed in destroying it again. American fascism will continue to have devastating implications worldwide, rendering ant-fascist education, among other things, in the United States and the rest of the world urgently needed.

3 Why the Middle East and North Africa?

There are two main reasons for dedicating a chapter to problematizing fascism in the Middle East and North Africa. First, the field of fascism studies has rarely addressed the region. Second, the forms of fascism in the Middle East are more similar to the fascism of the interwar period in more than one sense, such as open calls for violence against minorities, bold and widespread anti-Semitism, the Führer principle, and the normalcy of race talk in the public sphere. All these claims are backed up by analyses of examples of textbooks, newspaper articles, news reports, and social media, etc. from Turkey, Iran, Iraq, Syria, Egypt, Sudan, and so on. For instance, I have collected and analyzed data about anti-Semitism in social media, and the results could not be more shocking. I use social media analysis to investigate the problem of anti-Semitism in the MENA region. I also critically analyze the phenomenon of anti-Semitism in mass media to gauge the danger of the continual lack of non-Euro-centered and non-Eurocentric fascism studies.

Fascist practices, policies, and discourses remain unproblematized in the MENA region mainly but not entirely because of the ruling ideologies. There are some important scholarly works that address the question of fascism in Turkey and the Arab world, but within fascism studies overall, this remains a very under-studied area. To illustrate my point, I analyze multiple dimensions of fascist practices that involve racist ultra-nationalism, violence against minorities, leader cultism, and chauvinism. In a book titled *Fascism in the Middle East* (Bahozde 2025), I focus on another element that has not been noticed, let alone problematized. Namely, there is nothing about the state of oppression that would rule out fascism, and, in fact, oppression makes the emergence of fascist tendencies among any previously or presently colonized and racialized group likely especially in the absence of a popular progressive movement to lead social and political emancipation. More often than not collective grievances, whether stimulated by historical events or ongoing suffering, whether caused by genocidal colonialism or religious crusades, prepare the local atmosphere for the rise and reproduction of exclusionism, again, especially, in the absence of a strong popular and progressive front formed around a comprehensive philosophy of unconditional egalitarianism and universal emancipation, the most obvious historical example of which is, of course, Marxist communism in terms of the power of its appeal to the marginalized everywhere and the scope of its conception of emancipation.

4 Dialectics, Critique, and Negation

I want to emphasize that by no means do I intend to argue or even imply that the current crisis in the MENA region, or the rest of the world for that matter, is merely ideological in its nature. On the contrary, the roots of the ideological crises are to be found in the social reality. While this book focuses on ideology critique, it does not suggest that critical analyses of the ideological realm suffice to change the existing state of affairs. Despite the century-old aggressive campaigns to discredit dialectical materialism in favor of idealist frames of reference, we should not shy away from thinking and researching in terms of dialectical materialism. As Walter Benjamin noted, "the historical materialist" knows that "the subject of historical knowledge is the struggling, oppressed class struggle itself" and, at the same time, makes the exposure of the "historical continuum" possible precisely in order to materialize the revolutionary historical leap (2006, 394–396). In Marx's own words, "material force must be overthrown by material force; but theory also becomes a material force as soon as it has gripped the masses" (2010a, 182).

Just to further emphasize the materialist premise and the dialectical frame of reference, the following observation by Vijay Prashad is worth quoting here:

> If we look into the entrails of the system, we will find that its solutions do not lie within it. Its problems are not technical, nor are they cultural. They are social problems that require political solutions. The social order of property, propriety, and power has to be radically revised. That is without question. The issue is what must be the strategy, the tactics, the way forward to a place that is not what we have now. The global South is a place of great struggle, of various tactics and strategies experimented with on the streets and in the halls of government. It is an unfinished story—one that has to have a good ending. (2014, 11)

It is an idealist fallacy to assume that uncovering the truth (even if in its fullest materialist sense) would result in changing the world. Ultimately, it is the conditions of producing and reproducing untruth that must be changed in order for a historical, progressive, change to be brought about in human society. Once the social relations and actual conditions of people's lives change, once the inhumane circumstances are abolished, what is in the realm of ideas and values will follow suit. That said, the interactional changes between the two realms are continual. It is just that those who dominate the social means of power also dominate the ideological means of hegemony. Thus, undoubtedly the regime of truth and knowledge production is structured and maintained in ways that legitimize and perpetuate the existing regime of social relations of inequality. Therefore, emancipatory social transformation must aim at all realms, including the material and the ideological ones, as well as spheres that bridge them through various forms of labor.

There is another critical point to emphasize with respect to what makes an intervention such as this book necessary from a historical materialist perspective. The point is that ignorance is a dangerous social force. Even when it is innocent, it could actively and continually partake in actualizing violence. Ignorance in itself might not be a crime, but it is one of the most common conditions of criminality. An inhumane reality always includes ignorance as one of its substantial components. That is so because a social norm cannot be produced without some form of approval, if not participation, of the majority of the individuals in that society. It follows that in an inhumane social reality, ignorance is a structural condition continually reproduced within the perpetual cycle of societal activities in that particular historical era.

Therefore, we cannot do away with exposing and negating ignorance no matter how hopeless the situation may be in terms of actualizing historical change. There is a fundamental difference between truth as an assertion and truth as a negation of untruth. From a post-nihilist and dialectical-materialist perspective, what invokes revolutionary thought is not a promised land in the future or a truth metaphysically asserted before it is realized historically. Rather, what invokes revolutionary thought is the imperativeness of directly negating the reality that is founded on falsehood and radically intervening in history, which has been a history of suffering.[4]

Existentially, one might be tempted to believe that the world is not worth knowing, but ignorance is not necessarily identical to not knowing. What makes ignorance such a dangerous social force is that it does not assume a position of not knowing. Rather, it encourages assertions and oppressive actions in the name of truth, justice, and beauty. The danger of the political implications of religion lies precisely in this metaphysical assertion of truth, as opposed to the religious person's notion of spiritual life even though the two sides are only hypothetically separatable. It is a fatal form of naivety on our part to assume, as we have repeatedly, that ignorance is harmless if unprovoked. A more fatal mistake is to enter some sort of alliance with ignorance, embodied, for instance, as a theology, to advance a cause, such as the struggle against class and racial domination. Today, certain theologians might behave as faithful comrades of the rest of us within the same struggle against colonial domination in a particular place, but the moment they assume power, they will be anything but partners with others who fall outside the distinctly defined in-group, the community of brothers and sisters who not only believe in a metaphysical regime of truths and values but also see themselves as missionaries tasked to enlighten and save the rest of the world.

---

4 Marx's theses on Feuerbach and Benjamin's theses "On the Concept of History" can best be interpreted in light of such a theory of negativity (Benjamin 2006).

Ignorance of ignorance, therefore, is a recipe for repeating the disasters of the past revolutions, which were quickly hijacked by the most regressive elements, often leading to a reality much darker than the pre-revolution ones. We have no option but to be aware of ignorance, otherwise we may very well become tools of oppression, which is precisely the danger that necessitates both philosophical and historical awareness. Revolutions that do not make the world better make it worse. Also, revolutions in which fascists are allowed to take part and revolutions that are led by generals typically worsen the state of unfreedom and inequality. In West Asia and North Africa, any time right-wing forces were tolerated in the name of prioritizing struggles against imperialism, colonialism, or despotism, we ended up with a post-revolution era much bloodier than the pre-revolution era. Often right-wing movements highjacked the revolution, resulting in a much darker age of absolute terror.

The anti-Marxist intelligentsia have played a significant role in minimizing the sense of danger in all these scenarios. In fact, this is at the heart of the failure of all so-called republics across most of West Asia and North Africa. A newly born republic would abolish a monarchy only to replace it with an openly fascist and terroristic regime led by a general, or an assassin, who in no time would go through a metamorphosis to become a god-like figure impossible to be replaced by any means, a father figure who would treat his people as cattle while expecting them to treat him as the only one who could govern them now and in the indefinite future. As medieval and undemocratic as they may be, when it comes to inheriting the crown, monarchs have plans, customs, arrangements, and so on. A president of an Arab republic, on the other hand, cannot conceive of a future without himself at the top of the pyramid of power. At best, he would prepare one of his sons to become the new mafia boss mastering the strategies of sheer terror and unlimited manipulation.

An important dimension of this critical theory of fascism and critique of fascism studies is the global perspective, which entails consistent assessments of international relations in terms of fascism as a form of ideology and a category of idealist movements based on the racialization of class, homogenization of society, essentialization of perceived cultures. We are born into a racist world, so our standards and norms, whether in language, education, politics, ethics, or aesthetics, are racist. The racist institution's primary function is to distort the perception of the reality—that is, of class society. By constructing a racist mode of perception, racism also constitutes an objective reality whereby the institution of class becomes increasingly inseparable from the institution of race.

Most importantly, problematizing racism requires creating a distance between cognition and the sociohistorical reality rendering that reality open for questioning. Given the normalized racist frame of reference and the frustrating cognitive limitations it imposes on language, I am compelled to frequently include clarifying notes on my use of certain terminology within the critical epistemological system I wish to advance for the purpose of a comprehensive problematization of the existing reality and, thus, a meaningful struggle for negating the prevalent regime of truth, which is, insofar as it becomes a social reality, nothing but a regime of distortion, oppression, and falsehood perpetuating its own metaphysics and epistemology.

In my view, a scholarship that does not challenge the dominant systems of signification plays an organic role in the perpetuation of a totalitarian social regime under which marginalization and silencing go hand in hand. To ensure not to take the side of the ruling groups, everything from the ideological sanctification of the semantics of domination to the production of microaggression against the marginalized should be the target of negation. At the center of all this are the linguistic manifestations of the antagonism between the hegemonic regimes and the emancipatory movements that desperately try to produce spaces for freedom as a condition of experience and spheres of thought as an actual exercise of freedom.

The question of negation as the essential method within the revolutionary philosophy and as an emancipatory step toward a new horizon of possibilities is revisited directly in the final chapter. Everything in between is dialectical critique actively aiming to negate the systemized falsehood that is at the heart of both the reality of oppression and the oppression of reality. Thus, the challenges this book has already set for itself include refuting denialism, which dominates the intelligentsia, and problematizing fascism, which has been taking up much of the public sphere without being noticed at all, let alone as a problem.

On a personal note, this book, like the rest of my books, is not funded by any entity, group, or person. In fact, the work was carried out without the security of any academic vocation. Also, like the process of writing the rest of my books, at no point have I had the luxury of knowing where, on which continent, I would end up after a few months, or even, in most cases including this, after a few weeks. That said, as an exile without sentimental ties to any place in the world, I did not need to do much to obtain the distance needed for problematizing fascism.

Exile should not be romanticized because, especially in the capitalist world, it could mean an imminent threat to survivability. Put even more bluntly, lackness could mean that death is always too close. Yet, at the same time, in the slim chance that one survives, the absolute lack of property also entails not being owned, not being confined to the limitations of ownership. At least cognitively, complete exile is an essential condition for any worthwhile philosophy including especially an anti-fascist philosophy. Exile as elsewhereness, which is the topic of my upcoming book, *Exile and Spatiality*, can be the best epistemic condition for negativity as one's state of being and negation as one's primary intellectual scheme.

As I write these lines, I know that every book or article I have written so far has only decreased my chances of survivability. If I had any remorse about burning the bridges along the way of my philosophical, intellectual, and academic journey, I would stop writing. No apologia to be offered for the committed sacrilege; only more heresy all the way to the end. Being about fascism, certainly this book is the farthest from any reconciliation with any house of power anywhere. For the record, I think this book's power lies precisely in the fact that its author always stood outside and against establishments of power everywhere.

Chapter 2
The Rise of Fascism and the Futility
of Conventional Fascism Studies

Practically, there is a semi-ban on the use of the term "fascism" in the academy, except by experts in Italian Fascism (capitalized) and German Nazism. For some reason, scholastic anxiety about employment of the term seems to be far greater than any apprehension that fascist movement might be on the rise. Terms and concepts in political philosophy are usually subject to infinite redefinitions without too much concern for their respective original models, but "fascism" is somehow exempted from such critical and conceptual treatment. Definitions of fascism are measured against the "standard" two models despite the fact that even those two models are not compatible, either with each other or with the traditionally recognized criteria of fascism.

Let us go back to the first philosopher of fascism in the hope that his definition will help satisfy the orthodoxy who insists on a historical definition or imposes a set of criteria deduced from the two interwar models, which amounts to the same thing. As all scholars of fascism studies know, the first and more or less the only movement that adopted the term Fascism (capitalized) had a philosopher called Giovanni Gentile, who recognized Benito Mussolini as Il Duce. In order to avoid repeating the boring story of historical versus false definitions and interpretations of definitions, the following passages from Gentile are worth reproducing:

> The doctrine of Fascism is not a philosophy, in the ordinary sense of the term, and still less is it a religion. *It is also not an explicated and definitive political doctrine*, articulated in a series of formulae. The truth is that the significance of *Fascism is not to be measured in the special theoretical or practical theses that it takes up at one or another time*. As has been said at its very commencement, *it did not arise with a precise and determinate program*. Often, having settled on an immediate goal to be attained, a concept to be realized, a course to be followed, it has not hesitated, when put to the test, to change direction and reject as inadequate, or violative of principle, just that goal or that concept. *Fascism sought not to bind the future*. It has often announced reforms that were *politically opportune*, but the announcement itself did not bind the regime to their execution. (2002, 21 italics added)

Of course, this does not mean that fascism could be arbitrarily attributed to any and every opportunistic movement. While they tend to be pragmatically unprincipled, fascist movements are also idealist (as opposed to materialist), nationalist, conservative, and militantly and fanatically anti-communist. Speaking about the forefathers of what became Fascism in Italy, such as Manzoni, Rosmini, Mazzini, and Mazzini's disciples, Gentile asserts that "there is not a single materialist among

https://doi.org/10.1515/9783111609041-002

them—not one who does not sense the religious character of life" (2002, 7). Gentile, like many German nationalists, continually appeals to idealistic notions such as the soul of the nation, national character, blood, race, and, most importantly, culture. Today, in the era that started with the announcement of the alleged death of Marxism at the end of the 1980s, culturalism as the prevalent embodiment of idealism shapes the dominant mode of perception and discourse. Today's normalized form of racism and fascism is culturalism. This is evident in the fact that the word culture is so widely thrown around by not only anti-immigrants and Islamists but also self-proclaimed liberals and post-Marxist leftists (for more on this, see Žižek 2008; Ahmed 2015, 2022a, 2023a).

The second half of this chapter briefly discusses the main approaches to fascism studies. I especially focus on the futility of the prolonged debates around what should and should not be called fascist. Given the main confusion around fascism, some definitions are inevitably too broad while others are too narrow. This applies to most historical and generic definitions, with some significant exceptions in the latter group. I refute the historical, or orthodox, approach altogether because it simply fails to account for non-European and new-European fascist movements. As for the generic definitions, I discuss their merits and some of their problems, preparing the ground for the third chapter where I present the core of my critical theory of fascism.

Several recent books warn about the rise of fascism, but they repeat the same mistake of taking Mussolini's Fascism and Hitler's Nazism as the ultimate standards of fascism. Comparing Trump with Hitler is neither interesting nor useful. In fact, such comparisons seriously undermine the threat fascism represents today simply because they fictionalize fascism. Any Trump supporter would always be able to point to the genuine differences between the two personalities, thereby winning the argument. "Fascism" will always be useless for analytic purposes as long as it is treated as a term rigidly defined. Unlike a term, a concept cannot be confined to a dictionary definition. The endless scholastic debates around a potential definition of "fascism" are ill-founded. Searching for a definition to serve as a yardstick will not be able to accomplish more than the sheer repetition and accumulation of citations. Outside academic conferences and monographs, fascism has been taking multiple new forms across the world for more than a century.

1 Asymptomatic Fascism: A Sociopsychological Account

After fascism fell out of fashion following WWII, fascists in Europe developed discursive camouflaging to avoid immediate detection in the new public sphere (this does not necessarily apply to fascist movements and discourses outside Western and Central Europe).[5] For instance, most European fascists do not openly express hatred toward Jews or affinity toward Hitlerism, and in some cases, they simply shed that skin altogether when they realized Hitlerism had become a bad populist investment. Except for some small groups, they know that to gain popularity, they need to appeal to and reproduce the phobias specific to the time and place. Their strategists come up with discourses that correspond to their potential constituencies' current frustrations even though some of those strategies still feed on the same old collective phobias. For instance, to exploit xenophobia, anti-immigrant language proves to be more effective in a world where there are more and more refugees, and Islamophobic platforms pay off quickly when the Muslim Other appears more visible in Christian majority communities.

We will be witnessing a continual increase in fascist duplications of corporate models and commercial strategies. This also means more swift transitions from the business sector to politics; after all, thanks to the global triumph of consumerism in the post-Soviet era, market strategies can be used effectively in election campaigns to appeal to large numbers of de-classed and bourgeoisified people. All that a fascist demagogue needs to do is to give the frustrated masses reasons to justify their impulses and redirect their potential anger against their oppressors who make their life conditions miserable to the imagined imminent threat of the invading and implanted Other, an enemy. As a rule, when there is no actual enemy, fascism creates an enemy in the public imagination. The image of an outside enemy conspiring with alleged collaborators within provides an easily reproducible formula to be causally linked to the narrative of the supposed decay of the

---

5 For instance, among Iranian nationalists, old race talk, especially Aryanism and anti-Arab racism, are not uncommon (for more on this, see Ahmed 2017; Zia-Ebrahimi 2011). Pan-Arab nationalists, especially when addressing their own constituents, do not make much effort to hide their intolerance for perceived Jews. Islamists might differ on endless issues from the secular nationalists, but they have anti-Semitism in common (Ahmed 2017; see also Ter-Matevosyan 2015; Hanioglu 2014). Fascists are intolerant of Marxist communism because it advances the doctrine of universal inclusivity and equality as opposed to social hierarchy, racism, nationalism, clannism, etc. They also categorize people into distinct (perceived) groups according to a strict tribalist system of classification and an utterly racist mode of perception. As sworn anti-Semites, they see perceived Jews as nothing but members of a tribe whose essence in life, intentions, politics, values, motives, etc. are determined by their alleged tribal identity. Yet, at the same time, the same fascist mentality somehow manages to merge those two enemies, communism (Marxism, Bolshevism, socialism, internationalism, etc.) and assumed essentialist Jewish politics (Jewish nationalist politics, Judaism, metaphysical fidelity to Jewry, deterministic Jewishness, or whatever else the projected tribalist identity is supposed to mean). To this day, these fascists have failed to see how the conspiracy theory they have been reproducing for so long perfectly and scandalously exposes a lack of minimal intellectual ability to conceive the basic logical difference between inclusion versus exclusion, let alone to advance political platforms that claim to save their beloved nations.

moral and patriotic values and the ensuing existential threat to the nation.[6] In this way, the miserable are made to feel included, respected, and important while at the same time the exploitation of their lives and deaths, illusions and sufferings, rights and responsibilities, bodies and environment continues.

The psychoanalytic approach remains necessary not to reduce fascism to a psychological disorder but rather to avoid dismissing the dimension that has to do with alienation under capitalism. Fascism on the psychological level is a play on the human fear of separation from the original unity with the mother, the primordial peaceful oneness with the womb where security is absolute. Life, especially in the mechanized world of capitalist modernity, is a lonely undertaking. The alienation and reification that are built into the capitalist relations of production render a nihilist relapse into primordial tribalism extremely appealing. Therefore, in the absence of emancipatory movements based on a post-nihilist philosophy, the rise of fascism is always a real possibility (for more, see Ahmed 2022a). The crisis of alienation does not have individual solutions, and on some level most people sense that something else more profound is needed. In the absence of a popular universalist emancipatory movement, fascist ideologues and movements have the best chance of attracting millions of isolated and alienated subjects. Fascism speaks to the frustration of people and offers semi-religious and simplistic answers.

On a fundamental level, fascism's answers are based on an easy dualism that stems from both pathological narcissism and primordial fear of the outside world. The dualism is, of course, composed of the clan vs. the Other. The image of the Other

---

6 To provide a recent example, in 2021, Mark Levin, one of the right-wing stars of Fox News, published a book titled *American Marxism*, where he makes the Frankfurt School one of his main targets, blaming its members, along with Zionists, for the alleged destruction of "the greatest nation" in the world. Notice, however, that the Frankfurt School is not mentioned anywhere in the book because Levin believes it is called "the Franklin School" (2021, 82). At any rate, the opening lines of the book can serve as an example embodying the imagined enemy in the fascist imagination:

> The counterrevolution to the American Revolution is in full force. And it can no longer be dismissed or ignored, for it is devouring our society and culture, swirling around our everyday lives, and ubiquitous in our politics, schools, media, and entertainment. Once a mostly unrelatable, fringe, and subterranean movement, it is here—it is everywhere. You, your children, and your grandchildren are now immersed in it, and it threatens to destroy the greatest nation ever established, along with your freedom, family, and security. Of course, the primary difference between the counterrevolution and the American Revolution is that the former seeks to destroy American society and impose autocratic rule, and the latter sought to protect American society and institute representative government. (Levin 2021, 1)

Just in case his readers are losing patience to discover this fatal danger, Levin confidently adds, "The counterrevolution or movement of which I speak is Marxism" (2021, 1).

may change from one place or time to another, but its continual reproduction is essential for every fascist enterprise. Like most mythical traditions that were later reappropriated in the Abrahamic religions, the role of the evil demon is absolutely essential for both making the role of God indispensable and framing an identity on the basis of exclusion. The evil demon is both what glues the members of the in-group together and what ensures the internal power hierarchy. It is the fundamental source of the oppressive structure and absolutist order. Practically the in-group members trade their freedoms for a sense of certainty, autonomy for a sense of security, and intellectual potentiality for a sense of belonging.

As we learn from Erich Fromm's famous *Escape from Freedom* (1965), the state of freedom is scary because it requires autonomy of thought and full responsibility for the future. Also, as the existentialists of the 20th century, like Albert Camus and Jan Paul Sartre, realized, freedom necessarily entails never-ending anxiety. The *mobomassdividual* would do anything to keep that existentialist anxiety at bay.[7] The first technique to eradicate the existentialist angst is to submit to an authority, a father figure, whether found in religion or the tribal/national leader. Only if one submits, will the father figure have the psychological power of eradicating anxiety. Therefore, the fertile soil of fascism is the bourgeois world itself, the antipode of autonomous thought. In the absence of emancipatory movements, the more suppressed individuals become, the more their likelihood of joining a fascist crowd, and the larger the crowd becomes, the faster we fall into a dark age.

In our contemporary age, the vast majority of people inevitably experience forms of alienation due to a whole array of reasons that have to do with both lifestyles, which are drastically different than what we as a species have been used to for many hundreds of thousands of years, and life conditions, including working circumstances and their psychological consequences. When the compound sense of alienation, absurdity, individual insignificance, and purposelessness reach a certain point among people of any society, a societal change must take place. The agents of that change are the people themselves. The difference is whether the change they bring about will amount to (a) the invention of a progressive way forward toward more emancipation from the irrational, toward the realization of both individual autonomy and the universality of one's humanity, or (b) a fallback into primordial tribal space defined by the desire to return to the purity of the

---

7 I propose the term as a critical alternative to the term "massification," which has anti-democratic connotations. The base term, "mobomass," is meant to allude simultaneously to mob-mobilization, the bourgeoisie/bourgeoisified, and "mass/ification," to suggest that it is a reference to neither "the mass" nor a mob per se, but individuals who are ideologically bourgeoisified and depoliticized precisely in order to be instrumentalized for an anti-egalitarian political agenda—more on this in the next chapter.

mythical origin. In the absence of an international emancipatory project, fascism in one way or another prevails making total barbarism a reality. Once a fascist coalition becomes popular enough to seize the political ruling institutions, it will certainly create actual enemies through its own antagonistic policies. When the antagonized Other reacts, which is inevitable, fascism will have already placed us in its fatal reactionary cycle that will continue to eat away lives to reproduce itself.

Everywhere, fascism begins its campaigns of hatred against the most marginalized and defenseless groups. Fascists identify with the powerful precisely in order to reject all that subconsciously resembles their own sense of insignificance, weakness, and powerlessness. In dissolving him/herself in the shadow of the powerful, the fascist finds a strategy to abolish his/her paralyzing sense of purposelessness in life. When modernism destroys the collective myths and rituals, and the critical faculties of reason are not enhanced within emancipatory social projects, fascism becomes the new collective religious refuge to provide the suppressed and confused individual with a realm of meaning. The fascist space needs its own image of evil and never-ending sacrifices. First the most vulnerable will be targeted. As the madness of the ritual elevates and fascism totalizes its will over society, more and more people will be perceived as enemies. If it is not stopped, eventually nobody will be safe even when and if the fascist world collapses inwardly.

2 Ideology Critique

If there is one thing we must learn from ideology critique, it is the fact that ideology does not present itself as ideology, that is, as a way to perceive the world. In fact, it does not *present* itself at all insofar as its followers are concerned. It merely *describes* what it purports to be the truth and what it would have us believe is reality. Once one buys into the fascist version of the *truth*, only fascist action makes sense. True to their religious roots, today's dominant ideologies stand on the corpse of epistemology and point to the shining stars in their metaphysical space. If one looks in the direction where an ideology points, one has already fallen under the ideological spell. For instance, the moment one enters a debate in which the center of the dispute is whether black people have equal mental capacities as white people, even when one adamantly rejects the racist position, one is already crediting the racist worldview and reproducing its linguistically codified false logic. This is precisely the problem with the common anti-racist discourses that merely rely on the moral refutation of racism or other fascist claims. When anti-racists depict the problem of racist discourse as a mere moral wrong, as opposed to factual distortions, practically they continue to see the human world and every individual as if "race" had a biological weight, and, thus, they reproduce racism, albeit unintentionally. Therefore, we need to refuse to make racism something debatable by refusing to engage with racist discourses for the same reason any reasonable person would consider a debate about whether the earth is flat as intellectually offensive. Of course, respecting everyone's right to freely express their beliefs, we can still tolerate flat-earthers, obviously not as opinion leaders or educators. However, forms of denialism that cast doubt on the universal entitlement of all human subjects to human rights are not merely a matter of "free speech," as some naïve liberal arguments want us to believe; rather, such denialism is political through and through. It distorts the truth in order to justify otherwise unjustifiable inequalities and forms of dehumanization against populations who are already silenced and marginalized by the existing relations of power and knowledge production. By the same token, historical revisionists will continue to cast doubt on genocides and will do so in the name of reason and freedom of thought and speech, but precisely for the sake of reason and freedom of thought and speech, fascist discourses must be discredited publicly. In the meantime, critical problematizations of discriminatory ideologies should be supported in all the arenas of knowledge production and opinion making.

The norm is naturalized even if it is pathological. It is the marginalized who are named to be demarcated, to be further othered and pathologized. A dominant ideology does not hesitate to name everything other than its own assumptions, and of course it does not want to be classified as an ideology among other ideologies precisely because its legitimacy is based on its supposed metaphysical superiority and its presumed objectivity. There is one way to see the truth and many ways to interpret it, we are supposed to believe; thus, the ideologue merely makes the truth visible, and their political and moral judgments then follow logically. Racists, for instance, are genuinely unaware of the fact that racism is an ideological feature— let alone a completely flawed one that has been devised to legitimize the interests of ruling groups. For racists, to give voice to racism is simply to speak the harsh truth. Polite racists try to avoid using racist speech forms, at least in public, but they nonetheless continue to endorse the same distorting worldview.

The same applies to sexists in their perceptions of sexism. This is precisely why so many racists and sexists are adamantly opposed to liberal political correctness. Another common complaint of racists is that certain minority members habitually label the actions of majority members as racist. Sexists, likewise, frequently complain that feminists see everything as being sexist. The critical account we all need to hear in response to such objections is something along the following lines: *Yes, what is normally uttered is more likely to be racist/sexist because the entire history behind the value system we inherited had been shaped by racism and sexism. We are born into a social world that is deeply racist and sexist, so being non-racist and non-sexist necessitates a process of unlearning, which takes much more than good intentions.* In a similarly dismissive way, leftists have long been accused of carelessly throwing around the word "fascist." It does not occur to the accusers that fascism might indeed be all around us; even some self-proclaimed leftists can fall into their own forms of fascism, which they usually envelop in superficial rhetoric borrowed from Marxism or feminism.

If we classify ideologies according to their forms, as opposed to contents, fascism would be a form of ideologies, some of which go back to even before Mussolini, some that are contemporary, and potential ones that could emerge in the future. Two fascist ideologies could be completely opposing each other in terms of their political conflicts, nationalist and religious discourses, and any number of other specifications. Some fascist movements are Aryanists, others are not. Some identify themselves as Christian, Muslim, Hindu, or Buddhist while others proclaim secularism. Some fascist movements have antagonistic relations with each other while others have both ideological kinship and strategic shared interests. However, none of today's fascist movements that are worth noting in terms of their relative popularity identify as "fascist." Then, the immediate question that arises is whether there are any good reasons to use the term "fascism" to refer to the particular phenomenon we intend to designate.

"Fascism," as a concept, is needed for the purpose of naming and problematizing a phenomenon that is global but has local variations. Because chauvinism is a characteristic aspect of these movements, each one of them necessarily adheres to its own distinct ideology, with particular specifications such as the image of a perceived enemy. Chauvinism necessarily imposes bold particularities on each fascist movement, and in this sense, fascist movements entail more differences than similarities. However, what they have in common is precisely their exclusionary, xenophobic, absolutist, and irrational ways of perception, which result in various forms of violent discourses, politics, policies, and platforms. The rise of such movements is indeed a global phenomenon. "Fascism" captures the form of this class of ideologies better than any other attempted term including populism, authoritarianism, or extremism, each of which is either too narrow or too broad. Fascist movements are tribalist anti-communist, modern anti-modernist, instrumental-rationalist irrational, and totalitarian automatist. Whenever possible, they make use of democratic means pragmatically to attract the maximum number of people to reach state power, and once in power, they have little regard for democratic institutions and practices.

The formation of an international/ist anti-fascist front is long overdue. The new internationalist force can be inspired by the formulas invented by resistant movements who have been struggling against multiple forms of oppression without falling into a nativist, chauvinist, nationalist, fundamentalist, or capitalist trap. It is simply not true that the age of movements that are at the same time cosmopolitan, egalitarian, and inclusive is over. The social inequalities and political crises that gave rise to the communist and anti-fascist movement about a century ago have only intensified, so it is only rational to expect the persistence of such a movement but of course with new strategies and not necessarily in the same places. What we need to do is to pay closer attention to the margins of the margins to recognize, stand with, and be inspired by such creative movements.[8]

3 Stations in Fascism Studies

The purpose of the following discussion is to contextualize my proposition that fascism should be considered an *ideological form*, as opposed to an ideological system. It should be noted that most of the literature in fascism studies inevitably suffers from various forms of reductionism. For instance, rarely have Spanish, British, Portuguese, Italian, Dutch, German, and Belgian colonial practices outside Europe been considered in the literature about fascism, even though those practices, both historically and thematically, started before what is normally considered the emergence of fascism. Both Aimé Césaire and Frantz Fanon argued that the crimes the Nazis committed in Europe were not dissimilar to the crimes European colonialism had been committing outside Europe for a long time (Césaire 2001, 3; Fanon 1994, 166).

Even studies that trace fascism back to the 19th century do so from the perspective of the history of ideas. To be fair, the Marxian accounts tend to stand out for their consideration of the imperialist and colonialist dimensions of fascism. Despite the anti-Marxist testimonies that became fashionable especially in the late 1980s and throughout the 1990s, even today the Marxist theory seems to offer more robust accounts. For example, Karl Polanyi's *The Great Transformation* investigates the political economy of fascism and its connection with capitalism and capitalist crises (Polanyi 2001; originally published in 1944). To Polanyi, "it was a case of symbiosis between movements of independent origin" (Polanyi 2001, 250). Polanyi asserts, "the part played by fascism was determined by one factor: the condition of the market system" (2001, 250). Polanyi shows that fascist movements did not become strong enough to represent a serious international threat until the major crisis of the market economy took place. While I maintain that for investigating the rise of a fascist movement, the critique of political economy is indispensable, my objective here is limited, and it concerns a critical conception of the ideological aspects of fascism. That is to say, my attempt here is focused on fascism in the ideological realm, but by no means do I intend to imply that its causes are simply

---

[8] For more on this, see Ahmed 2022a.

located in the realm of ideology. On the contrary, every fascist ideology, like any other ideological species, is a product of sociohistorical circumstances. By the same token, resisting fascism requires a holistic project to negate the material conditions of domination and dehumanization in addition to political, intellectual, and educational anti-fascist struggles.

Horkheimer conducted a great deal of ideology critique in relation to fascist phenomena, but he also stated, "whoever is not willing to talk about capitalism should also keep quiet about fascism" (Horkheimer 2005, 226). The Frankfurt critical theorists were faithful to Marxist materialism throughout. In their co-authored book, Horkheimer and Adorno point to the systematic generalization of patterns of sameness as something directly related to the mind-numbing standardization within the capitalist modes of material production. They write, "the more superfluous physical labor is made by the development of technology, the more enthusiastically it is set up as a model for mental work" (2002, 167). Then, they add:

> If, even within the field of logic, the concept stands opposed to the particular as something merely external, anything which stands for difference within society itself must indeed tremble. Everyone is labeled friend or foe. The disregard for the subject makes things easy for the administration. Ethnic groups are transported to different latitudes; Individuals labeled "Jew" are dispatched to the gas chambers. (Horkheimer and Adorno 2002, 167)

In 1976, Terry Eagleton published an article titled "What is Fascism?" and it opens by stating that "Only a few years ago, an article with a title such as this would have seemed of merely historical interest" (Eagleton 1976, 100). Fascism, Eagleton maintains, "signifies a massive offensive by the bourgeoisie at a time when the working class is disorganised and defensive, betrayed by a reformist leadership, lacking a revolutionary alternative. The ingredients of fascism, then, are multiple: economic and political crisis, proletarian defeat, failure of social democracy, absence or impotence of revolutionary leadership" (Eagleton 1976, 102). Most importantly, Eagleton realizes that "What is common to all fascist formations, however, is the markedly high degree of relative autonomy which the formation grants to the ideological region" (Eagleton 1976, 106). He concludes his paper by stating, "if the notoriously loose and emotive use of the term 'fascist' common to some sectors of the left is a dangerous political imprecision, it can at least serve to remind us that fascism is never far beneath the surface of bourgeois democracy" (Eagleton 1976, 108). Eagleton's own statement can also *serve to remind us* that things have worsened so much that his own paper would most likely not find a home in today's world of peer-reviewed research thanks to the gentrification, if not outright rejection, of Marxist phraseology.

In the 1970s, the totalitarianism theory that had been widely adopted in the West for two decades started to become less and less defendable. Henry Ashby

Turner (1972) proposed that fascism should be defined as a reaction to modernization. In terms of his wording, Turner was careful not to sound too confident about
what his thesis could accomplish; nonetheless, that thesis soon became the new
theory of choice, especially for scholars who were not prepared to entertain the
idea of reconsidering their stance on the Marxist theory. Turner's definition also
became the subject of criticism even within the anti-Marxist camp. For instance,
through reference to some of the primary sources of the Italian fascists, James
Gregor argues that the modernization theory would not be applicable to Italian
Fascism (1974). Gilbert Allardyce, who along with Henry Ashby Turner, James
Gregor, and Ernst Nolte comes from the anti-Marxist camp, argues that the Nazis
would not be considered fascist according to the modernization theory because
they were very enthusiastic about industrialization (Allardyce 1979, 373). However,
Turner himself shows that a generic definition could not hold up to this kind of
analysis because even the two supposedly fundamental models of fascism could
not be grouped under the term fascism (1972).

One of Gilbert Allardyce's main grievances was that fascism had not been taken
seriously and that researchers had not listened to fascists themselves (1979, 368).
To Allardyce, there is nothing close to a set of common criteria to determine how
or why cases other than the Italian and German models should be considered versions of fascism (1979, 371). However, his observations could be used to arrive at
the exact opposite of the conclusion he puts forward. Namely, precisely because
"fascism" cannot be soundly defined as a universal ideology or international
movement, fascism should not be attributed exclusively to the interwar period in
Europe. Because the position that argues for a historical definition has never lost
its appeal in the field, those who argue for a generic definition sound unorthodox
in comparison. As I will argue in the next chapter, we need to go a step further and
leave behind this binary of historical versus generic definitions, which should be
considered an orthodox binary despite the critical significance of some of the projects. Instead of the search for a shared ideology called "fascism," we should think
of fascism as a set of characteristics of ideologies that otherwise might have very
little in common. Such an approach would provide a way out of what seems to be
a deadlock created by the endless, and to a great deal repetitive, debate around
historical versus generic definitions of fascism.

Most of the problems from the 1960s and 1970s have persisted in fascism
studies, and somehow the criticisms of the earlier approaches did not lead to an
end to the traditional search for a definition. For the last three decades, Roger Griffin's (1991) work has been widely quoted especially in works that avoid Marxist
analysis. Griffin claims to offer a solution for the problem of definitions, and he sit-
uates himself in a supposedly non-orthodox position, admitting that fascism could
take new shapes (Griffin 2018, 1). He offers what he calls a "palingenetic" account of

fascism based on a "definitional minimum" (Griffin 1991, 13, 50), but his work does not leave behind the reductionist/idealist approaches. Ultimately, Griffin offers yet another typical definition, and if anything, it is a narrow one. In his supposedly minimalist definition of fascism, revolutionism is included. Here is precisely where the anti-communist strategy surfaces in Griffin's work as well. Namely, it is the strategy of pairing communism and fascism as belonging to the "revolutionary" species. This strategy continues to provide scholars who tend to sound critical of conservatism but are nonetheless deeply revisionist and anti-Marxist with a convenient discursive avenue to come across, albeit falsely, as unorthodox, or at times even as critical, theorists.

Outside the scholarship that got into the propagandist and revisionist habit of pairing fascism with communism, Robert Paxton's work has been among the most influential. To Paxton, fascism is a "function," a recognizable and traceable political practice. Rejecting the common convention that assumes the existence of particular texts behind every (Western) political movement or phenomenon (Paxton 1998, 4–5), he maintains that "feelings propel fascism more than thought does" (1998, 16). Fascist movements adamantly impede prospects of both justice and freedom, which speaks to the anti-revolutionary feature at the heart of fascism. Also, fascists' grievance is that the bourgeoisie is not exploitive enough (Paxton 1998, 7). Despite the indisputability of these two points, i.e., the anti-revolutionary and anti-egalitarian features of fascism, not to mention the continual historical antagonism between fascists and communists across regions and countries, there have been overwhelming attempts to group fascism and communism together. It should go without saying that pairing fascism and communism has been one of the widely adopted strategies of the Cold War era, so the pairing itself does not say anything about fascism, but rather it uses fascism to target communism.

Other critical scholars have aimed to tackle the conventional underestimation of fascism and the prevailing conservative strategy that tends to dismiss the link between the capitalist political economy and fascism (e.g., Gandesha 2020b; Cox 2019, 2021; Ayers 2024). Alison J. Ayers quite rightly points to a new conservative strategy that has been utilized to obscure the problem of (neo)fascism in the age of neoliberalism (2024). Namely, Ayers maintains, populism has been deployed widely in reference to movements and regimes that in reality exemplify neoliberal fascism, such as Narendra Modi's Hindutva and Recep Tayyip Erdogan's neo-Ottomanism (2024, 414–415). Indeed, as both Enzo Traverso (2019) and Alison Ayers (2024) argue, populism obscures more than it could clarify, and by omitting the nuances entailed in the rise of the extreme right, it has also helped conflate the right with the left. The strategy of conflating the far right with the far left was commonplace during the Cold War era when the term "totalitarianism" was deployed precisely for that purpose.

While both the theory of totalitarianism, which dominated most of the scholarship in the 1950s and 1960s, and the theory of modernization, which was proposed by Turner as an alternative approach, have been frequently criticized for their shortcomings and invalidities, the Marxian accounts have been subjected to a far larger number of attacks in the decades following the end of WWII. By the 1990s, it was almost obligatory to at least go through the motion of denouncing the Marxist theory under various names and justifications. It is as if denouncing the Marxist theory suffices to prove the sophistication of the presented works. The works of Marxist anti-capitalist critics, from Lenin, Rosa Luxemburg, and Lukacs to Immanuel Wallerstein, Slavoj Žižek, and Etienne Balibar, including critical theorists such as Horkheimer and Adorno, remain indispensable. Indeed, that line of scholarship is essential for developing a critical theory of fascism as a viable alternative to the reductionist and orthodox theories that have been multiplying since the 1950s without making the breakthrough each attempt typically promises.

What may be recognizable in fascist doctrines are their relationships with the world. For instance, whether religious or secular, pan-European or pan-Slavic, Islamist or Hindutva, they are exclusionary, anti-egalitarian, retroactive, and semi-tribalist in terms of a sharp division between the perceived in-group versus out-group. There were substantial differences even between Italian Fascism and German Nazism in terms of their ideological worldviews, as has been explained repeatedly by historians. The rise of movements that have empowered Modi in India, Erdogan in Turkey, Viktor Orbán in Hungary, Trump in the United States, and Jair Bolsonaro in Brazil points to the presence of global conditions that have to do with the current phase of capitalism. Therefore, approaches that tend to ignore the political economy of fascism on both regional and global levels will only continue to distort the real threats of fascism and the fascist dimensions of the existing reality.

Chapter 3
A Critical Theory for Unmasking Fascism Everywhere

We have been witnessing a global rise of ultra-nationalism and fanaticism, rendering public awareness and critical analysis of fascism ever more relevant. Fascism, I argue, is an ideological form rather than an ideological system. I use *ideology form* to refer to overall characteristics that distinguish a class of ideologies from other classes of ideologies. The theory of *ideology form* is meant to enhance our capacity for recognizing, problematizing, and critically analyzing both existing and potential variations of fascism. Fascist movements in different sociohistorical and geopolitical circumstances vary in terms of their belief systems, strategies, and politics, so conventional comparative methods and approaches that deduce their criteria from a particular model have restricted the area of fascism studies. I argue for a trans-spatial and transhistorical concept with flexible theoretical applications. My central claim is that fascism denotes a class of ideologies that have a similar form, just as a concept such as egalitarianism, socialism, sexism, or sectarianism makes sense as a form of ideology rather than a particular ideology or philosophy.

Capitalism is a mode of the domination of production and the production of domination. The regime of cultural production is key to maintaining the relation of domination across various societal arenas, social institutions, and the biopolitical economy of space. The culture industry has been playing a significant role in the proliferation of social patterns of sameness. This sameness prepares the environment for right-wing populism and totalitarianism. Without such a totalitarian climate in society, fascism cannot become popular. This chapter concretizes a critical theory of fascism with analytic potentiality in various geographical contexts, whether in the West, Latin America, the MENA region, the Indian Subcontinent, or Far Asia. I reconceptualize fascism while constructing more useful analytic and critical means of diagnosing various aspects of fascist movements. What makes such a notion theoretically and instrumentally significant for the social sciences is its conceptual flexibility.

The point is that fascism has improved its means of camouflaging far more than anti-fascism has evolved its tools of diagnosis and resistance. The critical theory that is advanced here allows for examining movements, ideologies, and discourses and diagnosing fascism anywhere and anytime. As a project, this book and in particular this chapter aim to enable the public to diagnose fascism swiftly and effectively. Even in its most theoretical parts, such as this chapter, the book's main objective is to raise anti-fascist awareness and confront fascism with, by, and for the public.

https://doi.org/10.1515/9783111609041-003

1 Fascism as a Concept

Usually, political concepts such as democracy, socialism, sovereignty, etc. are not, nor should be, defined on the basis of their historical origins. To take the first example in the list, we do not define "democracy" exclusively on the basis of the model invented by ancient Athenians. Yet somehow "fascism" is commonly defined merely by the specifications of the first occurrences of fascism. For the most part, this has crippled critical debates and analytic applications of the concept. Just as we continue to reappropriate other political concepts, we should be able to enhance the conceptual boundaries of the term "fascism," without having to always justify its use in terms of the Italian and German models that emerged during the first half of the 20th century. There is good reason to recover the term as an analytical concept rather than treating it as something from the past.

By reconstructing the framework and reframing the conceptualization process, the theory of *ideology form* offers a way out of what has otherwise become a deadlock in fascism studies. To further clarify the theory's core idea and practical applications, let us start with examples other than fascism. Egalitarianism makes sense as a category of ideologies (and movements), namely, ideologies (and movements) that give social equality a central role in their signification system. The category would include ideologies that otherwise, e.g., in terms of philosophical sophistication, strategies, platforms, etc., may be vastly different if not incomparable. Feminism as a category of ideology denotes ideologies that put primary emphasis on the principle of gender equality, the negation of patriarchy, and thus the realization of women's emancipation. Some feminist ideologies differ extremely from other feminist ideologies, but the category remains valid because it merely signifies an ideological *form*, as opposed to philosophical development, historical compatibility, strategic validity, etc. Of course, a particular ideology could be classified under egalitarianism and feminism at the same time. Egalitarianism and feminism are just two examples of *ideology forms*.

Racism, as a third example, refers to all ideologies that perceive human society primarily from the perspective of "race." Similarly, the concept of "fascism" can and should be understood as a category for distinguishing ideologies that share a certain *form*. Many fascist ideologies may be categorized under racism as well, but not all racist ideologies are necessarily fascist. Once we establish the conceptual framework as an ideology *form*, we can move on to the conceptualization process to determine the *form* in terms of categorizable and reappearing traits of social movements. Precisely through developing conceptual means for recognizing the phenomenon we can comprehend how the term fascism can be used meaningfully. At the same time, the concept will enable us to diagnose a certain category of movements even if those movements emerge with extremely dissimilar slogans, belief systems, value schemes, and so on. That is to say, a movement could be called fascist simply on the basis of its orientation vis-à-vis society, the angle from which it perceives the reality and imagines the past and the future, regardless of the quality and the quantity of its epistemic distortions, violent actions, effective strategies, etc. Of course, each fascist movement could be further qualified, but for employing the word "fascism" or diagnosing a movement as fascist, grasping the ideological form in question suffices.

There are fascist ideologies and philosophies as opposed to a standard fascist ideology or philosophy. Let us suppose that we adopt this conceptual approach, but also suppose that we hastily decide that fascism as a category refers to the class of ideologies that have in common exclusionism, anti-egalitarianism, and intolerance for heterogeneity. Even with such a basic formula, we will be better equipped to diagnose fascist politics and movements wherever and whenever they emerge without having to deploy a conventional definition as a measuring device every time.

Ascribing a specific ideological content to fascism in order to define it as a term will inevitably amount to reductionism. To make the point clearer, it might help to consider the nature of the fallacy when committed in terms of other notions. Let us take "sexism" as an example. Sexism may be used to describe a general characteristic of certain ideologies, but it does not denote a particular ideology. We can speak of sexist ideologies, as opposed to *the* ideology of sexism. To assume that sexism is an ideology is to confuse the subject and the predicate. It would also be false to impose a birthdate or a birthplace on sexism simply because it is a *feature* shared by many ideologies and worldviews. Of course, fascism could refer to more than a mere ideological feature, and it could be claimed as an ideology, e.g., Italian Fascism. In this case, we could speak of both the ideological form (of fascism) and a specific ideological content determined in terms of historical and spatial particularities as well as political and societal objectives. In other cases, i.e., when fascism is not claimed as the name of a particular ideology, "fascism" does not denote a particular ideology or philosophy. Even in the case of Italy, it is misleading to analyze today's fascist movements as reoccurrences, duplications, and resurrections of Mussolini's Fascism. We capitalize the "f" when we use the word as a proper noun in reference to the brand Mussolini invented and named. In all other cases, i.e., when the signified is not the ideology of the movement that was founded by Mussolini, fascism is used as a term, and it can be conceptualized and reconceptualized like other terms. The monotheistic idea of god happened to also be called God, which is why we capitalize the first letter when the word is used as a proper noun. Otherwise, "god" is an indefinite noun that means "deity" but not any particular deity unless we use other words to qualify the word "god." To insist that there is only one deity, God, is to totalize the monotheistic (idea of) god, which is exactly what monotheists do, situating monotheism in a direct contradiction with philosophical logic.

Without necessarily adopting Plato's entire system of metaphysics and epistemology, it might be helpful to keep in mind the Platonic notion of "form" in order to make sense of the general noun that denotes a class of entities as opposed to a particular one. In this sense, "fascism" should be used as a categorical "form." Only when we specify the form, e.g., Japanese fascism, Aryan fascism, Iranian fascism, Christian fascism, or Islamic fascism, would we be speaking of a particular fascist ideology, of course, without implying that an identity, Japanese, Aryan, Iranian, Christian, or Islamic, is inherently fascist. Indeed, fascism is not unique to any particular region, nationalism, religion, or patriotism; rather, it (and, of course, resistance against it) could appear anywhere and among any particular population just as sexism or racism is not unique to certain ethnic, national, or religious groups. As Enzo Traverso asserts, "fascism has not only been transnational or transatlantic, but also transhistorical" (2019, 20). The realization itself is crucial but not enough; we need a theoretical conceptualization of fascism that reflects its transhistoricality and transgeographicality simultaneously. A definition that is not formulated around, and does not lend itself to, such a theoretical conception will necessarily fail to account for all cases of fascism even if it appears to accurately describe multiple variations.

As early as 1921, Antonio Gramsci (1978) emphasized that it is futile to try to explain fascism as a concrete ideological platform. For instance, he wrote, "Fascism has presented itself as the anti-party; has opened its gates to all applicants; has with its promise of impunity enabled a formless multitude to cover over the savage outpouring of passions, hatreds and desires with a varnish of vague and nebulous political ideals" (Gramsci 1978). Ironically, even though Gramsci deduced his conclusions from Mussolini's movement on the eve of the National Fascist Party's reign in Italy, and he did mean Fascism with a capital letter, his account captures what conceptually characterizes fascism better than most of the accounts that followed for decades, especially after WWII. Many of the later accounts insist on formulating their definitions considering the Fascist and Nazi programs and policies and Mussolini's and Hitler's personalities. In the same article, Gramsci warns against reductionist accounts as he also emphasizes the need for an approach that can best be described as a critical theory, broadly defined as a Marxian, materialist, multidisciplinary theory of society and social movements. Gramsci's work in general anticipates the Frankfurt School's Critical Theory that started to take shape in the 1930s in the works of a group of Marxists who were widely denounced politically and academically, at home and abroad.

Because fascist movements are discriminatory, chauvinistic, and exclusionary, we should not expect vast similarities between the contents of the ideologies of two fascist movements unless they have in common, say, the same racist agenda. Because "fascism" does not designate any universal set of philosophical principles, even what is universally agreed upon as a textbook case of fascism should be considered as a particular variation of fascism specific to particular sociohistorical circumstances and geopolitical contexts, keeping in mind that in a drastically different set of circumstances and contexts, the equivalent ideology would be drastically different. In other words, every fascism, including Mussolini's Fascism, is just a variation of fascism. Using one movement's ideology as a standard model does not help in conceptualizing fascism. Even within the same geography, e.g., Italy or Europe, just as racism has evolved its discursive means and strategies since WWII, we should not expect much resemblance between today's varied iterations of fascism and those from the 20th century. Most fascist movements are extremely pragmatic and adaptive, so focusing exclusively on historical definitions and origins does little to help in detecting fascism as a remerging or enduring phenomenon.

In fact, even the Nazis never identified themselves as fascists, and admittedly there were significant differences between Italian Fascism and German Nazism. Furthermore, if we were to apply the criteria of the definition provided by the inventors of the term, whereby totalitarianism is at the heart of fascism, Mussolini's Italy itself should not be called fascist because for many years it was not a totalitarian one-party state, which is something Hannah Arendt noted early in the debates surrounding totalitarianism and fascism (1979, 257). Therefore, molding our definition on the historical models would make the term useless as a concept. Theoretical flexibility, and, thus, potential plural instrumental uses, are essential for conceptuality. If the definition of fascism is restricted by a few historical references, it can only function as an ordinary word insofar as a word has a specific meaning and sense.

Because fascism is more of a modern tribalist impulse that manifests itself according to specificities of circumstances as opposed to a set of principles induced from a universal and philosophical worldview, it can best be understood as a form of modern exclusionary fanaticism, which can be secular or religious, and racist in the sense of biological or cultural racism. As mentioned earlier, Giovanni Gentile, the first self-identified philosophizer of "Fascism," makes the point that it does not denote a particular philosophy (2002, 21). Gentile also described the opportunistic and pragmatic nature of Fascism. As a matter of fact, it is the lack, not the presence, of principles that should be considered as one of the features that characterize fascist movements. However, in their attempts to define fascism as an ideology, scholars have continued to emphasize different criteria in various orders and combinations.

The field of fascism studies has been gravely limited by conventional methods that have led to the domination of reductionist accounts intermingled in repetitive scholastic cycles. Even though the conventional approaches may appear diverse, they adopt similar methods for defining fascism and diagnosing fascist movements. These methods amount to searching for and then deploying a particular set of criteria as a yardstick or what can be called a *fascismo-meter*. When these *fascismo-meters* are designed retroactively and Eurocentrically, often they prove to be dysfunctional in terms of their capacity to recognize vast variations of fascist movements. Therefore, I argue for moving toward critical conceptualization and away from traditional definitions. Normal definitions are for normal terms, and as such they could be relatively rigid, lacking theoretical grounding, dialectical viability, and critical potentiality. Concepts, on the other hand, are dialectically flexible because they are constructed through continual theorization. This flexibility also becomes evident and proves to be indispensable in the process of applying the concept in critical analyses of ideologies, discourses, events, and social and political phenomena.

The orthodox rigidity and historical reductionism have implications that reach arenas far beyond academia. What is at stake is not just elusive theoretical methods. The more serious problem is the political implications in terms of comprehending the threat of fascism in contemporary societies. Today, in multiple countries around the world, despite the variations in their influence and nature of democratic institutions, democratic principles are increasingly abolished through systematic violations of everything from laws to basic norms of the public sphere. Yet, we are less and less capable of being shocked by what happens. It is absurd that many of us are alarmed only when someone somewhere carries the swastika flag. It is not that a large number of people are indifferent about the rise of fascism; rather, the majority of people are falsely assured by public opinion makers, including some liberal politicians and educators, until it is too late for civil society to stop the fascist forces. Underestimating the threat of the rise of fascism is not merely the result of theoretical fallacies. Also, it is a fallacy to assume that theoretical fallacies are themselves not socially and politically produced. What we are facing is unconscious denialism within a broader ideological hegemony, which is in turn rooted in material interests and social relations of domination. Even without all the sound arguments that refute reductionist accounts of fascism, we should be able to recognize fascist movements and detect the rise of fascism. Of course, there are also anti-fascist movements, protests, and platforms in every society, but, with more critical education, anti-fascism could be more popular and more effective. The general public should be able to recognize the signs of fascism even in cases that carry little or no resemblance to previous models or current models elsewhere.

2 Fascism as *Ideology Form*

A critical theory of fascism necessitates a philosophical conceptualization of analysis. As a sociopolitical phenomenon with vague but potentially detectable features, fascism cannot be comprehended as a specific set of philosophical claims. A philosophy may be fascist, but there is not a universal philosophy of fascism. Like "totalitarianism," "fascism" does not denote a particular ideology or philosophy. Also, like "totalitarianism," "fascism" has commonly been reduced to something less than a useful theoretical concept precisely because most of the historians failed to break free from the discursive authority of state politicians. The definitional frame of totalitarianism was drawn mainly to mirror Soviet policies, thanks to Carl Friedrich and Zbigniew Brzezinski's book published in 1956, and to a lesser degree Hannah Arendt's classic published in 1951 (1979). Thus, "totalitarianism" was born dead. From the beginning, referential rigidity was built into the definition rendering it conceptually and analytically useless even though it has been serving effectively as an anti-communist propaganda tool. The similarity in the lives of these two terms is that they were deprived of conceptual flexibility from the outset.

Fascism is an orientation characteristic of ideologies that might have nothing in common other than their *form*. This is exactly why two fascist movements could fatally oppose each other in their politics. Indeed, it is more likely for fascist ideologies from different geographical contexts to contradict each other and fascist movements from different societies to be aggressively antagonistic toward each other, simply because each side desperately needs an enemy and qualifies to serve as an enemy simultaneously, for instance, Neo-Nazis versus fundamentalist Islamists, or Arianism versus Baathism. What makes the two opposing sides fascist is what they have in common in terms of the nature of their fanaticism, compulsivity, irrationality, intolerance, essentialism, and power-cultism, all of which are ideological characteristics as opposed to ideological specifications.

Therefore, critically examining the *form* of an ideology is sufficient to determine whether the ideology is fascist or not, regardless of the content of the ideology in terms of its particular similarities or dissimilarities, agreement or disagreement, with the doctrines of any other fascist ideology, including Italian Fascism and German Nazism. Of course, examining the ways in which the content operates can also be useful, but it should not be considered decisive in the diagnosis. For instance, whether the ideology demonizes the Other on the basis of perceived "race," faith, culture, nationality, or gender should be considered a specific qualification of a particular ideology rather than determining whether the ideology is fascist or not. By the same token, whether the essentialized Other in the ideology is Jew, Arab, Muslim, black, Catholic, Asian, white, Chinese, or some sort of combination such as native American women, Somali men, or Latin American immigrants, matters only insofar as we study the particularity of a specific case of fascism.

A typological discussion focused on the logic of classification and conceptualization is essential to make my distinction between an ideological form and an ideological system clear. I use "form" in the sense of the compositional frame of a category, i.e., the general configuration of entries (with corresponding entities). Each entry that is classified under a particular category/form should be more distinct as a sub-category, and, moving down, the divisions continue from the general to the specific. As the number of specifications increases, the ideological systems become more tangible.

A group of ideologies might be classified in terms of nationalism, but ultimately each nationalist ideology aims for a definitive content in terms of, say, the perceived identity of the "national self" or its other. Also, historically, each nationalist ideology could break into multiple, and conflicting, nationalist ideologies diverging from the original ideology in several ways and to various degrees. At the base level of the categorical divisions, the entries are necessarily different and distinct from each other. If A and B are identical, they should be signified through one signifier/entry. However, what makes a number of entries members of the same group of ideologies is what they have in common. Moving upward in the classification system should structurally correspond to a decrease in *content* commonalities and an increase in *form* commonalities.

The higher we look in the vertical classification system, the broader each "ism" is and thus the lower its rate of specifications. That is to say, the more we zoom out, the better our perception of the general frames at the expense of the detailed particularities. By the same token, the more we zoom in, the more tangible the identities, the signifiers, become. If we keep zooming in, we will enter a micro-level of resolution discovering that there are other endless units within each entity's unit and so on. Therefore, classification is meant to be a logical process of composition. The plausibility of any particular system of classification depends on its grasp of the actual compositions of the classified.

This proposition is conceptually straightforward and logically clear but essential to avoid orbiting in endless cycles of debates that are often doomed to endlessly bounce back and forth between semantics and observations, with the former often restricting the latter, thereby prolonging the lifespan of the dominant frame of reference. Often our political debates orbit within this kind of sphere, so awareness of the ways in which concepts are created philosophically is indispensable for both critical analysis and theoretical problematization. A term such as democracy, egalitarianism, or fascism should not be used as if it necessarily denoted one ideology. That would substantially restrict our theoretical abilities and analytic capacities and fatally limit progress in the relevant fields of inquiry. When we describe a system or an ideology as being democratic, we make a specific claim within a relatively general proposition. The system or ideology in question could, for instance, be a liberal democracy, a nationalist democracy, a socialist democracy, a direct democracy, etc.

The same goes for egalitarian/ism. Vastly different ideologies can be classified under egalitarianism, and it would be false to deduce that those ideologies are identical in terms of their contents. Their similarity is on the class level; it is a similarity of the general form. They all give substantial weight to "equality," each in a different way and to a different degree. A number of egalitarian ideologies could, at the same time, be classified under democratic ideologies, and vice versa. It is possible to designate or soundly argue for recognizing certain socialist ideologies also as democratic ideologies. There have been ideologies and systems described, whether rightly or wrongly, as socialist, but we cannot construct a universal scale of socialism based on socialist ideologies exclusively from a particular geography and history. Socialism continues to be conceptualized and reconceptualized within a large number of worldviews. No historical example of socialism can be seen as an authentic and definitive model.

Similarly, "fascism" can and should be conceived as a class name, a form of ideology, as opposed to a particular ideology or even a relatively small group of ideologies. Of course, the conceptualization concerns the size of the class. As in any other area of political philosophy, the concept-creation and theorization are strongly intertwined. There are many fascist ideologies, and there is an infinite number of other potential fascist ideologies, movements, forces, and systems that could emerge under other circumstances. Therefore, my theorization of fascism will include describing some specific ideological features, but they should be understood in terms of a description of the general ideological frame that contains fascist ideologies. That is to say, in addition to my arguments for *ideology form*, I will start by discussing what might distinguish fascism as an ideological form. The point then is not what fascist ideologies contain (that would be an impossible task), but what general features they have in common. What I aim to do here is to address the ideological manifestation of "fascism," not its origins or circumstances of growth, which would require adequate investigations in multiple fields. Methods that are based on the assumption that the origins of fascism and the reasons for its growth could be found in the so-called history of ideas could not be more misleading because they commit the typical idealist fallacy. Here, I am concerned with the ideological guises of fascism, which should not be conflated with the conditions that give rise to fascism.

3 Diagnosing Fascism

Fascism Signifies a Class of Ideologies

Insisting that an ideology is not fascist if it does not contain the same elements as those contained in Italian Fascism and German Nazism is at best analogous to a position that would recognize schist and gneiss as the standard metamorphic stones for deciding what stones could or could not be considered metamorphic. Some of the scholars who prefer a generic concept implicitly recognize fascism as a category, but more often than not, their conception of the category is too rigidly determined. The equivalent of that in the geological classification of stones would be something along the following lines. Even though marble and quartzite share certain characteristics with both schist and gneiss, they would not be considered metamorphic stones because of their other features. More to the point, what geologists have classified as metamorphosed limestones and metamorphosed sandstones would falsely be excluded from the class of metamorphosed stones.

In any society and at any point in time, a new fascist movement could come up with an entirely new essentialist category to draw the line between the in-groups and out-groups. If fascism studies cannot be useful in aiding us with analytic tools of diagnosis to enable us to recognize new fascist movements, something must be missing in fascism studies. It is time for the field to dispose of the *fascismo-meters* for good and, instead, allow for more critical theoretical analysis and conceptual creativity. This is especially crucial given the dangerous nature of fascist movements. Using Italian Fascism or German Nazism as the ultimate *fascismo-meter* or some sort of authenticity test kit will continue to undermine the usefulness of fascism studies. In addition to the theoretical deficiency, the social and political consequences are inestimable, especially at the current historical moment when exclusionary movements are on the rise in various parts of the world, and we are in desperate need of building international anti-fascist awareness.

To argue that fascism is an *ideology form*, as I suggest, should not be read as denying the existence of fascist philosophies, ideologies, and worldviews. To the contrary, a fascist movement has fanatic ideologues and dogmatic followers of a specific set of ideological beliefs and ideals. What my theoretical intervention refutes is the common perception of fascism as one specific ideology. I suggest reconsidering fascism within a system of classification and with a clearer comprehension of the kind of logic the classification of ideologies requires.

The concept of "fascism" should be placed in the first layer, that is the broadest level, of the classification system, on the same level as, for instance, democracy, egalitarianism, cosmopolitanism, socialism, feminism, and sexism. Initially, what distinguishes the ideological category called fascism is that it is necessarily non-cosmopolitan, exclusionary, essentializing/homogenizing, and anti-communist. Fascist movements can differ drastically in terms of their ideological orientations, but they have in common the above-mentioned traits. That is also to say, detecting that set of signs, i.e., non-cosmopolitanism, exclusionism, essentialism, and anti-communism, in any movement or ideology is enough reason to suspect it as a potential fascist movement or ideology.

Fascist ideologies are exclusionary but on different nationalist, racist, cultural-ist, and/or religious bases, which necessitates further break-down of the main category of fascism into smaller and smaller sub-groups. The more universal symptoms are linked to antagonistic tendencies toward ideological forms and movements that embody, adopt, or advocate egalitarian and inclusive universalism. Fascists in all historical and geographical circumstances tend to be patriarchal, anti-feminist, and anti-socialist. Some fascist movements may adapt their discourses and social façades to appear as not so antagonistic against feminism and/or socialism. They might even claim feminism and/or socialism. However, their essentialism and intolerance of egalitarian and inclusive universalism will always come across, thereby betraying their deep adherence to social inequality and their intolerance of the idea of a world without oppression, domination, and exploitation. A fascist force cannot claim to be socialist and internationalist, feminist and internationalist, or egalitarian and internationalist at the same time. Instead, when and if it claims an egalitarian perspective, e.g., feminism and socialism, it does so within the framework of the in-group, e.g., the nation. Needless to say, even if we take an expression such as "national socialism" at face value, it is a contradiction in terms, from a Marxian point of view.

Because Marxist communism is the historical movement that so profoundly and inclusively encompasses all the dimensions of social equality, every fascist ideology and movement is fundamentally anti-Marxist. This is to say, fascism's unmistakable anti-Marxist trait has to do with the irreducibility of the Marxist formula as a worldview and a revolutionary philosophy that is simultaneously feminist, socialist, and internationalist, embodying a form of egalitarian and inclusive universalism that captures and negates social inequality in all its complex and multidimensional constructs. Marxism is essentially socialist, internationalist, and universally anti-racist and anti-sexist at the same time. Even historically, fascism emerged as an anti-Marxist force with the clear objective of destroying the communist movement (Ali 2022, chap. 7). This is something Mussolini and Hitler strongly believed. As Tariq Ali (2022) explains, Churchill admired Mussolini and Hitler until 1937 precisely because of their anti-communist mission. Churchill and other Western leaders continued their support for fascist forces such as the Falangist regime in Spain and the Kemalist regime in Turkey as part of their anti-communist strategy.

The Fascist Double Bifurcation

The fascist depiction of the collective self and its Other could not be more con-tradictory. The collective self, the nation or the racial or religious community, is imagined as an extremely fragile being on the verge of the ultimate destruction at the hands of outside enemies and their collaborators, those among "us" who betray the nation, the community of faith, etc., the unpatriotic, the unfaithful, the immoral, etc. At the same time, however, there is always another depiction of the nation, the community, etc. as an indestructible leviathan with some sort of divine mission endowed with a super-historical or supernatural power to surpass all chal-lenges. The nation, therefore, is assumed to be so great even God put all his trust in it to carry out the divine mission on earth, but somehow it is also so pure and fragile that it could be ruined irreversibly even by a few miserable immigrants, leftist educators, or decadent writers and artists. Parallel to this bifurcation of the self-identity, there is another bifurcation pertaining to the fascist self's Other who is also assumed to be both powerful enough to represent an existential threat to "us" and so powerless that it could be no match for "us" in an open conflict of forces. In their study of the anti-Semite discourse in the United States of the 1940s, Löwenthal and Guterman note this "fantastic fusion of ruthlessness and helplessness" (2021, 69). This contradiction, however, is not arbitrary; rather, it is precisely the "power-lessness" of the marginalized that proves to be an irresistible object of hatred and enmity, as Horkheimer and Adorno also noted (2002, 138).

At the same time, to the fascist, there is nothing more appealing than sheer power. Whether mystified or vulgarly exhibited, power is the ultimate magical ingredient in every fascist recipe anywhere. The appeal of the father figure is rooted in this, and by politically empowering him, fascist followers fulfill their desire to exercise absolute power, to eliminate all that is powerless, including the marginalized groups whose presence provokes the suppressed, unconscious, indi-vidual self-image as hopelessly weak. The fascist is, therefore, exemplary of the narcissist-masochist character whose self-love and self-hate form a bipolar per-sonality pathologically addicted to denialist and suppressive patterns of behavior. The follower finds unique enjoyment in unconditional submission to the leader who provides a sense of moral certainty through the promise of absolute power. The leader intuitively understands the follower's painful narcissistic-masochistic chasm, so he symbolizes both the protective father toward his (the nation's) chil-dren and the unforgiving force against the intruding Other. The leader is a "great little man" (Löwenthal and Guterman 2021, 134, 149; Adorno 2001, 142; 2004, 226), someone who is perceived as one of the "people," a true son of the nation, and a father figure endowed with unique abilities to stand for the nation with utmost honesty and selflessness against both inside and outside threats. Whenever "the nation" gains more discursive significance than the state and the leader acts as if s/he has a national or divine mandate to claim authority over the state institutions, there is reason to search for other signs of fascism.

Anti-Semitism is one of the most common aspects of fascist movements, but even this denotes the form of the ideologies in question more than it indicates a similarity of definitive ideological contents. Anti-Semitism is common among fascist movements from different parts of the world due to the fact that historically Jews have been a minority in so many different parts of the world. It is hard to think of any other demarcation of a group of people who, as a result, have been subjected to discrimination so universally and for so long. It is only expected that most fascist movements, given that they are exclusionary, would be obsessed with anti-Semitism. The presupposed otherness of Jews has rendered perceived Jews a convenient candidate as the imagined enemy. Historically, anti-Semitic demonizing myths have accumulated leading to the creation of a terrific ready-at-hand candidate for the role of the Other. Another way to put it is that because fascist movements are desperate for the image of an enemy, anti-Semitism only intensifies in the age of fascism.

The perceived Jew is accused of being whatever the fascist in-groups imagine themselves not to be. For many fascists, Marxism is nothing but a creation of World Jewry to destroy capitalism. To isolationist fascists, Jews are the secret manipulators of both capital and global capitalism. If the fascist group is theistic, Jews may be depicted as the ultimate enemies of God. No wonder, Islamist fundamentalists and white supremacist groups, despite their enmity, could come together when it comes to anti-Semitism. A clear case of such an alliance can be seen in the *Journal of Historical Revisionism*, which published hundreds of anti-Semitic articles throughout its twenty-two years of life, 1980–2002. That said, it has become increasingly more common for white supremacist groups to distance themselves from anti-Semitism and, instead, draw their metaphysical dividing line between Judeo-Christianity and Islam, in order to essentialize perceived Muslims. In a similar manner Islamists assume absolute political despotism on the basis of metaphysical absolutism merged with racist and nationalist exclusionism.

While anti-Semitism is one of the most common symptoms of fascism, an ideology could be fascist without necessarily professing anti-Semitism. To reiterate, because Jews have been discriminated against across many regions and ages, it is not surprising that fascist groups reproduce and intensify the existing prejudices against perceived Jews systematically. The same is true in terms of patriarchism and fascism. Almost all societies have been patriarchal and sexist in the last five thousand years, so exclusionary movements tend to push their patriarchalism and sexism even further. Thus, while both anti-Semitism and sexism remain common among many old and new fascist groups, it is possible for fascist groups to condemn anti-Semitism and/or gender inequality, albeit superficially. In fact, there are white supremacist fascist groups who seem to have realized that toning down their anti-Semitism might serve the group well in terms of popularity and mass mobilization against the post-9/11 (imagined) enemy Muslim. While the intensity and criminality of anti-Semitism in Europe cannot be compared with anti-Muslim tendencies in today's Europe or the United States, the irrationality of the exclusionary mentality that has surfaced lately does carry some resemblance with the anti-Semitic discursive strategies (Ahmed 2021a, 2021b).

The Great Little Leader

Essentially, fascism is an obsession with the cult of power, which can be embodied, for instance, as the striving for the extensive exercise of power against the Othered. Often the leader is a "great little man" (Adorno 2001, 142; 2004, 226; Löwenthal and Guterman 2021, 134, 149), who functions as both the fetishized locus of authority and someone who (supposedly) understands and speaks the language of the common people. He is perceived as one of the "people," a true son of the nation, and a father figure endowed with unique abilities to protect the nation against both inside and outside threats. Whenever "the nation" gains more discursive significance than the state and the leader acts as if s/he had a national or divine mandate to claim authority over the state institutions, we should search for other signs of fascism and evoke a public debate about the issue.

Whoever plays the role of the "great little man" character will also have to fulfill the psychological needs of the followers. In this sense, the movement creates its own leader, even though each leader would of course have his/her own style of, say, bullying, vulgar exhibition of power, and staged authenticity. We could come up with lists of characteristics and behaviors of fascist leaders by analyzing the personalities of past fascist leaders, but ultimately it is essential to keep in mind that the Führer principle has a particular function in the fascist dynamics. Drastic differences with past examples of the Duce or the Führer should not deceive us in terms of diagnosing fascism. Also, a woman or a gay man within the movement could become the "great little" leader, and in fact, we have already been witnessing instances of such cases (e.g., Marine Le Pen's rise as a leading figure in France, and Ben Shapiro's potential rise to a position of political leadership in the far-right movements in the United States). Of course, all these movements tend to be extremely misogynistic and homophobic, but they can also be pragmatic enough to go through some deceptive and superficial liberal motions if that makes them more popular in a certain place and time. Having a (perceived) minority member in the position of leadership is an effective strategy to sustain the status quo, a change in order not to change.

The leader's role, almost like a job description, is quite literally determined by the movement itself in accordance with its anxieties and fears in that particular sociopolitical circumstance. Another disturbing part of fascist dynamics is that the democratic candidacy and selection processes function as a quest, a test, or a filtering device, so to speak, to determine who could best fulfill that role (in both the dramatic and the psychological senses of the word). In other words, the movement creates its leader democratically. If the leader is empowered as the country's leader, then his/her leadership will take the final step to undermine the very democratic means that brought him/her to power as s/he will translate the movement's totalitarian wishes into action whether through issuing executive orders, inciting insurrections, plotting an outright *coup d'état*, or triggering a counter-revolution to highjack the society at a moment of crisis. However, any such sudden development is a sign of a well-developed fascist movement.

The Fascist Power Complex

Usually, every fascist takeover is preceded by a long and gradual evolution in terms of the popularity of exclusionary discourses and groups that have been permitted through passive enablers, many of whom might even identify as liberals. The problem is that these petit bourgeois and bourgeois enablers are not alarmed by fascism precisely because they do not perceive the magnitude of exclusionary physical and symbolic violence that takes place every day. The real habitat of fascism's growth is not the would-be leader's head, as so many Hitler biographers try to have us believe. In fact, reducing fascism to the personality of a leader is one of the worst methods of reductionism. The real habitat for the growth of fascism is the normal social environment, under capitalism. There is arguably nothing more central to the ideological means of capitalism than depoliticizing and normalizing class violence, rendering it appear as nothing or anything else but class violence. Discursive strategies that reduce fascist violence to a problem of an evil genius (e.g., a bad leader), morality (e.g., bigotry), corruption (e.g., bad apples), or innocent ignorance about cultural differences are common strategies for masking class violence in order to deny it, often unconsciously. Fascist enablers are habitual denialists, and the reason behind denialism is not so mysterious when we take into account class relations and class politics.

The normalization of the exercise of power against the marginalized, the excluded, the silenced, and the Othered is at the heart of fascist dynamics. Capitalist relations of production tend to turn people into automated and alienated individuals, especially in the absence of a cosmopolitan project of resistance to negate the prevalent order as the best possible world. The fastest path for this alienated and disempowered individual to gain a sense of self-worth is one and the same as the mechanism that would enable him/her to assume a persona formed around sheer power precisely in order to deny the deep sense of fear, weakness, and insecurity. As Adorno puts it, the Nazi world "fulfilled the collective fantasies of power harbored by those people who, individually, had no power and who indeed could feel any self-worth at all only by virtue of such collective power." Adorno insists that "no analysis, however illuminating, can afterward remove the reality of this fulfillment or the instinctual energies invested in it." Then, he adds, "even Hitler's *va banque* gamble was not as irrational as it seemed to average liberal thought at the time or as its failure seems to historical hindsight today" (2005a, 95).[9]

The very powerlessness and hopelessness when suppressed will end up making the subject hate the powerless and hopeless Other precisely because the subject senses in that Other him/her own defeated and suppressed self. The fascist hatred directed against the minoritized, the immigrant, and other disempowered groups is rooted in this politicized sadomasochism. If revulsion of the powerless is one side of the coin in fascist psychology, idolization of the powerful is the other side. The fascist fetishizes the vulgar exhibition of power, e.g., a leader who acts like a bully, and the apparatuses of pure violence, e.g., armed forces.

Fascism is centered on the exclusionary dichotomy of in-group versus out-group whereby the popularized collective self-image intensifies xenophobic and narcissistic peculiarities. For instance, an already marginalized minority would be depicted as the fatal threat to "the nation" while at the same time "the nation" is supposed to be the greatest nation on earth. The in-groups would be told that "the nation" is the most powerful nation that ever existed, yet groups of desperate refugees would be depicted as invaders who, if not stopped, will destroy "the nation" and its "way of life." In another fascist movement, massacring the men and enslaving the girls and women of a religious minority are considered not only permittable but also moral. The latest instance of this was the genocide of the Yezidis at the hands of ISIS. There are patterns in the stories told by surviving Yezidi women about certain behaviors of their torturers and rapists, and those patterns are indicative of the role and ramifications of ISIS's ideology. Reoccurring behaviors by the jihadis suggest that they experienced a momentary sense of guilt prior to or after raping their victims, but they would cite religious decrees that permit raping the captured women of the "infidels," a term used in reference to groups that practice non-Ibrahimic religions.

---

9 Adorno closes section 34 of his *Minima Moralia* (2005b) by stating, "the almost insoluble task is to let neither the power of others, nor our own powerlessness, stupefy us."

What becomes apparent in these behavioral patterns is that perpetrators immediately resort to ideological resources to gain approval of acts that otherwise might be impossible for them to commit. This is indicative of the role of the ideology in normalizing what otherwise most human beings would find repulsive.

Mob violence is more easily born and justified by the members of the mob, and this is sufficiently explained by both Gustave Le Bon and Sigmond Freud. A fascist ideology's role is far more essential before the mob is physically formed, i.e., for and during the mobilization process. It is also an essential symbolic capital for the follower to resort to when he or she is about to commit violence in a setting where the crowd is not present physically to lend him or her the overwhelming moral support that may numb his/her sense of empathy for the victim. It is in such isolated settings where some sense of autonomous judgment, thinking for oneself, as Kant would say, might creep back into the subject's world. Precisely because of this, a full-fledged ideological system with catchy phrases, easily quotable assurances, sharp and visible distinctions between the in-group versus the out-group, and absolutist moral decrees is indispensable in any fascist movement anywhere.

Fascism and Anti-proletarian Propaganda

Ishay Landa's *Fascism and the Masses* (2018) convincingly argues against the common depiction of fascism as a "mass" movement. Landa explains how commonly, and falsely, historical fascism has been associated with the masses in most of the literature. His book is a valuable project that critiques the convention of blaming the underprivileged for the rise of extremist and violent movements including fascism. The masses, "the rabble," "the herd," were often openly looked down upon by the Enlightenment philosophers in Europe, including liberal philosophers such as Kant and Mill, let alone others such as Nietzsche and Herder. In fact, Marx and Engels, and those who later followed their lead, are the only 19th-century European philosophers who adamantly and universally reject that pejorative bourgeois and aristocratic use of the term "the masses." Marx reversed the use of "the masses" from a derogatory expression to what signifies a revolutionary subject capable of leading human society to its ultimate historical emancipation. Of course, here I am speaking about Marx's "proletariat," but due to Marx's influence, communist discourses across the world adopted a very progressive use of "the masses."

"Mass politics" first emerged in Europe in the early 19th century (for more on this, see for instance Hobsbawm 1996), and it was broadly speaking progressive because it was influenced by the French Revolution and the Enlightenment. More importantly, "mass politics" was the kind of politics that insisted on the democratization of state and public affairs. Therefore, the privileged groups and classes, to which most writers and philosophers belonged, delegitimized "mass politics." Authors played a crucial role in these campaigns simply because they were among the public opinion makers in the age of print and later technologies of mass communication. Of course, the bourgeois thinkers who advanced the Enlightenment project played a key progressive role in evoking democratic "mass politics," but the bourgeoisie as a social class quickly tried to solidify its own hegemony, so its political progressiveness steeply declined when the old aristocratic, monarchic, and theocratic hegemony started to fade away. Just as it is not surprising that "mass politics" came under hostile attacks from the outset, it is also not surprising that it took a modern communist project to defend the masses and their potential cosmopolitan emancipatory role.

While the Frankfurt School emigres did use "the mass" in an unfavorable sense, I think we should note that, unlike partisan Marxists, they did not use the term in reference to the disempowered, oppressed, and exploited majority under capitalism. Adorno, who is the most criticized Frankfurter for his (supposed) elitism, was concerned about the confusion the use of the term "mass" in "mass culture" might cause, so he decided to use "culture industry" (Löwenthal 1989, 49–50), which does not have any anti-egalitarian or anti-democratic connotations. Indeed, the culture industry is managed from above and does entirely fall within the capitalist modes of production. It is shaped around the principle of exchange, unlimited accumulation of capital, commodity fetishism, and so on. Moreover, the culture industry does feed into fascism through interwoven processes of standardization of perception, repetition of totalizing patterns of sameness, commodification of identity (as individuality, uniqueness, or difference), and fetishization of (national) oneness.

I would argue that even Arendt did not mean to use "mass" in reference to the working class even though Landa is completely justified to point to her ungrounded defense of Nietzsche and others. Arendt was not enthusiastic about the communist universal doctrine of standing with the working-class masses, and it is, perhaps, understandable why she would adopt the old language that is inherently biased against the marginalized majority. Nonetheless, Arendt's account of the term warrants a defensive argument on her behalf.

Arendt's use of "the mass" is not only not interchangeable with the working class but in fact stands in contrast to it. "The mass" is formed through *de-classing* people (Arendt 1979, 261). That is to say, the "mass politics," for Arendt, is premised on the depoliticization of class; the worker is not mobilized as a member of the working class; the totalitarian mobilization entails the liquidation of class and its replacement with "the mass" (Arendt 1979, 311–323, also see, 323–324). Class is an objective social identity founded on actual material conditions and, hence, the objective interests of people, whereas followers of a totalitarian movement are composed of alienated and automatized individuals mobilized against the universal interests of the working class.

Fascism is Counter-revolutionary

Fascists viciously oppose universalist politics of egalitarianism even though, socially, large numbers of them may come from the working class. Fascists may be, and often are, against capitalist modernism and bourgeois liberalism, but they are nonetheless modern creatures of capitalism fanatically mobilized against every actual and potential cosmopolitan project of egalitarianism. They may follow ideological systems based on racist, culturalist, nationalist, patriotic, and/or religious foundations; they may be pan-European or anti-EU, Americanist or anti-Americanist, Orientalists or anti-Orientalists, imperialist or anti-imperialist, pan-Arab or anti-Arab, Russophile or Russophobe, monotheist or secular, Hindu or anti-Hindu, Buddhist or anti-Buddhist, etc.; they may be climate change deniers or ecologists, misogynistic or gender-pluralists, consumerists or minimalists, hedonists or stoics, soldiers or poets, athletes or philosophers. In all cases, historically and sociologically they are outcomes of capitalist social relations.

Fascists might and often do call themselves revolutionaries, but if for nothing else than for the sake of anti-fascist revolutionaries, we should not attribute the revolutionary quality to any fascist movement. Fascist movements are counter-revolutionary in every sense. Primarily, as Žižek noted in his reading of Benjamin, it is precisely the failure of revolution that gives rise to fascism (Žižek 2008, 386). This was true of both the secular and non-secular first generation of fascist movements in the first half of the 20th century, such as Italy's Fascism, Germany's Nazism, and Spain's Falangism. In most cases, whether in Europe or elsewhere, only when the communist movements weakened, did fascist movements rise to power and manage to maintain their hegemony. As Traverso, among others, notes, anti-communism is one of the most common features of old fascism. To make his point, Traverso refers to Mussolini's own statement that fascism is a "revolution against revolution" (see Traverso 2019, 12). Even a right-wing scholar such as Ernst Nolte, who notoriously blames Bolshevik violence for the rise of Nazism and Asianic cultures for Bolshevik violence, admits that fascism is "counterrevolutionary" (Nolte 1965, 31, 39, 45, 62). Nolte is also right in his observation that fascism is "bourgeois and populist, modern and antimodern" at the same time (Nolte 1979, 394). Fascist ideologues mobilize sections of the working class for anti-proletarian purposes and utilize modernism for anti-progressive purposes. By the same token, they may adopt revolutionary tactics for entirely anti-emancipatory objectives in order to totalize social and political domination (while communism, by definition, is a revolutionary doctrine to end social and political domination). Therefore, the revisionist accounts that attribute a revolutionary characteristic to fascism could not be more misleading just as their pairing of fascism with communism could not be more contradictory.

Chapter 4
Fascism in the United States

American fascism has been growing at the heart of liberalism and become an effective and reproducible formula due to its adoptability and adaptability. From the beginning, American fascism did not have to constrain itself by pre-historic mythology. At the same time, it was founded on such a sophisticated biopolitical regime of racist classification and segregation, it had a substantial influence on establishing the Nazi legal regime of race. Unlike Germany and Europe in general, the US has never undergone the equivalent of de-Nazification aimed at uprooting fascism. To make things worse, communism, as the major anti-fascist movement, has always been exceptionally weak in the US. All this and American global hegemony, especially after the fall of the Eastern Bloc, have resulted in the rise and rise again of American fascism, with little challenge or problematization in the academy or among the intelligentsia at large. This, in turn, has kept the future open for the likely ultimate destruction of what is left of American democracy at the hands of a broad fascist alliance that has empowered one of its representatives, Trump.

The strength of American democracy lies more in the constitution and meticulous distribution of power across a wide but organically linked net of state institutions, which in turn benefited countless movements, including leftist and anti-racist ones whose advocates could have been subject to even more violence in the absence of the constitutionalized and institutionalized rights. That is also to say, for the most part, democracy in the United States is rooted in the political society, as opposed to civil society, to use the old liberal phraseology. This, of course, has its unique advantages for (1) the effective functioning of democratic institutions of administration on all levels of governance, and (2) the potential continual enhancement of democratic practices. One could argue that this is precisely what has made the American democracy both robust and capable of progressing at a substantial speed, in comparison to other Western democracies.

However, the downside of this is that if the state's democratic structure were to come under threat, there is no guarantee that civil society would have the will or even the capacity to prevent the fall of that structure. The fact that Donald Trump, who as president openly encouraged attacks on state institutions at several levels, continues to enjoy substantial support as of 2024 confirms the assumption that American civil society is prone to fascism. It seems that about half of American voters were not disturbed enough by the president's explicit disrespect for laws, public institutions, democratic practices including elections, and all the social contracts on which the state is founded including the Constitution. Add to those his sexist behavior, disrespect for scientific authority, banal denialism of basic logical

https://doi.org/10.1515/9783111609041-004

propositions, autocratic expectation for total loyalty, bullying personality, and a lengthy list of practices that suggest habitual corruption. Whether one wants to call Trump a fascist or not, the fact that Trump has substantial support among American voters suggests that the rise of a fascist leader is probable in the sense that the civil society is not democratic enough to prevent a fascist takeover of the state.

1 Trumpism and Fascism

While more American scholars and intellectuals have become alarmed by the rise of fascism since 2016 (e.g., Burley 2017; Stanley 2018; Churchwell 2020; Cox 2021), fascism had been present in and around American politics since the 1920s, and the conditions that allowed for its emergence and growth have much deeper historical, political, and ideological roots in the United States. To be clear, here I am not referring to organizations that tried to copy Italian Fascism or German Nazism, such as the Silver League of America (1934–1941). That is not to say that the threat such organizations represented was negligible, but there was and continues to be a much stronger spectrum of fascist movements in the United States that never identified themselves as fascist, just like most fascist movements elsewhere. H. Arthur Steiner (1905–1991), a professor of international relations and an officer in the Marines, in an article published in October 1935, in *The American Political Science Review*, admits that "our problem here is not to analyze the possibility of the introduction into this country of a foreign brand of Fascism. More immediately, the 'danger' is of an indigenous American reactionary movement, disguised behind the facade of democratic ideology" (Steiner 1935, 821).

In terms of the material conditions that are brought about by capitalism (Polanyi 2001; Horkheimer 2005; Eagleton 1976; Köves 1997; Gandesha 2020b; Cox 2019, 2021), including earlier capitalist forms of mass enslavement of people, it is hardly surprising that American fascism emerged as early as, if not prior to, European fascisms. As Sarah Churchwell, among others, argues, fascism has a long and uninterrupted history in the United States (2018). Let us bear in mind that the Ku Klux Klan (KKK) was founded in 1865, following the American Civil War, and as Paxton argues it was a foreshadow of fascism (2004, 49). In 1919, racist, anti-black, anti-Catholic, anti-Jew, anti-Chinese, anti-immigrant, and anti-socialist groups were on the rise, while the government was going after anti-war activists and socialist leaders such as Eugene Debs. Debs was imprisoned when the KKK was preparing a comeback. In its second wave, in the mid-1920s, at a time when the total population of the United States, including all age groups and racialized demographics was less than 115 million, the organization's membership might have reached five million according to some estimations (MacLean 1995, 10, 197; Pegram 2011, 3; Churchwell 2020), and going by the Klan's own account, there were six million Klansmen (Hernández 2019, 6). Somewhere around a quarter to a third of American protestant men joined the Klan (Churchwell 2020; also see Madison 2020, 4). The Republican Party was on friendly terms with the Klan with many Republicans being proud Klansmen. Today, in 2024, the Republican Party itself has become the camp that brings together hundreds of right-wing groups who are united in their support for Donald Trump.

The United States stands out globally for its continual intermingling of class oppression and racialization. Ideologically too, the American system of racialization has continued its production and reproduction of a climate that is fitting for the emergence and reemergence of fascism. Racialization has been deeply entrenched in the United States and, as Martinot shows, only its institutional expressions have changed, multiple times, in response to the economic and social circumstances (2008; also see Ngai 1999; Whitman 2017; Churchwell 2020). The rise of Trumpism could be interpreted as the latest chapter in the evolution of fascism from its early militaristic and imperialist stages to its current neoliberal and libertarian phase. It is grossly misleading to assume that American fascism is peculiar to the rhetoric, politics, and policies advanced by Trump and his "people," as he likes to refer to his close collaborators. To the contrary, Trump and Trumpism merely represent the embodiment of fascism at this particular historical moment. With or without Trump, fascism will continue to threaten not only marginalized groups and classes but the institutions of the state as well. Neoliberalism has given American fascism a historic boost precisely by "marketizing" the state, as Samir Gandesha strongly argues (2020a, 121; also see Köves 2004). As Gandesha contends, most of the studies on Trump and authoritarianism were unable "to connect up their analyses with the larger problem of the specifically 'damaged life' of neoliberal society" because "they focus rather too much on Trump himself—and figures like him—while overlooking the socioeconomic conditions that make such figures so attractive to a significant proportion of the electorate" (2020a, 121).

In his *Screens of Power* (2021; originally published in 1991), Timothy Luke detected the GOP's political orientation moving crucially toward the far right and anticipated a continuation of this slide rightwards under the influence of the neo-conservatives. In the articles included in his *The Travails of Trumpification* (2022), Luke tackles a form of right-wing politics he had indeed anticipated in 1991. He sees much of what happened during Trump's 2016–2020 presidency as "Trumpification" of the state institutions, policies, and politics on many levels. Judging by the general trajectory Luke had identified, what is coming will be even worse. The velocity of *fascist politics* is increasing, and it seems the tilting to the right has reached the point of freefall. While Luke does not address the question of fascism per se, his diagnoses of the rise of right-wing politics in the United States reinforces the argument about the rise of American fascism.

To Luke, the events that took place during the Trump's first administration and the social strata behind the new rise of right-wing extremism "indicate actually how limited the fascist frame of analysis from Nazi Germany is for interpreting the United States today" (2022, 148). This critique is sound when, as it is implied in the proposition, the frame of analysis is obstructed by rigid historical comparisons, but the application of the concept of "fascism" is, I think, more than useful if it is done within a frame of critical theorization that is not based on reductive standards, e.g., those based on traditional-historical definitions or mechanical-comparative methods so common in the area of fascism studies (e.g., Del Boca and Giovana 1970; Gregor 1974, 2006; Allardyce 1979; Griffin 1991; Kallis 2003; Stanley 2018). A conceptual frame of analysis is not feasible if we constrain our understanding of fascism by the positivistic definitions, whether historical or generic. Such methods are limiting precisely because they are limited, i.e., insufficiently conceptualized. After all, a statement similar to Luke's could be made with regard to the limits of a liberalist frame to analyze both the Weimer Republic and the United States without having to imply that only one of the two can be considered a liberal state. By the same token, if an argument is made about fascism in the United States, it should not be based merely on comparisons with the fascist models of interwar Europe.

2 Revisiting *Prophets of Deceit*

As early as 1949 Leo Löwenthal and Norbert Guterman showed that fascist agitators do not abide by any specific ideological system, arguing that American fascism in particular is broad (2021). Bear in mind that the Nazis borrowed a great deal from the American racial regime of legitimation and legislation, which together made the American racist order the most sophisticated in the world. Hitler and others among the most extreme Nazi leaders were thrilled to reproduce a race-based regime, of course, with adjustments that fit the Third Reich's German-Aryan-ism (see Whitman 2017). Furthermore, James Whitman notes, "when Nazis rejected the American example, it was sometimes because they thought that American practices were overly harsh: for Nazis of the early 1930s, even radical ones, American race law sometimes looked too racist" (2017, 5).

American fascism has a unique elastic nature, unlike Nazism or old Italian Fascism. Löwenthal and Guterman figured that the American fascist "has no pre-liberalistic tradition on which to fall back; he does not find it expedient to pose as a socialist, and he dares not explicitly repudiate established morality and democratic values," adding, "he only indirectly and implicitly assumes the mantle of charismatic leadership. He works, by necessity rather than choice, within the framework of liberalism" (2021, 153). While Nazism and Italian Fascism contained mythical assumptions about mythical terms (e.g., race and nationhood), rendering European fascism of the interwar period semi-religious and as such difficult to reproduce elsewhere, American fascism has always been more pragmatic in terms of reappropriation and reproduction.

Löwenthal and Guterman realized that even in terms of rhetoric, American right-wing agitators came up with a fascist formula that is far more transmittable than the Nazi version (2021, 154). For instance, "the mythical notion of the pure-blooded Nordic Aryan German superman would have to undergo many profound changes before becoming an effective appeal in this country [the United States], but the agitator's Simple Americans could be used in other countries as Simple Germans, or Simple French, or Simple Britishers, and so on" (2021, 154). The American fascist discourse is a "standardized and simplified version" of the Nazi discourse offering a much wider scope in terms of its appeal to general and vague popular feelings regardless of the nature of political circumstances and nationalist mythology (2021, 154). However, Löwenthal and Guterman should have also considered the fact that the American established norm had already been racist segregation and violent racialization for a long time, so racist ideologues in the academy and racist demagogues in the opinion-making industry, including radio show hosts, worked (and continue to work) in an environment that was (and is) quite receptive of fascism. To make things even worse, Marxist communism and communist anarchism, which have been the main anti-fascist movements almost anywhere fascism has emerged, have always been widely demonized and at times criminalized in the United States.

American fascism is able to lend itself to reappropriation (or adaptability), adoption (or reproducibility), and camouflaging (or renewability). While American fascism has never faced a campaign of uprooting or criminalization, the term "fascism" fell out of fashion just in time for American fascists to quickly camouflage their political persona through new, post-WWII, discursive strategies, such as those shaped around culturalism, as opposed to biological racism, and anti-communism, as opposed to segregationism, racist classism, or class apartheid. So much so that many American fascists shamelessly and without a sense of irony even claim libertarianism. That said, there is indeed a presence of libertarian themes including hostility toward the so-called "big government," which is a distinguishing characteristic of American fascism. Many libertarians have an open affinity with Trumpism and other right-wing movements, which is, at least partly, rooted in the anti-abolitionist hostility toward the Union. The anti-abolitionists argued that the state should not intervene in the right to property, because from their point of view, the white man had an intrinsic right to claim ownership over not only land but also people as slaves to work the land for him.

Generally, when historical progress moves toward a greater realization of social equality, the privileged sense acutely that the circumstances are potentially or actually threatening their privileges, which is in turn perceived as a threat to them as individuals, families, communities, and as a "nation." The aggregate of fears and anxieties results in the rationalization of irrational political reactions. Under capitalism, class violence against the under-class is already widely normalized (e.g., starvation, homelessness, etc.), legalized (e.g., disproportionate imprisonment and policing of marginalized bodies), and naturalized (e.g., national borders functioning as rotating doors to exclude the impoverished among the marginalized and racialized). Therefore, the already biased common sense in the bourgeois public sphere does not become alarmed by the rise of fascism. Instead, even when faced with undeniable cases of violence against the underprivileged, it habitually exceptionalizes the cases to minimize their political significance. In the meantime, it amplifies every individual case of violence committed by a perceived Other in order to conceive it and present it as culturally and politically representative of the collective Other. In short, fascism is a normal product of social relations of class and racial segregation in the age of nation-states. Only when fascists take over the political system in a country, does the bourgeois public sphere experience some shock. It should be a matter of disbelief that most opinion makers were taken by surprise on January 6, 2021, when Capitol Hill was attacked by right-wing militias. Even those who follow political news closely and those who are directly involved in political affairs of the state were shocked by the events, as if racist militias had only just emerged. What we are dealing with now is the kind of inaction that stems from denialism.

Denialism will assist rather than prevent the ultimate destruction of the American democracy's institutional structures at the hands of fascist forces. If this sounds like a cliché, so be it; as long as the same mistakes are repeated across ages and geographies, some statements will also be remade without losing their truth value. While it is true there is a world of difference between the American political system and Nazi Germany of the 1930s, the American intelligentsia should also keep in mind that in the United States racism and fascism at large have never been delegitimized as they were in Germany following WWII. In fact, the politics and culture industry of *mobomassification* of the proletariat (that is, the bourgeois manipulation of the dominated class destroying any remanence of class consciousness and instead erecting a mob mentality centered on the demonization of the disempowered class and idealization of the powerful exploiters) has continued in the United States even more aggressively since WWII.[10] The *mobomassification* of the working

---

10 I propose the term *mobomassification* as a critical alternative to the term "massification," which has anti-democratic connotations. The base term is *mobomass*, which alludes to the process of the mobilization of people to make them act as a mob according to a bourgeoisified form of politics. That is to say, the term refers to individuals who are ideologically bourgeoisified and depoliticized

class has reached a point where the takeover of fascism has become unstoppable. The most central aspect of the rise of fascism in interwar Europe was to stop the increasing popularity of the communist movement.[11] The communist and the broader leftist movement in the United States has never been weaker, so, at least in this sense, fascism has already been ruling. Trumpism just represents the latest act of the fascist play.

3 The Peculiar Adaptability of American Fascism

The American version of fascism has been incredibly flexible and uniquely built around hegemony as a means of societal control, rather than militaristic control as a means of accomplishing hegemony. Even the idea of race was freed from the constraints of nativism, which is not surprising given that, for obvious reasons, the European settlers could not capitalize on what the German *Volkish* movement or Italian nationalism founded in terms of claiming the right to the racially denoted fatherland. American fascism, therefore, has always centered on the individual as the genealogical locus of race and the ultimate representative of the collective, the nation. While from the perspective of German Nazism, the unity of the nation necessitated the submission of the individual, in the case of American fascism, the sanctity of the nation is deposited in a semi-absolute form of individualism. More to the point, in the American fascist worldview, the European colonizers and settlers that crossed the Atlantic necessarily became the ultimate inventors of the new nation, and, therefore, the essentialist aspect of the nation is not only mobile but also entirely dependent on the innovative, adventurous, and autonomous individual hero. In place of the doctrine of blood and soil, the American right, from the beginning, adopted an entirely different version of the nationalist construction of the in-group self, which is based on an image of a distinctly singular subject who is also extremely individualist. If the mystery of Germanness for a German fascist is embedded in perceived and mystified *Volkish* roots, in the American fascist worldview, uprootedness is precisely what distinguishes the national hero. Fascists in Europe always called for a new revival of the old, the imperial might, the united collective, and so on. In the United States, on the other hand, the fascist discourse has centered itself on a return to the old-new. Since "America" has always already been "the new world" discovered by the first white settlers and, because after the Amer-

---

precisely in order to be instrumentalized for an anti-egalitarian political agenda (this is explained in Ahmed 2023a).

11 For a recent and powerful discussion of this rather underestimated aspect of the origins of Italian Fascism, see Chapter 7 of Tariq Ali's *Winston Churchill: His Times, His Crimes* (2022).

ican Revolution, the United States was legally conceived by "the founding fathers," American conservativism has a modern beginning point, and its ideal hero does not need to seek any credentials outside his or her own whiteness, which was deposited in him/her very personhood as a free individual in charge of creating new spaces and making wealth in the new world. Even in terms of Christianity, thanks to the tribalism in which Protestantism had already started to result, there was no central religious authority to limit the uprootedness of this new hero in this new world. The rural areas became a breeding hub for white, armed men claiming ownership of whatever they could appropriate from the native Americans. American law enforcement was founded to, among other things, protect so-called private property, which for the most part designated white men's claims to rightful ownership of everything from occupied native American lands to enslaved black bodies.

American fascism does not need to claim anything about pre-history or a collective spirit to advance its political projects publicly and populistically. Its old is considered the real new, and its call for unity is a call for re-securing unlimited privileges for the white individual vis-à-vis the republic as a super-institution that embodies sovereignty inclusively on behalf of the country's general public, the government as the legitimate executive authority accountable to all citizens, and the public institutions that aim to safeguard equality under the law. In addition, and more importantly, intrinsic in the right to unlimited private property is the capitalist endeavor to exploit all so-called natural resources and a racist desire to control the determining factors of social relations of domination. Indeed, one of the earliest episodes of the clash between white supremacists and the state is what has become known as the American Civil War. To reiterate, many white slave owners on all levels of political and civil society adamantly refused to recognize the abolition of slavery, considering the Union's decision to ban slavery as an intrusion into their individual rights and freedoms. Ironically, this contradictory (racist, exclusionary, and oppressive) frame of reference has been definitive of the libertarian conception of freedom in the United States.[12] Bearing this in mind, it is not surprising that today there is an open alliance between libertarians and ultra-conservatives. In fact, in the United States, libertarianism makes up a cornerstone of the fascist

---

12 George Fitzhugh (also cited in Martinot 2008) wrote a book arguing that the slavery system in the Southern states was in the interest of the enslaved. He uses Christianity as the absolute moral system to justify slavery, or total control over the "weak" by the "strong." Interestingly, because he defends slavery against what he calls capitalism (not to mention socialism), he admits several times that the only source of capital is labor. Under proper slavery, he argues, slaves are taken care of, but under capitalism a laborer is a slave without a master, minimal allowance is given to him while being maximumly exploited. The capitalist gentlemen are "cannibals all," which is also the title of the book (2011, 7).

discourse that aims to appeal to the white majority. This also explains why ultra-nationalists so habitually refer to rhetoric and doctrines that are traditionally part of the liberal project, such as the right to freedom of speech and freedom of inquiry. American fascism does not have a fundamental problem with liberalism, but what it cannot stand is democracy. Roberto Esposito points to an important contradiction between liberalism and democracy, arguing that the former is centered on particularism while the latter demands egalitarianism (2008, 641–642). But to Esposito, there has never been such a thing as a liberal democracy. Liberal democracy, in other words, is a contradiction in terms just as totalitarian communism is a contradiction in terms.

The right's attack on the mainstream media and what has become known as "cancel culture" also stems from the deep tendency to revive unlimited white privilege, or the particularism granted to the white man in liberalism. What upsets most of the elites in this regard is not the age-old liberal gentrification of the public sphere, which in fact has amounted to naturalizing a regime of censorship against egalitarianism, especially communism. Rather, what upsets them is the standards that have been put in place through political correctness. Political correctness could, and should, be seen as problematic but for the opposite reasons; it has functioned mainly as a means for the gentrification of the public sphere in the sense of masking the ongoing regimes of inequality and thereby perpetuating oppression. Put bluntly, liberal political correctness tries to maintain egalitarianism as a form and a formality, and by doing so it reduces the arena of politics to the public sphere, which is inherently bourgeois and virtual, as opposed to inclusive and spatial. Hence, from a Marxist point of view, liberal political correctness is a reductive project for the idealization of what is in reality material. In its very defense of the public sphere, it universalizes the bourgeois reductive account of freedom and equality as mere ideals, as moral maxims.[13]

In this regard, the role the Habermasian project of de-Marxification of critical theory has played is not insignificant. As a critical theorist, I bring this up in order to emphasize the significance of the dialectics of space, which has a material

---

[13] Even Hannah Arendt, who was by no means a Marxist thinker, and, therefore, her adoption in the academy has been considered safe, realized the immediate link between the bourgeoisie and fascism (for more on this, see Ahmed 2023a). Consider the following:

> The mob man, however, the end-result of the "bourgeois," is an international phenomenon; and we would do well not to submit him to too many temptations in the blind faith that only the German mob man is capable of such frightful deeds. What we have called the "bourgeois" is the modern man of the masses, not in his exalted moments of collective excitement, but in the security (today one should say the insecurity) of his own private domain. (Arendt 1994, 130)

dimension, as opposed to a sphere, which disregards the essentiality of the actual conditions of life and the spatial relations of power. The doctrine of ideal communication is appealing to scholars who want to associate with critical theory but not Marxism, and the struggle for democracy but not necessarily for egalitarianism. Habermas, along with John Rawls, Richard Rorty, and Charles Taylor are perhaps the most effective figures to come to the philosophical rescue of liberalism in our age. Their projects have provided liberalism with a moral, positive, and idealist set of philosophical tools and doctrines to gentrify the politics of dissent in the West and further marginalize Marxism in both the academy and the streets and, in effect, depoliticize the social space of power, thereby contributing to the broader campaign the bourgeoisie desperately needed to render the revolutionary discourse of class struggle seem outdated, irrelevant, inadequate, and so on. Other effective strikes against critical theory in its broader, Marxist, framework came from:

1. the ideologues of neoliberalism, such as Milton Friedman and other American disciples of the Vienna school of economics, particularly Friedrich Hayek;
2. some political scientists such as Francis Fukuyama and Samuel Huntington who shamelessly sugarcoated American imperialism in the name of the triumph of liberalism;
3. and last but not least culturalists, including multiculturalists, or moralists who reduce the white man's other to homogeneous groups essentially defined by their supposed cultures, as conceived by a racist episteme that ironically celebrates difference, multitude, non-binarity, and so on (for more on this latter point, see Ahmed 2022a, especially chap. 5).

Notice how for instance there is barely any talk of anti-racism in universities, and instead positive terms such as diversity, equity, and inclusivity have become part of the dominant norm for reasons that exceed the strategic planning of public relations and marketing. Using anti-racist terminology so widely would of course amount to admitting that racism is a prevalent problem. What liberal institutions often tend to do is to replace negative concepts with their respective positive antipodes, the language of critique with mass-produced rhetoric of celebration, and critical praxis with meaningless claims about critical thinking, which more often than not serves a form of nihilism that shamelessly advances religious or semi-religious claims and casts doubt on all forms of scientific authority. The discursive strategies and rhetorical tools of racism have evolved so much and been normalized so much that in today's world anyone with a basic level of Western liberal education could easily pass as a diversity-loving citizen and multicultural advocate. Of course, there are still plenty of racists who either lack that basic liberal education or simply refuse to let go of the old racist language, but these voices also help further the illusion of a *liberalist* struggle for defending diversity when in reality the liberal camp has only invented more effective ways to internally silence the marginalized by sentimentalizing, idealizing, and positivizing the perpetual and systematic processes of othering.

At the end of the 1940s, Löwenthal and Guterman anticipated that American fascism would spread more swiftly than the German version. Today, American fascism is adopted and adapted outside the United States, in places such as Canada, Brazil, and even some of the birthplaces of old fascism in Europe. Among the latest signs of the global appeal of the American model of fascism is the right wing's rejection of some of the most fundamental conditions of democracy, such as elections as a legitimate means for distributing representation and political power. That said, attention should also be paid to the strategic ideological nuances that have resulted in such a broad de-democratization of politics, which in turn paved the way for the rise of fascism. As the Marxist front has become increasingly weaker in the West since the 1950s and 1960s, there has been an intertwined ideological strategy of depoliticizing the political and politicizing the non-political.

4 Fascism as Reverse Politics

Growing at the heart of capitalist liberalism and providing an effective formula in terms of its adoptability and adaptability, American fascism has always been more resilient than its European counterparts. There are two intertwined sociopolitical phenomena that fatally weakened liberal states' immunity against anti-democratic movements and *ideological forms* like fascism: the systematic depoliticization of the political and the politicization of the non-political. A prime embodiment of the latter is the biopolitical subjugation of the marginalized. For instance, abortion has become increasingly political in the worst possible sense, i.e., as a question of governmentality. On the other hand, the bourgeois public sphere is increasingly becoming more indifferent to some of the most urgent crises such as conflicts between the world's two main nuclear powers. Depoliticization of the political is also evident in the prevailing discourses surrounding the ecological crisis, which, at best, moralize and, hence, privatize the problem or, at worst, deny it altogether.

Anticipating the ecological disasters that would result from the normalized and depoliticized economic form that is capitalism, in *Capital III*, Marx notes:

> From the standpoint of a higher economic form of society, private ownership of the globe by single individuals will appear quite as absurd as private ownership of one man by another. Even a whole society, a nation, or even all simultaneously existing societies taken together,

are not the owners of the globe. They are only its possessors, its usufructuaries, and, like *boni patres familias*, they must hand it down to succeeding generations in an improved condition. (2010b, 763)[14]

The global hegemony of neoliberalism is simply the totalization and globalization of private ownership, and this is done in the name of non-ideologicality in the age of alleged post-ideology with the help of a regime of knowledge production that purportedly rejects advocacy in education. This is fascism in its most advanced form; it is the imposition of universal discrimination, systematic exclusion via inclusion, endless exploitation of labor and nature, and unlimited exercise of power, or, in one word, totalitarianism. Everything political is deliberately de-politicized while everything that is non-political is systematically politicized.

At the same time, what is supposed to be indisputably individual is hyper-politicized, dictated through collective exercise of power that is inherently oppressive and totalitarian. Take for example the issue of abortion in the United States where the inherently individual space of the female body is allocated to the collective for political deliberation, which in turn will determine which of the two main political parties should enjoy authority over the entire political space, including the now politicized female body. Thus, an issue as personal as pregnancy is decided upon collectively through voting processes that are not even specific to the issue. Abortion is merely one of the *political* issues raised in the conservative-liberal false duality. The voting process is conducted *democratically*, but what is dismissed is the fact that *what is voted on* is inherently anti-democratic. The procedure, therefore, amounts to political coercion and social suppression. To grasp the nature of this imposition one needs to imagine a scenario in which every personal affair is subjected to political deliberation, legislative ruling, political administration, and policing. As if it is not bad enough to turn a woman's decision regarding her pregnancy into a collective issue determined by millions who do not know anything about her and her life, the male half of the society also take part in the decision making, for every woman, now and in the future.

We need to note that even claiming that there had been a moment of emancipation and universalism, even in the idealist/false sense is in fact too generous of a reading of liberalism. Unlike Marx, the philosophers who are considered the founding fathers of liberalism never rejected slavery unconditionally, and yet this is something deliberately hushed in university textbooks. Here, perhaps it suffices to cite the following lines by Losurdo who appropriately cites a number of the founding philosophers of liberalism to make the point:

---

14 Also cited and discussed by Domenico Losurdo (2016, 41), in his excellent book titled *Class Struggle: A Political and Philosophical History*.

No one would wish to include in a textbook of civic education the pages where Locke regards slavery in the colonies as self-evident or where he invites readers to feel no 'compassion' for the Irish 'papists', who at the time were the target of ferocious persecution and a veritable policy of colonial extermination. And no one would wish to include the pages in which Jefferson theorizes the natural inferiority of blacks, or those in which Mill demands 'absolute obedience' of 'races' deemed to be in their 'nonage' (or semi-animal), or where he celebrates the Opium War as a crusade for liberty. (2015, 298–299)

5 The Broad Racist and Capitalist Lines of American Fascism

Despite its long history of evolvement, American fascism has barely been problematized let alone challenged. According to the theory of *ideology form*, fascism is a form of ideology thereby encompassing a wide variety of ideologies, each of which may imply specific discourses, mechanisms, strategies, and tactics that pragmatically respond to the peculiarities of historical and geopolitical circumstances in which the movement in question emerges (Ahmed 2022a, 2023a; also see Chapter 3 of this book). American fascism emerged and developed in circumstances that in many ways made it extremely adaptable and reproducible. The complicated history of racism, colonialism, and imperialism, which is entangled with the history of the United States, helped the formation of American fascism as a model of fascism that is not only unthreatened by but in fact, at least in many ways, is dependent on bourgeois liberalism.

As noted earlier, American fascism adopts two main strategies: (1) the depoliticization of what is otherwise utterly political, e.g., the environment, and (2) politicization of what otherwise should be utterly non-political, e.g., the right to the body, which, even according to the principles of liberalism should be an indisputably sanctified personal right. With Donald Trump, the intertwined strategy reached a new stage whereby some among the ruling class wanted to dispose of the politician as the middle person between capital and the state. Trump's wager is centered on something much more fanatic than the traditional conservative objective of so-called "small government." Trump represents a camp within the ruling class that prefers the ultimate annexation of the government to the business and financial sector. To this new bourgeois camp, it is not good enough that the state serves the interests of the ruling class; they want the state to be under the direct command of the one percent of the one percent. This is precisely why someone like Elon Musk comes out in full support of Trump who, in turn, promises Musk a position in his new cabinet. What this means is that even the attempt to expose official politics' allegiance to the ruling class has become redundant.

Ironically, despite being a pathological liar, Donald Trump is right to accuse the political establishment of dishonesty, hypocrisy, and so on. The deeper irony is that Trump's message unwittingly entails exposing not only politicians as agents of the top capitalists but also top capitalists as the patrons of politics. Basically, the Trump doctrine amounts to bringing the capitalist to the front—as the puppet-master, to be the government, to become the state—as opposed to merely monopolizing things through state employers. Trump's popularity already shows that about half of the American public consider his doctrine as honesty (being oblivious of the fact that what he is honest about also betrays his own dishonesty as a member of the ruling class). The other half or so of the American public, who support the Democratic Party, also miss the point. They are too consumed by Trump as a scandalous figure to grasp the bigger scandal, i.e., the fact that with or without politicians as middlemen and middlewomen, capital rules. The difference between the Democrats and the Republicans at this stage comes down to the method rather than nature of control. The Republicans under Trump's leadership seem to believe that it is better to have capitalists control electoral politics directly by claiming the position of the head of the state while the Democrats seem to prefer the old way, i.e., through so-called donations. Either way, it is the one percent of the one percent, e.g., Jeff Bezos, Bill Gates, Donald Trump, and Elon Musk, who call the shots. The difference is that some, such as Bezos and Gates, prefer to focus on business and mandate professional politicians to handle the political, whereas others prefer the short cut, that is, to have members of the 0.01 percent, such as Trump and Musk, at the head of the state.

Trumpism is just a stage in the development of fascism in the United States, which has continued since long before the term fascism was coined. The American brand of fascism, unlike its interwar European counterparts, calls for small government. However, when it comes to social conservatism and the use of police apparatuses against racially minoritized groups and immigrants, fascists on both sides of the Atlantic are not only illiberal and anti-democratic but also militaristic and totalitarian. American fascism is against the state in so far as the state could impose restrictions on the bourgeoisie's unlimited control of natural resources and labor. For American fascists, individual rights are sacred except they adamantly refuse to perceive the racially othered and immigrants as individual rights holders. To deny racially minoritized persons individual rights, American fascists have invented an array of discursive, moral, patriotic, nationalist, religious, and legal strategies and tactics.

The same movement that supposedly defends individual liberties against the potential tyranny of the state historically has been an aggressive opponent of recognizing the individuality and the liberty of large segments of the population. In the established regime of social, political, and economic apartheid the individual right to freedom and property entails racist totalitarianism. When the Spanish, Dutch, and English expeditions "discovered" the "new world," from their perspective, everything was up for grabs. This entailed not only robbery and destruction of the social ecology on the continent but also mass enslavement and mass murder. When they wanted to turn the colonized lands into permanent sources of wealth, they established the biggest institution of slavery and the largest intercontinental slave trade in human history. As a fundamentally racist mechanism of unlimited exercise of power, capitalism established a multilayered system of trade and production that combined (a) total exploitation of the natural resources on the de-populated American continent, and (b) total exploitation of the African as brutally transformed and transported labor. The same system, simultaneously, established another cross-Atlantic trade route between the Americas and Europe. The capital that was created from this intercontinental mass murder (of the American populations) and mass enslavement (of African populations) rendered the imperialist capacities of the Spanish, Portuguese, British, French, and Dutch elites global.

By the 19th century, a racist world system of capitalism was in place, but, having let go of much of its grip on America in favor of the new American ruling elites, the white ruling elites in Europe began redesigning their colonial enterprises in terms of both scope and strategy. While Asia, including India and China, became targets of multiple European colonial powers, it was the potential booty in the African colonies that increased the risk of clashes among a relatively large number of European elites. To unentangle their overlapping interests, and to prevent any further white-versus-white wars, such as the American War of Independence, the tyrants of Europe felt the need to produce an agreement among themselves, which culminated in the Berlin Conference of 1884–1885.

By the early 20th century, the barbarism engendered by elites had already committed multiple genocides in various parts of Africa and Asia, and at times their imperial expeditions clashed, but they remained relatively faithful to their racist notion of kinship, so they continued to preserve their genocidal barbarism for Africans, Caribbeans, Asian, and indigenous Americans and Australians. However, growing imperial ambitions could no longer be contained, and thus the Great War broke out in 1914, leading to the irruption of multiple fascist trends on the European continent and Britain, thereby bringing home the barbarism and genocidal tendencies of the ruling elites and their *mobomassified* followers and armies. An opposite movement based on class consciousness had been growing across Europe, which not only opposed colonialism and the 1914–1919 war but also put up a struggle against fascism everywhere in Europe, most visibly in Russia, Hungary, Italy, Spain, Yugoslavia, and Greece. If there is a fascist landmark, it is the anti-Bolshevik crusade in every geographic setting since the Bolshevik Revolution.

The war against the internationalist movement often brought rivals together. What Mussolini, Franco, Hitler, Churchill, Roosevelt, and Stalin had in common was their intolerance of internationalist communists. In terms of racist mentality and language, Churchill and Roosevelt were not different from Mussolini and Hitler. Just as Hitler's crimes cannot be understated or relativized, the racist tradition that gave rise to Hitler and the post-WWII strains of fascism should not be underestimated under the pretext that they are dissimilar to Nazism. The lenses through which Hitler looked at human beings are the same as those adopted by the ruling elites from Locke to Mill and Jefferson to Churchill.[15]

The history of capitalism is the same as the history of modern racist colonialism. The British colonization of India and America started with the expeditions of the East India Company, which was founded in 1600, and the Virginia Company of London, founded in 1606.[16] Thomas Jefferson, the main author of the American Declaration of Independence, the philosopher and scientist among the founding fathers, and the third president of the republic, believed that Africans and native Americans were inferior to white Europeans in terms of what he, borrowing Kant's philosophical terminology, called "the faculties of reason and imagination" (Jefferson 1787, 153). Further clarifying his racist hypothesis, he writes, "the blacks, whether originally a distinct race, or made distinct by time and circumstances, are inferior to the whites in the endowments both of body and mind. It is not against experience to suppose, that different species of the same genus, or varieties of the same species, may possess different qualifications" (153).

Despite all their conflicts, these ruling elites did not differ in terms of their deep belief that the racially perceived white man was entitled to rule the world. Their differences, where there were any, had to do with particular imperial interests within the same racist system of capitalism. Meanwhile, despite all their disputes and conflicts, they adopted similar forms of fanatic antagonism against the communist project. Fascism is the concept that aids us in understanding this broad fanaticism that re-couples and infuses race and class. When the ruling class goes into survival mode, that is, when the bourgeoisie's grip on total power is threatened, fascism emerges to intensify intertwined mechanisms of racist bourgeois control and bourgeois racist hegemony. When the deployment of democratic means fails

---

15 On the blatant racism in the writings of the Enlightenment philosophers, including Hobbes, Locke, Kant, Mill, and others, see Eze 2001. For Churchill's racism and fondness for Mussolini and Hitler before the war, see Tariq Ali's recent biography of him (Ali 2022). As for Jefferson, one could argue that in terms of legitimizing racist mentality within and without politics, his role was more influential than the roles both Mussolini and Hitler would play in the 20th century. Jefferson uses the philosophical and scientific language of his time not just as a politician but also as a knowledge authority to establish the fascist world of Mussolini and Hitler. See for instance Jefferson's *Notes on the State of Virginia* (1787), which I cite again below.
16 For a concise history of colonizing what is now the United States, see Zinn 2015 and Srinivasan 2017.

to totalize the bourgeoisie's hegemonic monopoly, fascism may emerge to preserve the bourgeoisie's total control.

To the Klan, the United States belonged to "native-born" white Protestants. The white supremacists then, as now, were well aware of the genocide of the native Americans, and in fact made a point of openly claiming that the so-called one hundred percent Americans, i.e., white protestant Americans, would be eliminated like "the Indians!" Thus, in their very nativism, they admitted the genocide their white clan had committed against the population of the continent, and somehow, they saw themselves as the only fully entitled Americans. It is not that white racism had ever lost its dominant status in American social, economic, and political arenas; the Klan was simply a movement that emerged out of the white anxiety that the privileged might be compelled to accept concessions after they had been used to exercising unlimited power on the raced and disadvantaged Other.

There are still many debatable points about the Klan's history, but according to all accounts and the KKK's own documents, the movement from 1920 onward was fanatically anti-communist. Aside from their racial and religious targets, which include, Catholics, Jews, immigrants, blacks, Asians, and whoever is not white enough, the only movement and ideology they repeatedly designate as their prime enemy is communism. Thus, just like fascism in Europe, American fascism took it upon itself to fight communism at any cost.

Fascists, whether they abided by Catholicism, Protestantism, Islamism, or secularism, have had in common anti-communism. As they have also been anti-Semites albeit to different degrees, many of them conveniently portrayed communism as a Jewish conspiracy. Thus, the very people who were portrayed as a tribe and nothing besides were simultaneously and without a sense of irony also deemed responsible for initiating and leading the most internationalist, universalist, inclusive, and egalitarian movement known in all human history. Similarly, as detailed in the next chapter, most fascist movements in the Middle East, who otherwise feverishly disagree on almost everything, have in common a hysterical enmity against communism and racialized Jews. They too commonly denote Marxism as a Jewish conspiracy and at the same time perceive Jewishness as a tribal identity. The lack of basic reasoning to, at least, avoid committing such elementary contradictions is a common fascist trait. According to this view, one group of people is somehow responsible for both capitalist monopoly and world communism, the historically longest fanatic tribalism and the ideologically, philosophically, and politically largest and most radical movement of anti-tribalism.

Chapter 5
Fascism in the Middle East and North Africa

An old form of fascism has been enduring in the Middle East and North Africa (MENA) region. Showing that fascism in the region remains extremely under-studied, this chapter emphasizes the urgent need for critical research to expose the prejudices and false premises within the relevant fields of inquiry. Thus, the main objective is twofold: showing that fascism prevails among certain ruling elites and critiquing the dominant modes of knowledge production for failing to problematize fascism. To illustrate that fascism has not been challenged adequately by the intelligentsia, I elaborate on the strong presence of multiple features of fascism, such as ultra-nationalism, leader cultism (or the Führer principle), and violent persecution and demonization of minorities. In addition to critical argumentation against the dominant mode of knowledge production, the chapter critically analyzes multiple examples of discourse that are advanced in the public sphere by the ruling elites. Problematizing fascism in the MENA region is essential for, among other things, giving anti-fascist social and democratic movements in the region the scholarly attention they deserve. This is a much-needed investigation especially because there has been an overwhelming rise of fascist movements since the 1980s across countries, including Iraq, Syria, Turkey, and Iran. The recent global rise of discriminatory extremism only makes this kind of unorthodox research more indispensable.

In this book and elsewhere, I have adamantly argued against the comparative and conventional methods that are so widely practiced in fascism studies. However, for problematizing fascism in the Middle East, where fascist discourses have not been compelled to develop camouflaging strategies, revisiting the interwar period forms of fascism in Europe is advantageous. Indeed, the fascist discourses in the Middle East are to this day explicit in their racism and habitual glorification of war, blood, and soil. After looking into the history of several waves of nationalism and their affinity with the older forms of fascism, we may be able to better appreciate the challenges with which resistance movements are faced.

There are some important scholarly works that address the phenomenon of fascism in Turkey and the Arab world, but within fascism studies overall, the area remains extremely under-studied. In the absence of such debates, the marginalized majority have been brutalized in the region for decades, and some of the most creative movements of resistance have been ignored by the intelligentsia. As explained earlier in this book, I treat "fascism" as a form of ideology, not in the historically and geographically limited sense. This should not be interpreted as undermining historicality in this or any other area. As a theory historical dialectics is meant to be

https://doi.org/10.1515/9783111609041-005

most perceptive of both continuity and change, endurance and rapture, realization through rationalization and rationalization through realization, forces of homogenization and prospects of negation, etc.

On the level of the sociology of power and production, capitalism reshaped Europe and European colonialism reshaped the world accordingly. The domination of capitalism, on the ideological level, entailed the hegemony of nationalism as a mode of perception. Capitalism was a universal force from the beginning, but what it has universalized is not the ideal of freedom or equality, as we are often told by the spokespersons of liberalism. Rather, what capitalism has universalized is *total* power, which is a new formula of metaphysical, epistemological, moral, social, and political power. Capital is the totalization of control and capitalism is the globalization of capital, which started from the initial stages of modernity.

Within the same process, capitalism universalized a mode of perception that is inherently anti-universalist, which was essential to counteract the grave it dug for itself. The creation of the new universal sphere was inevitably going to create a horizon for universal egalitarianism, but to prevent that, capitalism needed an ideological regime that would re-tribalize human society, rapidly, deeply, and aggressively. Nationalism has become that force for homogenizing societies inwardly and tribalizing them outwardly. Just as the capitalist mode of material production globalized sameness and objectification, on the ideological level nationalism carried the seed of fascism to all corners of the world.

What all fascist movements have in common is anti-communism, and that is exactly the role each fascist movement has assumed often with the blessing of the larger capitalist establishment, including so-called liberal democracies. The outcome of WWII was the destruction of Nazism, not fascism at large. The Western bloc did not fight the Spanish and Portuguese fascist regimes for a single day, and in fact they were integrated into the larger anti-communist camp. The Portuguese fascist regime remained in power until 1974, that is, six years after Salazar's death. In Spain, the fascist regime, which had been secured militarily by Mussolini and Hitler, persisted until Franco's death in 1975. In Italy, the fascists were reintegrated into the system while the communists, who fought against the fascist regime from day one, were systematically disempowered despite their enormous popularity. In Greece, the fascists and their collaborators were supported adamantly by Britain as the communists were still fighting the Nazi occupation. France barely put up any resistance against the Nazi invasion. While for decades anti-Nazi French resistance was magnified by the official propaganda of the French Republic, we now know for a fact that more than half of the resistance fighters in France were non-French immigrants, including East European Jews, North African Arabs and Amazighs, Armenian survivors, and others who, for the most part, were hardcore communists. In the meantime, Britain and France, like Italy, Portugal, and Spain, continued their colonial campaigns. After 1945, just like before 1945, these campaigns were fascistic by every standard. The European powers and the United States now went on supporting endless fascist forces wherever they could to stop the spread of communism. This included supporting Islamists and juntas from Arabia to Indonesia. Contrary to the propaganda claims, this campaign in Africa, Asia, and Latin America was characteristically anti-democratic. The single reason for this global anti-democratic campaign that was conducted throughout the 20th century was the same as the original goal the first self-proclaimed fascist movement set for itself, namely, the purging of the communist project.

Today, about a hundred years after the first official rise of fascism, fascism is more prevalent than ever. It has indeed eliminated the internationalist communist movement and successfully outdated Marxist terminology and discourses replacing them with full-fledged racist, culturalist, tribalist, and mythological terminology and discourses. Following WWII, German liberalism launched an official process of de-Nazification, which was impressive even though it was far from uprooting the fascist mode of perception. Internationally, however, liberalism merely further empowered and utilized fascism within the anti-communist crusade. In the Middle East and North Africa, where communism was once by far the most popular political movement (see Bahozde 2025), the Frankensteinian breeds of fascism, the rabid anti-communist creatures, whether secular or religious, exemplify the current dark age, which, according to neoliberal prophets such as Francis Fukuyama and their intellectual brownshirts and academic enablers, was supposed to be the Hegelian end of history.

1 The Fascist Moment in the Dialectics of Enlightenment

To problematize the politics of exclusion in MENA, the nationalist bourgeoisie and fundamentalist religious ideologues should be *historically* held accountable, not the majority of ordinary Turks, Arabs, or Persians, even if and when relatively large numbers of the masses are mobilized, militarized, and used as a means of coercion against the Other, who are often represented by the more marginalized demographics. Nationalist and fanatic mobilizations around racist and sectarian identities result in the reproduction of inter-societal and cross-societal violence. The elites who control the means of the culture industry are to be blamed for the false consciousness that makes the economically exploited commit violence against those who are exploited economically and demonized racially and/or religiously at the same time.

Regardless of the validity or invalidity of my conceptualization of "fascism," the main argument regarding the need for wider and more critical public debates about problematizing exclusionary ideologies, politics, and policies that perpetuate discrimination and violence is sound. Furthermore, the cases that are analyzed are actual rather than hypothetical, so the plausibility of the main point advanced is not contingent on any particular conceptual validity or invalidity. For instance, the critical analyses and conceptual applications of fascism as an *ideology form* might not be persuasive enough for traditional scholars of fascism. However, definitional disagreements about fascism do not affect the educational value of what the chapter shows in terms of the unjustified cases of discrimination and what the chapter argues for, namely the imperativeness of the critique of all cases of unjustified discrimination.

The problem (of fascism or whatever it may be called) is not unique to any particular nationality, ethnicity, or religious sect. An identity, whether Turkish, Arab, Persian, Kurdish, Sunni, Shia, or Sufi, can be the perceived identity of perpetrators or victims of violent oppression depending on the particular temporospatial context. Of course, in the world of nation-states, the stateless are more prone to be subjected to fascist violence. That said, there is nothing in victimhood or statelessness that would rule out the possibility of the rise of fascism among former victims or former stateless groups. In fact, if anything, narratives of victimhood are often used as effective in-group justifications for advancing the group's own fascist ideologies and practices, especially within the frame of an assumed political sovereignty. *There* is a high probability of fascism being born and grown domestically but unnoticeably among the previously colonized groups. It is not improbable for fascist movements to emerge even among currently colonized groups, especially when that group identifies with a broader, expansionist, and imperialist identity, whether on the basis of religious or ethnic politics.

Fascist elites in MENA have been exploiting the false culturalist dichotomy of West-East to disguise their continual violation of the rights and dignities of the ruled majority in their countries. More to the point, by exploiting the oversimplified but common anti-imperialist discourse and the moralist Eurocentric belief according to which imperialism is exclusively associated with whiteness, fascist elites in MENA have been able to advance their imperialist, racist, and at times even genocidal agenda in the name of resisting Western imperialism. Meanwhile, the post-Marxist left in the West has for the most part believed the culturalist lie of racism. In the 1970s, the left, for instance in West Germany, had no problem calling the Shah of Iran a fascist. Today, thanks to the widespread culturalization of politics and politicization of culture, both the left and the right in the West seem to believe that Khamenei is indeed the supreme spiritual leader of Iranians and that he is indeed fighting imperialism! Meanwhile, for the last forty years, Iranians from all backgrounds have tried everything not only to show their rejection of the ruling regime but also to bring it down. Even armed struggle has continued throughout the last forty-three years, yet in this culturalist era, it has become possible not to hear Iranians and instead believe a ruling elite that is by all accounts criminal (e.g., Amnesty International 2017). Similarly, under Erdogan's ruling party (Amnesty International 2020; HRW 2021), democratic and progressive voices have been persecuted brutally. However, Erdogan's claim to collective/cultural representation and his appeal to the culturalist mentality outside Turkey have been by far more effective than the plight of the oppressed in Turkey, including Turks and Muslims not to mention Kurds and non-Muslims. Even when thousands of scholars and educators were persecuted across Turkey and many were forced to escape the country to the West, boycotting Erdogan's regime was never considered in the European and American civil society associations, to say nothing about governments.

2 Fascist Ideologies, Geographies, and Phases

While the theory of *ideology form* is helpful to diagnose some of the contemporary Western forms of fascism that acquired new discursive strategies of democratic camouflaging, in the Middle East, for better or worse, the forms of fascism have continued to display clear affinities with the older forms of fascism, which are openly racist and vulgarly antagonistic to the essentialized and homogenized Other. The broadly justified principle of armed struggle against colonialism resulted in the domination and continuation of the language of violence in the political spaces and public spheres across MENA. In contrast to the communist discourse that emphasized the politicization of the working class and the construction of proletarian class consciousness that was meant to be inherently democratic, the nationalist parties increasingly undermined the role of the civil society and the foundational principles of democratic participation replacing the paradigm of class and its objective denominators with the paradigm of "the nation," which in turn helped mystify all the crucial loci of political power.

Suddenly, it became morally and politically acceptable for newly formed states to pick up governmentality where the colonial powers had left it. Oppressive politics, including the deployment of excessive force against every movement of dissent and brutalization of entire populations in the name of national unity and security, became commonplace. The outcome, namely, the creation of a political world in which the exercise of power is universalized, producing monster states strongly tied to the interests and fate of oppressive governments is not surprising. In the meantime, even those who in the name of emancipation founded armed struggle movements to, whether rightly or wrongly, fight their colonizers started to sanctify violence. Specially in the 1970s and later, across the Arab world, a great deal of literature, music, and visual arts started to glorify the image of an assault rifle and idealize the figure of a Palestinian fighter with his keffiyeh. Legendary singers such as Umm Kulthum and Fairuz sang about war with the same, if not more, passion with which they sang about romantic love. Their voices, along with the voices of countless poets, novelists, playwrights, and other intellectuals, had an immeasurably profound effect on millions of young men and women, many of whom would readily see in a new enemy, Israel, the cause for all their sexual, emotional, social, and political disappointments. Quickly, the image of the general, the national hero, the father figure who will supposedly come to reinstall the lost glories of the ancient times gained extraordinary psychic powers over millions of *mobomassified* people rendering any talk of class consciousness obsolete among large sections of the working class from Iraq and Syria to Morocco and Algeria.

In the 1970s, a similar wave of romanticization of guns, shooting at the enemy, and the image of Peshmerga proliferated in Kurdish lyrics, plays, novels, and songs in Iraq and Iran. To this day, even after thirty-two years of the deeply corrupt and oppressive Peshmerga rule in parts of Iraqi Kurdistan, the word "peshmerga" remains for the large part sanctified especially among Iranian Kurds, which is a sad commentary on the reproduction of violence vertically and horizontally in the Kurdish society and personality in the name of resistance. Somehow, the image of the armed man took over the general imagination, rendering every aspect of political, communal, and intellectual life secondary to the appeal of guns. Sadly, the state violence that was supposed to be resisted has given birth to a world exclusively signified in terms of the symbolism of violence.

In the Arabic-speaking public sphere, even a group like Hamas, which has repeatedly proved that it does not have the slightest regard for any lives, including and especially those of Palestinians, remains widely exempted from any critique across most of the Arab media. Any critique of Hamas is immediately dismissed as siding with the Israeli colonial project. Under Hamas rule in Gaza, it may be understandable why more Palestinians do not speak up against Hamas's devastating politics, but, unfortunately for the Gazans, it is mostly those who do not live in Gaza (and do not experience what Gazans go through) who sanctify Hamas as a movement of resistance. What is even more disturbing is the fact that there is a near complete absence of a minimal level of rational argumentation in the public sphere to assess Hamas's acts. Hamas's strategy of hostage taking is simply based on two premises: (1) Israel does not give up on the lives of its citizens, and (2) Palestinian lives have little value for Hamas. Only with these two premises deeply rooted in the Islamist mentality of Hamas's leadership can that leadership's catastrophic decisions be explained. This is why, to Hamas's leaders, taking any number of Israeli hostages is worth the loss of tens of thousands of Palestinian lives.[17]

---

17 For more on this, see Ahmed 2023c.

In the war Hamas started on October 7, 2023, within less than sixty days, more than 3 percent of the residents of the Gaza Strip lost their lives, many more were injured, and about 80 percent were displaced. Some days, within a twenty-four-hour period, the number of Palestinian civilians who were killed was twice the number of the Israeli hostages in Hamas's captivity. Based on Hamas's own reports, on average 200 Palestinians were killed per day by Israeli fire,[18] not to mention Palestinians who lost their lives because of the collapse of the health system and starvation or those who were injured for life. None of that made the Hamas leadership release the 120–130 Israeli hostages. Had Hamas intentionally collaborated with the ultra-right Israeli elements to ensure the destruction of Gaza, it would not have acted any better for that purpose. Ultimately, the Netanyahu right-wing government took military steps to destroy life conditions in most of the enclave. At the same time, Egypt, Jordan, and other states made sure the Palestinians who were trapped in Gaza would not be able to leave the enclave despite months of continual bombardment, starvation, and homelessness. Hamas is not unique in its complete disrespect for the lives of the people it supposedly defends. All Islamist movements disrespect human lives, especially the lives of the people who are unfortunate enough to be under their rule. The problem in many ways exceeds Islamist movements to also include secular nationalist movements in the Middle East, as the long list of dictators have proven over decades.

There is a problem in MENA, and the problem might be better diagnosed if we look into the notion and history of fascism. Whether or not exclusionary movements discussed in this book should be called fascist is of secondary importance. The main point of this chapter is that without problematizing ideological forms that celebrate violence and fanatically reject otherness, exclusionism will most likely continue to be part of the political scene for a long time to come. Indeed, even in its classical sense, fascism has never been widely problematized anywhere among the Middle Eastern and North African intelligentsia or academia. New intellectual, academic, and public conventions must therefore be established precisely to interrogate every nationalist and religious political front from an anti-fascist perspective. Hopefully, problematizing fascism on multiple levels will prepare the path to a world where the individual right to life and freedom is sanctified and Otherness is strongly protected.

---

18 Thomas et al. 2024; Elaph 2024.

3 The Rise of Fascism

The rise of fascism in Europe in the 20th century was not merely due to an unfortunate turn of events in the 1920s and 1930s; rather, as Horkheimer and Adorno realized in their co-authored masterpiece, *Dialectic of Enlightenment* (2002), it was a historical point at which the political power of the reactionary forces that started to take shape and momentum right from the beginning of the Enlightenment project reached its peak, forming a decisive front against progressive cosmopolitan forces that descended from the Enlightenment project. The Middle Ages already had prepared sufficient grounds for chauvinism and political anti-Semitism to give birth to something as violent and catastrophic as Nazism. That is also to say, while nationalism comes to the stage in late modernity, it is only reasonable to think of its roots in the earlier centuries not so much as the Hegelian notion of the progression of reason but precisely as a turning point in the development of regression or unreason, at times as a continuation of the religious irrationality and at times as a reaction to the revolutionary project of the Enlightenment. Therefore, blaming the Enlightenment as such, as is fashionable now due to both wrong-headed versions of postmodernism and the rise of religiosity, is precisely an expression of persistent irrationality, which amounts to the ultimate submission to the age of fascism as the ultimate end of history.

As the Frankfurt School critical theorists insisted, instrumental rationality is at the heart of fascism, and it is the Enlightenment that gave birth to such an irrational rationality. However, it is crucial to emphasize that the Frankfurters remained faithful to the progressive Marxist doctrine, and as such they were careful not to commit any romanticization of the Middle Ages, including and especially the political influence of religion.

While fascism was undeniably an outcome of European nationalism, which in turn emerged from the Enlightenment project, fascism did not amount to the ultimate end of the Enlightenment project. In other words, despite the rational unjustifiability of any attempt to attribute some sort of an emancipatory teleological inner rationality to historical events that include Auschwitz, in the very will of the survivors themselves the bright side of the Enlightenment endured. Thus, the fascist era did not mean all hope was lost with the Enlightenment project. If anything, "for the sake of the hopeless ones" to use Walter Benjamin's phrase (2004, 356), for the sake of the victims of reactionary forces including fascism, we have no other option but to continue the struggle.

Europe has something tangible, namely the catastrophic rise of Fascism and Nazism, to lean on in order to reach the shores of a non-fascist, non-tribalist, and rational world. Unfortunately, it has not succeeded as it betrayed the most fundamental principles of the Enlightenment by tribally isolating itself while at the same time allowing Islamism to become stronger within and without Europe. Today Europe relies on mercenaries—and states that use mercenaries—to guard its gates against the non-white Other. Today the values of the Enlightenment project are desperately fought for in the cities of Afghanistan, Turkey, Syria, Iran, Egypt, and Sudan, rather than European and American institutions. However, in order to defend such a polemical claim and shed light on the significance of relatively popular but extremely underrepresented social movements in the MENA region, first we need to comprehend the nature and scope of the challenges facing the oppressed majority in the region. For that purpose, this chapter focuses on the crisis of fascism in the MENA region.

Fascist idealogues in the Middle East have not been compelled to disguise their aggressive racist and extremist worldviews. Rather, for the most part, the dominant ideologies continue to be discursively vulgar and openly violent. Since its historical emergence in the first half of the 20th century, fascism has never ceased to be prominent among nationalist elites in the Middle East. For the most part, the frenzy of nationalism that was intensified by European colonialism and the European invention of nation-states created a landscape in which fascism was the natural outcome. Long centuries of the hegemony of religious orthodoxy, patriarchal domination, and widespread violence against the underprivileged only further normalized the fascist political climate of the post-European-colonial era. Of course, there are often significant differences from one regime to another, but many of them have fascism, as an *ideology form*, in common.

It just so happened that at the end of World War I (WWI) an Italian right-winger would coin the term "fascism" and Mussolini's movement would adopt it. By the 1930s, the term was used to describe similar ultra-right-wing movements elsewhere in Europe. When the Axis powers lost WWII, the term fell out of popularity and gradually became derogatory for most people.[19] Even at the peak of the interwar fascist era, most fascists outside of Europe, including Japan, never actually identified themselves as such. However, this did not prevent political theorists from labeling the Japanese regime of the 1930s as fascist. In the Middle East, the dominant ideologies of the ruling groups are fascist par excellence, even by conventional standards of fascism studies. They are racist, ultranationalist, puritan,

---

19 As Umberto Eco writes, "Italian fascism was the first right-wing dictatorship that took over a European country, and all similar movements later found a sort of archetype in Mussolini's regime. Italian fascism was the first to establish a military liturgy, a folklore, even a way of dressing—far more influential, with its black shirts, than Armani, Benetton, or Versace would ever be. It was only in the Thirties that fascist movements appeared, with Mosley, in Great Britain, and in Latvia, Estonia, Lithuania, Poland, Hungary, Romania, Bulgaria, Greece, Yugoslavia, Spain, Portugal, Norway, and even in South America" (1995, n.p.).

chauvinist, totalitarian, anti-individualist, anti-communist, illiberal, intolerant of minorities, violent, expansionist, exclusionary, irrational, and often apocalyptic. They glorify violence, sanctify racist wars, produce fraternity-mentality, metaphysicalize the "national" identity, dehumanize and demonize otherness, popularize myths and mysticism, *mobomassify* workers, idolize the father figure, continually produce images of conspiring enemies, and victimize the collective (ethnic and/or religious) self. The ultranationalist and Islamist discourses systematically call for the unity among all in-groups to uproot imagined internal enemies and defeat fictive external enemies. Precisely because these are so common among the ruling regimes and the elite groups that support those regimes in the Middle East, fascism has barely been problematized or criticized.

Like many other scholars, I am careful not to write what could be used to further the daily and systematic discrimination against Muslims or any other group wherever they might face discrimination as a minority. Ironically, American white supremacists and European neofascist movements commonly use the expression "Islamofascism." I believe it is crucially important for people to realize that white supremacist ideology and Islamism belong to the same category despite the fact that each side, usually, not always, points to the other side to induce fear and hatred on which their own popularity depends for the most part. Fascism studies should play its role in clarifying that just as Aryan fascism is a political ideology that cannot be generalized to all those who are perceived as so-called "Aryans," Islamism is an ideology that is not endorsed by the majority of Muslim believers. Not despite but because of that, we are in need of serious fascism studies that could address Islamism in its various ideological, social, and political genealogies.

Avoiding the subject of fascism, whether religious or secular, would only make the despicable racist charges against millions of people more, not less, probable. In the meantime, religious authorities, whether Islamic, Christian, or Hindu, must not be sanctified wherever they commit discrimination against any particular population. Muslim, Islamic, and Islamist are different terms with different references. As intelligent beings, we are capable of rejecting two wrongs at the same time. We can, and should, reject anti-Muslim neofascism and Islamism at the same time just as we should be able to reject anti-Christian violence and Christian fascism at the same time. Without such awareness, there is always the risk of supporting a fascist camp in the name of fighting fascism.

Even when it comes to Islamist fundamentalism, the mainstream liberal and left in the West has refused to go beyond the habit of perceiving everything that has to do with Islam as the Other of the West. While the perception on the surface claims altruism and sympathy when the Muslim Other is systematically portrayed as a victim of the European man, it is deeply Orientalist and Eurocentric for it is not able to recognize the subjective autonomy of the perceived Muslim or the simple fact that a Muslim majority society, like other societies, contains various right-wing and left-wing orientations, politics, and forces. As a result, the far-right white nationalists and Islamophobes are left to freely exploit and abuse this gap that is caused by the lack of critical studies and formation of proper political alliances with the liberal, progressive, feminist, and democratic forces of the MENA region. Instead, often well-intentioned Western liberals and leftists unknowingly fall into the trap of supporting fascist movements and regimes in the MENA region, falsely assuming that they stand in solidarity with the victims of Western imperialism.

There is a desperate need for critical studies of fascism that would not exclude the MENA region. The fact that there are only a few studies in this area is itself alarming. Limiting fascism studies geographically to Europe and the Europeanized world may, superficially, suggest Euro-self-critique, i.e., holding Europeans alone responsible for fascism. On a closer analysis, we should be able to realize that such a view, just like clearer forms of Eurocentrism, is problematic. The implied assumption is that non-Europeans do not have a superiority myth. This might sound alright until we raise questions such as, "why is such an assumption made in the first place?" and "what makes non-white societies immune to the emergence of supremacist ideologies, supposedly?" It seems to me that the Eurocentrism of fascism studies is rooted in a rather racist assumption according to which only Europeans can suffer from racist arrogance, implying that non-Europeans cannot even be fascists.

It is definitely not that other societies are assumed to be free of confused, misguided, and irrational groups. It is just that even in *their* forms of confusion, misguidedness, and irrationality, as the unspoken assumption goes, they do not produce supremacy myths. And why not? This is where the mental racist structure can be exposed. Even though racist supremacy is always a myth, just like any other myth, it is the product of a false subjective reading of an objective reality. That is to say, the nature of the subjective falsity is still dependent on the nature of the objective reality. The only explanation for why it is assumed that non-whites are not at risk of constructing superiority myths is that it is assumed that everyone in all non-white societies are always already living with an unmistakable sense of inferiority. Therefore, the unconscious prejudice beneath the politically correct assumption that fascism is a white racist phenomenon is itself a white racist prejudice. To assume that fascism is a white phenomenon does not entail that non-whites are universally and metaphysically so good that they would not produce fascist movements. Rather, the unconscious assumption is that the non-white cannot even be a fascist. After all, fascism is a political notion and as such to be fascist presupposes subjecthood, personhood, autonomous individuality, and the ability to be wrong.

Political terms are not attributed to beings who lack subjecthood, personhood, individuality, and autonomous faculties of judgment. We do not describe a cat or a horse as liberal, socialist, or fascist, for instance, simply because a cat or a horse is not a political actor. For the dominant Eurocentric modes of ideology, non-Europeans' social and political lives are traditionally and culturally determined just as the behavior of cats and horses are determined on bases other than autonomous faculties of rational and moral judgment.

Throughout the rest of the book, there will be other occasions to revisit this oblique form of racism, or culturalism, and further problematize it, but now an overview of fascism in the Middle East is in order. However, what follows is not a conventional account of political groups that identified themselves as fascists. Such an account would be based on the conventional definitions of fascism, which are not effective for diagnosing fascism beyond a particular history and geography. Moreover, the political weight of self-identified fascist groups in the Middle East has been negligible anyway; what is more important is to examine dominant movements and ideologies in search of symptoms of fascism, which is the objective of the rest of this chapter.

Turkey

If we do not conflate the first emergence of the term of fascism with the rise of the first type of movement that could be called fascist, we could maintain that Turkish fascism actually predates both Italian and German fascism. This claim might sound odd to scholars who continue to consider Italian Fascism the starting point of fascism, even though Italian Fascism would not meet the most important criterion of fascism as defined by Giovanni Gentile himself, namely, totalitarianism (1995, 54). While Kemalism as a model of fascism has been largely ignored in fascism studies, finally a few illuminating works became available in the last ten years, including Stefan Ihrig's extensive and rigorous historiographic research that shows Kemalism's influence on Italian Fascism and the formation of Nazism (2014). Ihrig's work shows beyond any doubt that if we were to place the beginning of fascism in the 20th century both as an ideology and a regime, it should be Kemalism. The fact that Ataturk provided the first fascist example is clear even from direct references made by both Mussolini and Hitler. For instance, Mussolini called himself "the Mustafa Kemal of a Milanese Ankara" (quoted in Ihrig 2014, 106), and the fascist monthly *Gerarchia* headlined its last issue prior to the fascist March on Rome "*La luna crescent*," which was the title of an article on "Kemal Pasha's March on Izmir" written by the Duce himself (Ihrig 2014, 106). Hitler proudly admitted this fact, for instance, when he said "Atatürk was a teacher; Mussolini was his first and I his second student" or "Turkey was our model" and Ataturk was a "star in the darkness" (quoted in Ihrig 2014, 116).

Vahram Ter-Matevosyan makes a strong case for criticizing the dismissal of Kemalist (Turkish) fascism in fascism studies (2015). Ter-Matevosyan bases his approach on Sternhell's account, according to which the beginning of fascism in the history of ideas is the 19th century. He then traces back the origins of pan-Turkism to the late 19th century when Turkish elites came under the heavy influence of German and French racist nationalists and social Darwinists (Ter-Matevosyan 2015), and by the turn of the century, nationalist "writers began to emphasize the superiority of the Turks over other, especially Muslim, Ottoman ethnic groups" (Hanioglu 2014, 9). Ter-Matevosyan then observes that "once in power from 1908 to 1918 (with a brief interlude in 1912) and particularly after 1913, the Committee for Union and Progress had the chance to experiment with some of the constitutive elements of the fascist ideology, although the word came into existence later" (2015, 213). The fascist policies only intensified in the following decades, both influencing and being influenced by Italian and German fascism, but even in the years prior to the establishment of the Turkish Republic, the nationalist movement succeeded in the "spontaneous application of many policy features (pan-Turkism, unification of all Turks to build the Turkish father-land, expansionist ambitions, homogenisation, assimilation, resettlement of population)" (Ter-Matevosyan 2015, 213).

Other than the invention of the name, there is barely anything in Italian Fascism in 1920–1921 that could render it a more developed form of fascism than Turkish fascism both then and now. In fact, one can argue that Mussolini's movement never made it to the level of hegemony, totalitarianism, militarization, and mass racist mobilization of society enjoyed by Turkish nationalism. Therefore, Hitler's claim that he and Mussolini had been Ataturk's disciples was anything but metaphoric. While the Duce's goal to revive the glories of the Roman Empire and the Führer's dream of a Third Reich were semi-mythical at best, Kemal Pasha, who eventually named himself the Father of Turks, "Ataturk" in Turkish, was actually one of the generals of the empire. However, he wanted a more homogeneous and modern state with one absolute will, language, and pan-Turkish ideology led by himself. In other words, Kemalism was already incomparably a more developed fascist ideology than either Fascism or Nazism would ever become. Not to mention the fact that Ataturk's fascist regime and ideology are still alive and well more than a century after its birth.

Today, thanks to Erdogan's neo-Ottoman amendments, Turkish fascism leads not only pan-Turkic nationalism but also Sunni Islamism with a strong imperialist agenda stretching its colonialist ambitions from Central Asia to North Africa, from Italy's and France's former colonies to the gates of Europe itself. Also, very much like the Duce and the Führer, Erdogan shows little respect to anyone except for other powerful absolutists, such as Putin and Trump. In the meantime, Erdogan has successfully bullied European political leaders, exploiting their xenophobia and bad faith in the universal human rights, to pay his regime billions of Euros in order to keep refugees outside Europe. Erdogan is a typical fascist leader especially in terms of his strategy to smash every perceived and potential opponent in the order of vulnerability starting from the most vulnerable, and to maximally exploit those who show signs of relative weakness. Therefore, he will continue to make the most out of Europe's bad faith. While his proxy wars and Islamist expansion continue to create more and more refugees, he makes himself increasingly indispensable as the only man who holds the key to the damn behind which there is what Europe perceives as the single most fatal threat, the "refugee flood." It seems as though the horrors of the 1529 siege of Vienna has not left Euro-imagination, but this time around the European leadership knowingly wants to mistake the victims for the invaders and Recep Tayyip Erdogan for John III Sobieski. Jihadis supported by Erdogan have been roaming around turning almost every civil war in the MENA region into another ISIS-like nightmare, while the EU states, without any sense of irony or guilt, continue to support Turkey with money, military logistics, and weapons.

Chauvinism is a core characteristic of every fascist movement. As Sarah Churchwell puts it, "all fascism is indigenous, by definition" (2020). That said, the rise of fascism is a cross-national and cross-continental phenomenon. Fascist movements enable each other by capitalizing on and exploiting various provincial, racist, and sectarian xenophobia. The point to be emphasized here is not just that fascism has never left the Middle East since its inception but also Europe has never securely moved beyond fascism. The racist distrust of the Muslim Other of Europe has fulfilled the xenophobic prophesy by empowering Islamists and creating millions of refugees. At the same time, that very mentality has contributed to the realization of the worst possible outcomes for Europe's perceived Other. Namely, it has further disempowered the victims of Islamism, i.e., the vast majority of ordinary people in the MENA region, including those who become refugees escaping violence and its consequences.

By the 1930s, Kemalism "introduced the absolute superiority of 'Turkishness' (understood as something in between Nation and Race) and its revolution; which, in turn, legitimized the pyramidal rule of the Chiefs, headed by the Eternal Chief" (Bozarslan 2014, 34), and Kemal Ataturk had already become the worshipped figure whose images had occupied the foci of all public spaces. The racist policies of Turkification and the Kemalist personality cult as two clear signs of Turkish fascism still continue in Turkey, only supplemented by religious fanaticism and neo-Ottoman imperialism under Erdogan.

The Armenian genocide provided the model for the Nazis' determinate intention to commit the Holocaust (Ihring 2014). As the head of the state and the idealized absolute leader of Turkish nationalism, in the 1930s, Kemal Ataturk had

Turkish scientists design and publish biological research supposedly proving the superiority of the Turkish race (Hanioglu 2011, 162–171). Kemalism waged its genocidal campaigns against all those who were not considered Turks in Anatolia long before Nazism became popular in Germany, and the enduring power of fascist discourse in Turkey's political sphere clearly underlines the fact that Kemalist fascism has largely outlived Nazism and other European fascist regimes. Unlike Nazism, Turkish fascism has continued to enjoy virtually uninterrupted support from Western democracies. The West tends to view Kemalism against the Islamic Middle Eastern backdrop, as opposed to the liberal European milieu. From that perspective, all that matters ideologically is that Kemalism stands out as both secular and pro-Western. The continual genocidal campaigns against non-Turkish Anatolian peoples, most notably Armenians, but also Assyrians, Yezidis, Greeks (from 1915 to 1923), and later Kurds (starting with the Zaza and Alevi Kurds of Dersim in 1937–1938) have never been factored into Western democracies' diplomatic calculations. While the rise of the French National Front and the Freedom Party of Austria, understandably, spurred panic throughout Europe, Turkey remained an indispensable ally of Europe and the US. Of course, Western complicity over the last century has only served to further legitimize and normalize Turkish fascism.

Just as in Italy until the 1940s and in Spain until the 1970s, in Turkey anti-fascist Marxist and other leftist social movements have always been strongly present despite the violent suppression to which they have been subjected since the 1920s. Most recently, with the emergence of the Peoples' Democratic Party (HDP), a new movement has appeared that is supported by progressive Kurds, Turks, Arabs, Alevis, Christians, and others, which may be a hopeful historical turn whereby all forms of exclusionary discrimination are challenged in the interest of an inclusive political environment and an egalitarian social climate. The HDP is the only political party that (1) enjoys relative popularity in not only the Kurdish-majority cities but also in some Turkish-majority cities, and, at the same time, (2) explicitly rejects fascism and all forms of discrimination, including discrimination against politically oppressed peoples such as Kurds and Armenians, and discrimination against societally marginalized groups such as women, children, and LGBTQ+.

The HDP is part of a larger movement in Turkey, which is in turn part of an even broader regional post-national movement that is uniquely egalitarian, inclusive, feminist, secular, and pluralist. The Rojava experiment in Syria is the strongest manifestation of the same movement.[20] Recently, that same movement's central

---

20 For more on the history, philosophy, and politics of this movement and the ways in which it rejects nationalism and fundamentalism, see Öcalan 2013, 2017; Knapp and Jongerden 2014; Tax 2016; Ahmed 2019a, 2014a, 2014b.

slogan, *Jin, Jiyan, Azadi* (women, life, freedom), has been adopted by the popular Iranian anti-regime protest movement that (in less than two weeks after its first spark following the killing of a Kurdish woman, Mehsa Jina Amini, in Tehran at the hands of the regime's morality police), in addition to the Kurdish-majority Kurdistan, reached every corner of the country including the Persian-majority area in the center, the Arab-majority Arabistan, the Baloch-majority Balochistan, and the Azeri-majority Western Azerbaijan (Ahmed 2022b).

The Arab World

Turkish nationalism also inspired the "spiritual father of Arab nationalism" Sati Al-Husri, who was an Ottoman official and a fanatic supporter of the Young Turks (Tibi 1997). Al-Husri (in)famously drew from the ideology of the Young Turks to cultivate Arab nationalism in Syria and Iraq, particularly in his fascist construction of the education systems. During WWII, he openly advocated the Nazis in the Arab world. In April 1941, with the help of Mussolini and Hitler's regimes, Al-Husri's followers in the Iraqi army carried out a military coup against the monarchy in Iraq and installed Rashid Ali al-Gailani who was also a pro-Nazi pan-Arabist. Al-Gailani's regime was removed in May by the Regent of Iraq, Abd al-Ilah, with the help of the British forces.

However, this fascist coup gave rise to the bloodiest campaigns of the 20th century against Iraqi Jews in Baghdad up until then. The nationalists accused the Jews of aiding the British Army in retaking Baghdad and they mobilized the masses who attacked Jewish families across the city, killing hundreds of Jews and looting Jewish properties in the infamous pogrom known as *Farhud*, to which most other ethnic and religious groups would be subjected during the decades that followed. Al-Gailani fled to Nazi Germany and Al-Husri was deported to Syria. However, Al-Husri became the most influential figure in shaping the Arab League from its early days in the mid-1940s and the engineer of nationalizing the education systems in both Syria and Iraq (Tibi 1997, 121–122), both of which remain extremely fascist, especially in their portrayal of world history, international politics, Arabhood, and the adoption of anti-Semitism.

After Al-Husri's generation, Jamal Abdul Nasser and the founders of Baathism were the next generation of Arab nationalists. Egypt, especially under the celebrated Nasser, became a welcoming refuge for surviving Nazi officials. As Del Boca and Giovana explain, many Nazi officials who came to Egypt were even given prestigious and influential positions in the government (1970). Most notably, Nasser hired Johann von Leers, a major Nazi ideologue and propagandist, as his own adviser, who thought Nasser made a better leader than Hitler (Del Boca and Giovani 1970, 401). Praising Nasser's fascism, the French fascist Maurice Bardéche wrote:

> Nasser and his friends have discovered that the whole of Fascist mysticism is to be found in Islam, which is their past and, in the wider and more comprehensive sense of the term, their culture—that is to say, not only their source of inspiration, but something that conforms very closely with their nature and their instincts [. . .] Although it is just as inimitable as Hitler's Germanism, Nasser's crusade is, like National Socialism, confined to the men of one nation. But its geographical situation and the moment of its emergence endow it with the greatest significance. Of all the Fascist mysticisms it is probably the one which will leave the deepest mark on history on account of its enduring consequences. (quoted in Del Boca and Giovana 1970, 401–402)

Ironically, here we witness a relatively early instance of post-WWII culturalism, only used to make the racist case in a fatally positive sense. Apparently, to Maurice Bardéche, the perceived Arab primitiveness makes Arabs more successful material for the fascist project. The liberal antithesis of this view completely excludes Arabs from fascism studies, assuming that fascism is a European phenomenon. But we should not miss the irony here: both views are Eurocentric and racist because they are premised on the deeply rooted mentality of cultural racism. That is to say, the contrast between the two seemingly opposing positions is superficial. The difference simply stems from the two different political platforms or agendas.

While Bardéche sees in Arabs natural fascists in need of some organization and mobilization, which was, allegedly, taken care of by Nasser, the liberal position is not prepared to elevate the perceived barbarity of Arabs to the level of the ideological sophistication of fascism. Since fascism is indeed a modern phenomenon, reaching modernity, even in the reactionary sense, is a necessary prerequisite for forming fascism. Because Arab societies are perceived to be pre-modern, it is assumed that no movement in those societies can obtain the ideological sophistication of fascism, or other forms of post-Enlightenment ideologies for that matter. Thus, at the root of both views, culturalism is strongly present. Needless to say, for that precise reason, among others, both views are false. It should go without saying, contemporary Arab societies, like all contemporary societies, are exposed to the spectrum of modern ideologies from the far right to the far left, of course with respective geopolitical specifications. In my work, including this book, I aim to problematize and refute culturalism in all its implicit and explicit, illiberal and liberal, antagonistic and moralistic, applications, thereby rejecting the false dichotomies produced by Eurocentrism. Regardless of its geographic and historical circumstances, a society must neither be demonized nor romanticized. When nationalism became the dominant ideological form of the age, Arabs, like Turks, Persians, and others, were not exceptions. Also, like other nationalisms, Arab nationalism produced its own fascist tendencies.

Nasserism's rivals in Syria and Iraq were the Baathists.[21] Both Nasser's Arab Socialist Union and the Arab Socialist Baath Party relied heavily on the German National Socialist model not only in their propaganda (Joseph Goebbels is still quoted by Baathists), but also in their anti-Semitic discourse, depictions of the leader as the savior destined to restore the glory of the nation, and, of course, calls for national purity and a "final solution" for all those who failed to meet the nationalist criteria. In fact, concentration camps for political dissidents, defectors, rivals, and minorities figured prominently in the Baathist regime in Iraq. The regime perfected the politics of elimination by completely erasing every trace of all the victims of *al-anfal* in the late 1980s. There is a chapter in the Quran called *Al-anfal* "The Spoils of War" that urges believers to behead "infidel" men. Saddam Hussein chose the term *Al-anfal* for his genocidal campaign against Kurds in the late 1980s that claimed hundreds of thousands of lives. As far as I know, to date, not a single picture of any of those concentration camps has been found, and no former Baathist soldiers have revealed any information about the methods used to eliminate so many people.[22]

The Islamist and secular Arab nationalist alliance with Nazism has yet to be renounced in the Arab world, and anti-Semitism has arguably increased since the 1940s, as it is clear to any observer of the region's dominant political and religious discourses in which often Zionists and Jews are used interchangeably and sometimes Zionism, used vaguely, is the main object of antagonism.[23] Arab nationalists

---

21 For a concise but thorough presentation of the striking similarities between Nasserism and Mussolini's fascism, see Chapter 7 of A. James Gregor (2006). Gregor is among the scholars who use the term fascism very conservatively, staying faithful to the so-called generic definition of fascism, which is based on the characteristics of Italian Fascism. Therefore, it is particularly important that he makes the case about Nasserism's resemblance to Italian Fascism. His account of Islamism in the same chapter is equally informative.

22 In 2020, a former official of the Iraqi secret police, named Sabah Al-Hamdani, in an Arabic interview, admitted the indiscriminate arrest of Kurdish women, children, and men from rural areas and their mass murder by the Saddam Hussein regime in 1988 (see UTV 2020).

23 The Arabic website of *Aljazeera* published an article titled "The Role of the Arab Regime in Empowering Zionism" by a prominent journalist who is also the managing editor of a well-known magazine. In his narrative of the main events in the Arab-Israel conflict, the author emphasizes what he considers to be the missed opportunities of a historic victory of Arabs over Jews when the jihadis managed to blockade 100,000 Jews in Jerusalem at some point during the 1948 war. The Arabs committed what the writer sees as a fatal mistake when they accepted the UN ceasefire resolution, which gave the Jewish forces a chance to regroup and bring water and food to the Jews in Jerusalem, according to the writer (see Shaban Abdulrahman 2014). Anti-Semitic charges in the public sphere are not restricted to the coverage of the conflict with Israel. In 2018, an Iraqi news website published an extremely anti-Semitic article under the title that would be translated as, "How did the Jews control the porn industry to destroy human society? Discover it yourself."

and Islamists have been exploiting the Israeli-Palestinian conflict from its very beginning to further justify and popularize their anti-Semitism among ordinary citizens.[24] While some of those who remember their Jewish neighbors look back nostalgically to the past, few Middle Easterners outside Israel have had any contact with Jews because most Jews were forced to leave their countries in the late 1940s and early 1950s. Therefore, for the generation that grew up in the 1960s and later, there was nothing to counter the official anti-Semitic discourse that targeted Jews, universally holding them responsible not only for the statelessness of the Palestinian but also for more or less the continual state of crises whether wars, civil unrest, or economic underdevelopment and poverty. Perhaps what is most indicative of this typical anti-Semitic mentality, according to which there is always at least a Jewish conspiracy at work, is the ironic phenomenon of rivals accusing each other of Zionism. The premise is that Zionism is the worst possible crime, so if party A succeeded in convincing the public that party B has an affiliation with Zionism, nothing more is needed to be done to make party B collapse automatically as a result of the public's unforgiving reaction.

Throughout the Arab Spring uprisings, one of the most common accusations made by governments against their opposition was the alleged Zionist plot carried out by the traitors in order to destabilize the nationalist and patriotic government that proudly stood in the face of Zionist plans (Al-labwani 2019). Similarly, the opposition would regularly accuse the rulers of working for Zionist interests and thereby securing the support of Israel and American imperialism (e.g., Hamdi 2013). Secular elites, including national socialists, and Islamists are usually fatal enemies, but they have anti-Semitism, and other forms of racism, in common. The movements of the Arab Spring did not change that anywhere from Tunisia to Yemen. By drawing attention to the disturbingly widespread anti-Semitism I do not mean to attribute fascism to the majority of ordinary people. Rather, I think the Arab intelligentsia is mainly to be blamed for consciously advocating fascist ideologies, in some cases, and for not problematizing fascism, in other cases. The problem is that, if anything, the anti-Semitic policies of Nazism made it more, not less, popular among opinion makers in the region. The degree to which fascism is not problem-

---

Without any sense of irony, the piece was posted under the "Research and Reportage" section of the website (Alsaid 2018).

24 Of course, anti-Semitism here and elsewhere in this chapter is to be taken in the commonly used sense, i.e., racist hatred against perceived Jews. Otherwise, it is well known that race theorists and historians, including Arab nationalists, consider Arabs as a Semitic "race/nation." The Baathists have always been open about their anti-Semitism, anti-Jewish racism (for instance, see Al-Arzuzi n.d., 23).

atized by the intelligentsia and the normalcy of unmistakable anti-Semitic fascism exceeds the boundaries of academic concerns and jargons.

I made a conscious choice not to discuss the Israeli-Palestinian conflict and its role in spreading anti-Semitism for the simple fact that I do not want to contribute to the mentality that dismisses the magnitude of the problem of anti-Semitism by falsely associating its origin to that conflict. The mentality that searches for reasons in the deeds of the victims, or those rightly or wrongly associated with the victims, is itself a racist mentality. Racism always entails self-justification, and that justification is always false. Certainly, the Israeli-Palestinian conflict has intensified anti-Semitism among opinion makers in the Arab societies, but we should be able to address the problem of anti-Semitism without necessarily making that conflict central to the research. The Nazis strongly believed their anti-Semitic policies were a reaction to, or rather a solution for, what Jews allegedly had committed, or "the Jewish question." Today, the anti-Semitic mentality has not changed in terms of blaming the victims or those associated with them, or else anti-Semitism would have ended long ago. The Jews who were brutalized, robbed, or murdered in 1941 and those who were hanged on the electric poles of Baghdad in 1969 were as Iraqi as anyone could be and had nothing to do with Israeli politics and policies (note that the state of Israel was founded in 1948). The same goes for the many millions of others from various nationalities and backgrounds, including Arabs and Muslims, who became victims of the same fascism over the decades that followed.

That said, perhaps this deep anti-Jewish sense of enmity will start to change if the most recent diplomatic normalization projects between Israel and some Arab monarchies succeed in creating a shift in the public climate of opinion in Arab societies. What makes this somewhat probable is the fact that both Baathism and Nasserism, as the two extremist versions of Arab nationalism, have lost the popularity they enjoyed for many decades. Ironically, the Arab monarchies, including the Saudis, but with the exception of Qatar, have created a front against Islamism while Baathists, once adamantly secular and anti-Islamist, have joined the two main Islamist camps. Iraqi Baathists have merged almost entirely with Sunni Islamist movements, and the Syrian Baath sold its soul (along with Syrian state sovereignty) to the Iranian Islamist regime and Hezbollah. Arab nationalist elites, whether secular or Islamist, have lost their leadership to the Islamist camps led by Erdogan's Ankara and Khamenei's Tehran. The bloody conflicts in both Syria and Yemen reveal the hegemony of non-Arab players. In Yemen, the Houthis openly represent the Iranian regime's front against the Yemenis supported by the Kingdom of Saudi Arabia and the United Arab Emirates. In Syria, while the regime is supported by Iran, the Sunni Arab opposition has become a Turkish proxy fighting other Syrians to annex more land to the Turkish-ruled territories. These are indications of the ultimate failure of Arab nationalism to reach any of its goals regarding national sovereignty, and

Arab unity, let alone the revival of what to the nationalist mindset was once an Arab civilization. Not surprisingly, once more, those who want to make it great again have only succeeded in bringing about catastrophes, mass murder, suffering, and humiliation for their societies.

Under fascism, the Other is seen as an obstacle that must be neutralized, even if that means physical elimination. The majority's language, culture, and values are of course seen as natural and universal, at least within the geographic borders claimed by fascist nationalists. In stark contrast, the language, culture, and identity of the othered minority, are considered sectarian, tribal, backward, strange, irrational, primitive, and so on. Thus, when the majority imposes its language and values on minorities, it is only for the sake of the minority's interest, supposedly. Unfortunately, this way of thinking continues to be indicative of how minorities are treated throughout the Middle East.

The minority is always expected to accept oppression unconditionally in order to demonstrate that they are not conspiring to overthrow the glorious nation, or simply to prove that they deserve the right to live. It is as though the minority's only task in life is to painstakingly try to win the ruling elites' trust. Yet, it is virtually impossible for the nationalist elites to ever really trust certain minorities, if for no other reason than because one "bad" action by a minority member is deemed representative of the entire minority group—while there is a tendency to underestimate the magnitude and significance of systematic acts of violence against minorities. And since it is sociologically impossible for all members of a minority group to act in the same "harmless" way, it is impossible to meet the (politicized) majority's conditions for earning trust.

The majority-minority relationship is very much analogous to the husband-wife relationship in the most misogynistic of societies. Typical of Middle Eastern fascism, fascist leaders often try to evoke familial emotions to both agitate the largest possible number of people among the majority and appease minorities. Because family is the locus of suppression in patriarchal societies, it makes sense to see state fascism as a broader development of the micro-fascist and chauvinist dynamics of the family. A particularly demonstrative example can be seen in Iraq, where Iraqi nationalist elites have responded to calls for independence in the Kurdistan region by repeatedly analogizing Kurdistan to the wife who seeks separation from her husband (Arab Iraq). Notably, this analogy is never phrased the other way around, which highlights how Kurds have been seen all along by nationalist Iraqi Arab elites. Just as the wife in a patriarchal society is habitually exploited and abused but is nonetheless expected to fully accept the authority of her husband, Kurds and other minorities in the Middle East are expected to bear the brunt of fascist regimes without complaint.

On September 25, 2017, Iraqi Kurds voted for independence in a referendum that was vehemently opposed by not only the Iraqi government but also the Turkish, Iranian, and Syrian governments. On the following day, Iraqi newspaper *Al-Nahar*, on its front page, published a picture of five black men in underwear standing behind a couch and staring at the young blonde girl sitting on the couch. The image clearly indicated that the girl was about to be raped by the five men. The word printed on the chest of each one of the men read, Iran, Syria, Turkey, Iraq, and Jordon, respectively while the word "Kurdistan" was printed on the image of the female figure. Notice the newspaper used the image of five black men, which speaks to another layer of racist stereotypes at work, namely depicting black men as instruments of rape. The message, of course, was that Kurdistan was about to be raped by the five countries. Most of the remaining space on the page was dedicated to headlines and columns that indicated Turkish and Iraqi threats against Kurdistan.[25]

The state of Balochs in Iran and Pakistan, the Amazigh in Morocco, and native Africans in Sudan and Mauritania are just a few other examples of nations whose very existence is seen as a threat to the imperial nation-states that oppress them. Asian and African countries immediately became imperialist at the very moments of their independence from their European colonizers. The assumption that the state is the political expression of the nation, which is in turn imagined to be culturally homogeneous and "racially" pure, has not been challenged widely enough in the region. During the period between the two world wars and the 1950s, communist movements represented the only relatively popular anti-fascist force throughout the region. Then, the brutal suppression of the communist parties along with Moscow's betrayal of the movement prepared the region for the reign of fascism unchallenged until the Arab Spring.

The Arab Spring, however, precisely because of the absence of a popular left, was hijacked by Islamist forces in every country because they were the only movement that was organized enough to be able to determinately seize power, of course with the support of established Islamist regimes. During the first year of the Arab Spring, it already became clear that liberals would be neither able to seize power nor prepared to transform the uprisings to a revolution to rearrange the wider social relations of power and privilege (Ahmed 2011). Islamism dominated the stage so swiftly that the Arab Spring was halted before reaching more than half of the Arab-majority countries. People had legitimate reason to cling to the existing

---

25 For a screen shot of the front page of the newspaper, including the image, and a commentary in English, see Middle East Eye Staff 2017.

autocratic regimes as opposed to opening the door for the Islamists whose kingdom of God was nothing but a common doomsday.

In times of crisis, which have been more or less continual throughout the Middle East over the last hundred years, the perception of stability is associated with the notion of a strong leader, a patriarch who can discipline everyone in the family. Fascist leaders, in turn, excel at playing the role of the father who can use excessive force, but only for the sake of everyone in the family, for creating unity and stability. Just like God, the leader is both merciless and merciful. When he appears to be too severe, it is only because he knows best. The leader does not have to explain anything because his wisdom is beyond the people's comprehension; his judgment is trusted as a matter of course.

Given the intellectual impoverishment of the fascist leader, this arrangement works perfectly well. The leader's strength lies in his manipulation of physical force, and whenever he speaks, his statements are easily quotable and relatable for the *mobomass* individual. With the passage of time, and surrounded by an ingratiating inner circle, the leader comes to believe the lie that he is a sort of divine being, which quickly gives him the confidence to talk about everything. The follower reads this development as the leader's incredible modesty, insofar as he is willing to engage with issues of concern to the average man. However, this habit of talking about everything is in fact a clear symptom of old-fashioned totalitarianism. Fascism, in Giovani Gentile's words, is "a total conception of life" (1995, 54). The leader, as the embodiment of divine wisdom, becomes the authority in all arenas of social life and knowledge. He could pass judgment on anything from personal hygiene and eating habits to clothing choices, raising children, education, ethics, and medicine.

Saddam Hussein, for instance, had no reservations about advising all women that they should shower twice a day. In the same speech, he would also make statements about imperialism, the enemies of the nation, and the glorious future the revolution would secure for the nation. Every word he uttered would be reported by the media as sacred text. In the same vein, Khomeini in his *Little Green Book*, which is a collection of his fatwas and is religiously esteemed by his faithful followers, unflinchingly provides detailed instructions for the proper way to defecate and clean oneself afterwards (Khomeini 1985, §21).

In the old versions of fascist ideologies, there is always a fascist figure who is treated as a divine being. Insulting this leader is considered a serious crime on the level of blasphemy, for he symbolizes everything the nation aspires to be. He is the teacher, the father, the leader, the philosopher, and, of course, the hero. He gazes at everyone in the nation through his images and statues positioned at the very center of public spaces. It is because of him—not the miserable marginalized souls who build the infrastructure, farm the land, and clean the streets—that the nation thrives. From birth he was fated for a sacred mission, for making the nation free and powerful. He is above and beyond mistakes or misdeeds.

The fascist leader symbolizes force, and it is typical of sadomasochistic personalities to identify with the powerful and resent the marginalized, as we learn from Wilhelm Reich (1970, 63). Identifying with the powerful amounts to disguising the broken personality that has suffered from prolonged humiliation and suppression. Crushed and degraded, the authoritarian character, "the personality structure which is the human basis of Fascism" in Fromm's words (1965, 186), perceives power as the magical redemption for everything, but above all power is the main path to negating their own feeling of insignificance. The fascist movement, regardless of its religiosity or secularism, offers the mobs a religious experience of euphoria and a sense of purpose. What makes this source of power and purpose especially appealing is that the fascist doctrine articulated by the leader is extremely simplistic, containing strong elements of mysticism. Expressions such as "the spirit of the nation" or "the greatness of the nation," as both Mussolini and Hitler were well aware, designate nothing but a myth that is intended to stimulate the irrational drives of the followers. As such, they give rise to a violent movement eager to attack at the slightest provocation, which is usually supplied by the leadership and the fascist propaganda machine. The role of the charismatic leader is essential for mobilizing the mobs, which in turn is essential for the formation of fascist totalitarianism, Arendt noted (1979, xxxii).

The failure of Arab nationalism to fulfill any of its promises including the realization of Arab unity and emancipating Palestine has divided the popular bases of pan-Arabism along Sunni and Shia sectarian lines, which are exploited to their full political potentialities by the rulers of Turkey and Iran respectively. The retrogressive fallbacks into nationalism and then into Islamism were rooted in the demise of the communist movement, which was once a main if not the main emancipatory orientation in Egypt and Iraq. Relative to the size of the respective populations, the number of revolutionary communists in Egypt was substantially larger than the number of Bolsheviks in Russia on the eve of the October Revolution (Laqueur 1956, 277).[26] The Iraqi Communist Party (ICP) was by far the most popular political party in the country until the Baathists took over power and banned political parties (Laqueur 1956, 277; Franzén 2011). Bloody campaigns against the commu-

---

26 Walter Laqueur may be right that nationalism arrived in the Middle East without its liberalizing and democratic objectives, but his portrayal of European nationalism as successful models, if anything, is indicative of his own biases. Those biases become clear from the first few pages of the book as he insists on grouping communism, in the Middle East and everywhere else, as inherently illiberal and anti-democratic, just like Islamists and chauvinistic nationalism (1956, 7–9).

nists at the hands of police states from Tunisia, Egypt, and Sudan to Yemen, Syria, and Iraq continued for decades until the movement was almost eradicated, leaving the stage for two retroactive protagonists. Arab nationalism transfigured most of the Arab republics into what could be considered textbook cases of fascist dictatorships. Bashar Al-Assad is the last surviving member of that class of nationalist Arab leaders who have never failed to bring upon their peoples every imaginable form of division, suffering, and humiliation on multiple national, regional, and global levels. Baathism and Nasserism were the two main lines of Arab nationalism, and both were the equivalents of German National Socialism. Nasserism started to lose its hegemony after Nasser's death in 1970 when Baathism had just started its absolutist reign in both Iraq and Syria. The Syrian Baath has been in power in Damascus since 1963, and Baghdad fell under Baathism from 1968 to 2003. Both Baath parties, in Syria and Iraq, kept their mother party's slogan: "A single Arab nation with an immortal mission." Today, the Iraqi and Syrian societies are among the most devastated and brutalized societies in the world.

The nationalist leader felt entitled to eternal authority due to his actual or alleged role in the anti-colonial past struggle and positioned himself as the new god on earth in a disturbingly fascist style that mixed republicanism with a prototypical notion of dynasticism, citizenship with the absolute oneness of "the nation," and patriotism with the unconditional allegiance to the oneness ultimately embodied by the leader (in the same way the king was believed to be an embodiment of divinity in Ancient Egypt and the Europe of the Middle Ages). The so-called post-colonial republics not only repeated the European experiment of nationalism but in many cases duplicated the worst, namely the fascist, models. More or less, from Iran and Turkey to Libya and Algeria, each republic had its own Führer or Il Duce with pictures and statues of him occupying the focal points of both public spaces (and private spaces, which could only ironically be called private thanks to the police regimes that expanded the frontiers of the exercise of power to all arenas including people's living rooms). Indeed, the leaders in the so-called republics were by far bloodier and more totalitarian than both the past and enduring traditional monarchies across MENA. In fact, also like Il Duce and the Führer, the nationalist leaders were most obsessed by their utter enmity against the internationalists of their respective countries and had no tolerance for those who were deemed unfit to be part of the great nation, whether in Turkey, Iran, or the Arab republics. While in Europe Italian Fascism and Hitler's Nazism were criminalized and problematized in the post-WWII era, in the MENA region, fascism continues in its old form. This is to say, fascists in the MENA region have not been compelled to shrink in size or somehow mask their openly racist language in the interest of an opaquer fascist discourse.

Iran

Pan-Persian Aryanism is an evident case of the dominance and continuation of the interwar model of fascism. While pan-Turkish fascism gained momentum around the same time as Italian Fascism, and pan-Arab fascism was under the indirect influence of both Turkish nationalism and German Nazism, Persian fascism from the beginning was directly linked to Aryanism. In fact, Aryanism is still the normal discursive model among the pan-Iranian intelligentsia. Iranian nationalists do not seem to see any issue with taking pride from the Persian so-called race's so-called Aryan origin. Even worse, in the Persian-speaking public sphere, one gets the impression that there is no sense of concern regarding the political incorrectness of Aryanist mythology and rhetoric. References to the "Aryan race" constitutes the normative aspect of pan-Iranian nationalism and patriotism. That said, luckily, there is a number of Iranian scholars whose works focus on problematizing this issue. The quantity of such works, in comparison to those who maintain the racist norm, is still extremely small, but hopefully their influence will increase quickly among the general Persian-speaking Iranian intelligentsia. Below, I will touch on some the relevant works of anti-fascist critical research that are conducted by Iranian scholars.

Mostafa Vaziri's pioneering book, *Iran as Imagined Nation*, originally published in 1993, offers a comprehensive account of the mythology, orientalism, and racism surrounding the history of Persian pan-Iranian nationalism from its early emergence in the late 19th century and early 20th (2013). Vaziri's critical analysis of the rise of nationalism is praiseworthy for its deconstruction of not only the Iranian nationalist narrative but also European nationalism. He traces the early European attempts that resulted in the invention of the Aryan race and sheds light on the place Orientalists gave to a homogeneous Iran in their supposed Aryan world. Vaziri offers a much-needed challenge to the normalized nationalist frame of reference and the Orientalist mode of perception that continues to dominate the regimes of knowledge production in Iran and elsewhere.

Adding to this line of critique that demystifies the pan-Persian myth of superiority and exposes the direct racist and fascist European role in the creation of Persian Aryanism, Afshin Matin-Asgari takes issue with the institutionalized and normalized historiography that has been reproducing Iranian Aryanism (2018). Like Vaziri, Asgari exposes the mystifying nature of nationalism in its European origins and the direct involvement of European Orientalists in the invention of the myth of Iranian Aryanism in the 1920s, which increasingly intensified during the 1940s and even after the defeat of the Nazis in 1945. Iranian nationalism benefited from and aided its European counterpart, both by capitalizing on a supposedly superior racial origin and by distinguishing them from their perceived Other or those they classified as non-Aryan. For Italian Fascism, the perceived Others were mainly Arabs, Moors, and, later, Jews; for German fascism, Jews; and for Iranian fascism, Arabs and Turks.[27]

European ideologues of race within and without academia found in Iran (and India) the perfect missing puzzle for Aryanism while Iranian nationalists found in Europeans their supposed kinship, helping both sides to place the collective self in the myth of a mysterious time and place while looking down on large sections of their own societies and other peoples near and far. In this regard, Alireza Asgharzadeh published a book interrogating both the hysterography of Persian Aryanism and rejecting the fascist nature of pan-Iranian nationalism.[28] To Asgharzadeh, many in the intelligentsia are accomplices in the ongoing fascism in Iran, whereby non-Persian self-expressions in Iran are systematically and habitually tribalized and minoritized.[29] Anti-Arab, anti-Azeri, and anti-Turk hate speech are not uncommon among Persian nationalists. This hatred is rooted in some old and modern Persian literature and the normalized Aryanist ideology.

The early stages of Iranian fascism go back to the period of the rise of Turkish fascism only with a different path of development. Unlike both Turkish and Arab nationalism, Iranian nationalism drew its inspiration directly from German fascism on the basis of the racist myth of Aryan superiority. Supporting the historiographical research conducted by Mostafa Vaziri, Alireza Asgharzadeh, and Afshin Matin-Asgari, Reza Zia-Ebrahimi also revisits the direct link between Iranian nationalism and the myth of Aryanism in the worldview of European Orientalists. One of the early Persian nationalists is Mirza Aqa Khan Kermani, who seems to be the first writer who in the late 19th century claimed that Persians belong to the so-called Aryan race (Zia-Ebrahimi 2011, 454). Kermani is considered one of the founding fathers of Persian nationalism and is still widely admired by the Persian bourgeois intelligentsia without any problematization of his utter anti-Arab racism, often likening Arabs to beasts and parasites. For instance, he writes, "I spit on them [. . .] naked bandits, homeless rat-eaters [. . .] vilest humans, most vicious beasts [. . .] camel-rider thieves, black and yellow scrawny lot, animal-like and even worse than animal" (quoted in Zia-Ebrahimi 2011, 465). In one of his letters, Kermani, in one of his typical racist rants, rails against Arabs just before making an embarrassingly bad philological argument and then concluding that Persians and the French are from the same parents. He simply refers to the similarity of eight words in

---

27 For more on Iranian Aryanism, also see Soleimani and Osmanzadeh 2021.
28 Asgharzadeh 2007.
29 For instance, see Asgharzadeh 2007, 23, 93, 138, 146, 150–151, 160, 164, 198, 212; also see Vaziri 2013, 125, 219, 227, 230.

Persian and French to assert that both languages have the same origin. Then, in the same sentence, he concludes that the Persian and the French were brothers (whatever that means), but that they departed in opposite directions, the East and the West. Still in the same sentence, which, typical of his demagogy and preaching style, is a long paragraph, Kermani tells us that the brother who went Westward "achieved progress, civilization, prosperity, statehood, magnificence, and moral sublime" whereas the brother who headed to the East, the Persian, was cursed by "old thieves, parasites, wicked camel-eaters, greedy lizard-eaters, villains [. . .]" who stripped him of all perfections, ethics, and beauty and instead "covered him with lice, ticks, and dirty Arabic cloth" (Kermani n.d., 126).

Iranian nationalism, in both its secular and its Islamist versions, perceives Arabs as its main Other but Europeans, especially Germans, as its blood kinship, which has produced what Zia-Ebrahimi termed Iranian Self-Orientalization. By adopting mythical narratives of racism produced by European Orientalists, Iranian nationalists had already committed self-Orientalization, and to make things worse they made every effort to suppress their sense of racist inferiority by claiming genealogical, genetic, spiritual, and cultural kinship with the greater race of the Aryans. In fact, according to the nationalist narrative, the word "Iran" is derived from "Aryan" and is supposed to mean the land or home of Aryans (Zia-Ebrahimi 2011). Some of this Aryan mythology has also been picked up by many Kurdish nationalists, except those in Iran for reasons that have to do with discursive strategy (to differentiate Kurds from the perceived Persian Other).

A group of nationalist intellectuals influenced by Kermani published a newspaper called *Kaveh* between 1916 and 1922, launching an ideological crusade against all that ties Persians with Arabs (Zia-Ebrahimi 2011, 455). After the foundation of the Imperial State of Persia by Reza Shah Pahlavi in 1925, these and other nationalists became influential in the royal court, contributing substantially to the Shah's pan-Iranianism. At the same time, German nationalists, including Nazis, provided the Iranian elite with cultural and propagandist support through various means. These included thousands of books, a radio station that aired its programs in German, and invitations for multiple delegations to visit the Reich to deepen relations in a world where the Nazis were desperately in need of new allies to be able to challenge the British and French traditions of imperialist influence in the region and beyond (Zia-Ebrahimi 2011). Three-quarters of a century after the fall of the Third Reich and its mythology, unlike Germans, Persians hold on to Aryanism as some sort of common sense.

Zia-Ebrahimi's illuminating account of an event that took place in 2004 in Tehran sums up the problem of popularized Aryanism. He summarizes the event after describing the antagonism with which the Iraqi football team was treated in 2001 even after they lost the game and headed back to the airport:

Yet when the German national football team landed in Tehran on 7 October 2004 to play a friendly match, a wholly different reception was awaiting them. 1,500 Iranian supporters gave the German team a "triumphal welcome," and chanted "Germany, Germany" and "welcome to Iran." The manager of die Mannschaft declared: "It is unbelievable to be welcomed in such a way when you are the visiting team." "I had never seen such a thing" added one of the players. The game took place in the Azadi Stadium in Tehran in the presence of 100,000 supporters. The Süddeutsche Zeitung reported the "absurd popularity of the German national team in Iran," while the team's manager described the ambiance of the stadium as "incredibly emotional '[. . .] positive fanaticism."

The Iranians' enthusiasm was expressed when the German national anthem was sung. Right from the beginning, a large number of Iranian fans stood up and gave a collective Nazi salute to their German guests, while others brandished posters of Nietzsche, all this before the astonished eyes of the German supporters. The ZDF TV commentator took notice: "Luckily we only see it briefly, some perverse slips; some people stood, many even, and showed the Hitler salute."

Undoubtedly, these large numbers of Iranian supporters were not expressing sympathy for Nazism or the horrors it committed. Iranians are not as familiar with this period of European history as most westerners. The unusual welcome given to the German team at the airport indicates rather that they were trying—although in an unfortunate way—to convey their sense of sympathy to the Germans. That in the annals of Iranian football this sympathy was demonstrated only to Germans indicates that the message of the so-called Aryan brotherhood inculcated by German propaganda decades ago still finds an echo in Iran. (Zia-Ibrahimi 2011, 471)

When it comes to the racist myth of Aryanism, both the secular royalists, who support the Shah dynasty, and Shia Islamists who support the current regime, are in agreement, even though the royalists tend to emphasize it more.

4 Nationalism's Farcical Promise of Liberation

There is a good general argument about not blaming the victim, or, in this context, the minoritized victim. That is to say, it is absurd to critique the national liberation movements of a stateless group of people who have been brutalized by a state that treats them as second-degree citizens. Such an argument, however, should not be interpreted as a free pass for nationalist ideologues who capitalize on the plight of a minoritized group or as some kind of moral exceptionalism vis-à-vis the production of exclusionary modes of perception and oppressive politics. Most importantly, homogenizing any group of people on the bases of national or nationalist identity is misleading regardless of whether the group in question is privileged or underprivileged in terms of the existing race relations. Within racially minoritized groups, there are class and other relations of power, and usually those who lead a nationalist or a religious movement are among the privileged even if they come from underprivileged families.

Because the elites are relatively removed from the everyday reality and life conditions in which the majority of the people they supposedly represent live and because the elites develop their own interests within the parameters of exercising power, they tend to produce exclusionary ideologies that are not fundamentally dissimilar to the ideologies of their alleged enemies. Like the nationalist elites of its rival front, the nationalist elites who speak in the name of the minoritized group end up transcendentalizing race, personifying and homogenizing perceived national groups, and deploying an ethnocentric mode of perception vis-à-vis their community and the rest of the world. This fallback into racism is indicative of the ultimate triumph of coloniality, or colonialism as the dominant mode of perception and as an ideological form with potential overlaps with the fascist form. The nationalism of the minoritized could be interpreted as a transition from political otherness to epistemological oneness, from the position of an othered subjectivity, but subjectivity nonetheless, to a shadow of the colonizer. In the meantime, and within the same process of nationalism, the worldview of the racist oppressor is internalized by the oppressed in a process of *reversed psychoanalysis* instigated by the nationalist ideologues of the racially minoritized group.[30]

Those who do not submit to the regime of nationalist fetishism are often subjected to symbolic, or worse, attacks that are even more aggressive than the attacks against the members of the alleged enemy nation. Wherever there is martyrdom, there is much more vilification. Nationalists have a long history of manufacturing and distributing death on the basis of racist mythologies of good and evil. Victimhood may be an outcome of racist oppression, but it is never a guarantee against the reproduction of racism. Both Zionism and Arab nationalism started as progressive movements motivated by the sense of injustice, but as ethnocentric movements, they were bound to become oppressive and exclusionary. Sure enough, immediately after their respective takeover of formerly colonized countries, they became colonial powers vis-à-vis minoritized groups in the ethnically defined and claimed

---

30 Some of the Frankfurt School's Critical Theorists defined fascism as "psychoanalysis in reverse" (e.g., Löwenthal 1989, 51). The way I understand this is through the classical definition of psychoanalysis as *making the unconscious conscious*. If we go by this classical Freudian definition, then the reverse would amount to *making what otherwise is (false) conscious unconscious*. Also, let us recall that according to Freud, "a prominent feature of unconscious processes" is that "they are indestructible." "In the unconscious," Freud asserts, "nothing can be brought to an end, nothing is past or forgotten" (2010, 576). Thus, if we extend the hypothesis of *reverse psychoanalysis* to nationalism, we could argue that nationalism of the minority effectively borrows the view entailed in the nationalism of the majority from the realm of political disputes to implant it in a timeless realm thereby unwittingly and utterly naturalizing the worldview of its alleged enemy.

homeland. Some Jewish and Arab intellectuals quickly realized the dangerous trajectory of their respective nationalist movements and defected to become communist internationalists, while others defected the communist movement to join the nationalist parties, which are, needless to say, formed according to (explicit and/or implicit) racist terms.

In the case of Israel, Palestinian Arabs from Muslim and Christian backgrounds have been treated as colonized subjects, leading to prolonged hostilities, mass relocations, indiscriminate violence, etc. In the case of Arab nationalism, across MENA but especially in Sudan, Egypt, Syria, and Iraq, the nationalist regimes and militias committed every imaginable colonial and racist act against their racialized Others, or minoritized populations. Considering everything, the rulers of these states and the Arab nationalists in general are not in a moral position to reproach the Israeli administration and right-wing Zionists. Ironically, Arab nationalists started their exclusionism with Jews even before the establishment of the state of Israel. Most noticeably, Iraqi Jews were brutalized as a result of direct fascist politics supported by Nazi Germany. After the mass exodus of Jews from the newly formed Arab states, other minoritized groups such as Kurds and native Africans became the target of exclusionism. These bloody historical chapters may be ignored for a long time, but they cannot be denied.

That said, the point I want to emphasize is my contention that nationalism is necessarily exclusionary and therefore oppressive even if it emerges on the basis of legitimate grievances. Unfortunately, when leftism is weakened, the reaction to a discriminatory and oppressive power is another discriminatory and oppressive movement. One of the grievances of minority intellectuals in MENA, quite understandably, is that in the name of internationalism their identities were tribalized, racialized, and localized while the identity of the dominant ethnic group was naturalized as if it were inherently more compatible with the civilizational and universal inspirations of "the nation," which, if anything, is deeply racist, exclusive, and so on.

In 1991, I escaped Saddam's Iraq to the Kurdish controlled areas in Kurdistan, and in 1999, for the last time, I escaped the Kurdistan region of Iraq as well to end up in Al-Assad's Syria for two and a half years. When I was living in Damascus, I conducted a series of debates with Arab philosophers including two Marxist Palestinian philosophers, Ahmad Barqawi and Yusif Salamah, both of whom were teaching at Damascus University at the time. Ahmad Barqawi, and to some extend Yusif Salamah as well, made a point, that only years later, in Canada, did I start to fully appreciate.[31] Namely, after pointing to the contradictions of the pan-Arab

---

31 The original manuscript was in Arabic, but I have never had a chance to publish it. However, in 2008, I published the Kurdish translation (see Ahmed 2008). I express my deep gratitude for

discourse vis-à-vis the minoritized groups such as Kurds and Amazigh, Barqawi agreed with me that Arab nationalism is fundamentally irrational, but he added that "the problem is that reason is absent in all sides." That is exactly my position today about MENA; the identitarian ethos is irrational and fascistic. I further argue that in the absence of a popular leftist atmosphere, most often reactions to fascist regimes do not amount to the rise of anti-fascist movements but rather the emergence of other fascist forces.

Kurdistan

Here, I return to the case of Kurdish nationalism to subject it to the critical parameters developed thus far in this chapter. Kurdish nationalism is criminalized in the four countries where most Kurds live—Turkey, Iran, Iraq, and Syria. However, the movement itself fanatically demonizes Kurds who are not supportive of it, leaving many ordinary Kurds with no choice but to take a side either with the state that treats Kurds as a colonized group or with the Kurdish nationalist movement that strives to repeat the same racist experiment within a Kurdish state.

Recently, in the aftermath of the 2022 uprisings in Iran, citing tangible examples such as the disturbing yet normalized discourse of blood and soil and the popularized ideal of martyrdom, I raised my concern about the fascist tendencies of Kurdish nationalism. The overall reaction only further confirmed my hypothesis. For the Kurdish nationalist elite, their supporters, and countless goons, the identity of Kurdishness is absolute and determinate of all values of righteousness, honor, etc. While Kurdishness designates the so-called ethnicity, in terms of the political filtering and ranking of individual Kurds, complete and unconditional allegiance to an ethnocentric doctrine called *Kurdayati* is deemed imperative. Internally—that is, vis-à-vis Kurds—the enterprise of *Kurdayati* is no less chauvinistic than the colonial nationalist enterprises. For instance, Kurds who speak a language other than the two dominant Kurdish languages—Sorani in the south and Kurmanji in the north—are marginalized. People who speak Luri or Hawrami as their mother tongue are expected to speak Ardalani, which is very similar to Sorani, while there are barely any Ardalani (or Sorani)-speaking intellectuals and politicians who bother to learn any Luri or Hawrami. There is a similar relationship between Kurmanji and Zazaki, even though the speakers of both languages have been severely marginalized by

---

Ahmad Barqawi and Yusif Salamah and hope they are well and safe. I am also grateful to Dr. Sarbast Nabi for introducing me to Dr. Barqawi and Dr. Salamah in the early months after my arrival in Damascus.

the Turkish state (for more on this, see Çiçek 2017). If we divide the Kurdish liberation movement in terms of left and right parameters, the PKK movement, which emerged in Turkey but has supporters among Kurds in Syria, Iraq, and Iran as well, represents the largest force in the leftist camp. The communist organizations and groups make up the rest of the Kurdish political left.

There are two main clusters of Kurdish right-wing movements: the Islamists and the nationalists. There are Kurdish nationalist parties in Turkey and Syria too but without considerable militia, unlike those in Iraqi and Iranian Kurdistan. In Iraq, due to the corruption of the two main Kurdish nationalist parties, PDK and PUK, and their brutal suppression of the communists, there has been a rise in Islamism (see Ahmed 2018b). While PDK and PUK historically claimed the Kurds' right to self-rule to be their fundamental objective, and their grievances have been centered on the oppression of Kurds by the Iraqi state, they have shown little respect for the individual and collective rights of the mostly Kurdish population they have been ruling since 1991. The Iraqi Kurdistan Regional Government (KRG) is an empirical example of the failure of Kurdish nationalism, something Iranian Kurds know too well if for no other reason than because of the way Kurdish refugees from Iran have been treated by the KRG and Iraqi Kurdish militias. Yet, the Kurdish peshmerga, the central persona of *Kurdayati*'s hero or freedom fighter, continues to enjoy a sanctified image in the psyche of many Kurds in Iran.

To start to get a sense of the ideology of Kurdish nationalism, comprehending the impact of the rhetorical devices and the central terminology of the nationalist discourse is essential. The literal meaning of peshmerga is "the one who proceeds death," which emphasizes readiness to be killed for the cause. The word is the combination of *pêş* (before or prior to), *merig* (death), and *e* (to be). Peshmergayati (*pêşmergayetî*) is the state of being devoted to the patriotic project by living as a fighter, as a peshmerga, within the armed struggle of *Kurdayati*. *Kurdayeai* stands for the historical and ongoing movement of national liberation from an ethnic (Kurdish) perspective. While *Kurdayati*'s ultimate hero figure is the peshmerga, and its sanctified struggle is peshmergayati, *jash* is the antipode of peshmerga and *jash-ayeti* is the antithesis of peshmergayati, the opposite of patriotism, or the ultimate treachery. The literal meaning of *jash* is "a little donkey," and the term is meant to degrade the Kurd who collaborates with the occupier, the state. *Jash* is used in reference to Kurdish paramilitary forces who are armed and funded by the state to fight peshmerga. For the same reason, it comes in handy for each group or militia within the *Kurdayati* camp to accuse its rivals of committing *jashayati*, that is, the ultimate betrayal of *Kurdayati* (more on the terminology later as the discussion of Kurdish nationalism advances).

One of the common grievances of nationalist Kurdish intellectuals is that the privileged Persian groups and the Iranian state treat Kurds and other non-

Persian-speaking groups as ethnic tribes. Yet, ironically, Kurdish nationalists more than anyone else treat Kurdishness as a matter of puritan clannism. So much so, they regularly degrade their rivals by calling them bastard Kurds (*zole Kurd*). Another irony is that they take offense at being called Iranians, but they also take offense when state officials do not treat them as Iranians. Some of the Kurdish nationalists argue that "Iran" is a recent construction by Persian nationalists and, therefore, as the argument goes, such a state does not have any legitimacy from the Kurdish perspective. Just as the Young Turks assumed the Turkish political perspective, will, and leadership, and just as Baathists assumed the Arab political perspective, will, and leadership, the Kurdish nationalists have regularly assumed some kind of undisputable mandate to represent all that is supposedly authentic and faithful to Kurdishness. Indeed, when they express their views in the Kurdish language/s, they use the word "Kurd" as a singular collective, as in Kurd *wants* etc.; Kurd *was* treated unfairly; Kurd should do such and such, etc.[32] The nationalist takes this singular collective entity *Kurd* for granted and typically assumes a position of guardianship toward it. The closest translation to this supposed entity, *Kurd*, is "the nation." And, as always, what characterizes and in fact what makes the nation as an entity conceivable is precisely its supposed homogeneity or collective singularity.

Kurdish nationalists are not satisfied with "Iran," but obviously they would have been even less satisfied if the old imperial name of the state, Persia, had been retained. In the meantime, the nationalists deny their fellow Kurds who see themselves as Iranians any right to representation in the assumed political enterprise of *Kurdayati*. Thus, in their envisioned project, only nationalists may be recognized as legitimate rights holders, so *Kurdayati* excludes not only non-Kurds but also ethnic Kurds who do not abide by the predetermined notion of a good, faithful, trustworthy, and honorable Kurdish personality. Those who disagree with *Kurdayati* are automatically considered to be against *Kurd*. Indeed, even within the camp of *Kurdayati* in both Iraq and Iran, every party has been accused of betraying *Kurd* and, therefore, of *jashayati*, by some other parties within the camp. A member of a peshmerga group would be called a *jash* by followers of rival peshmerga groups.

It is as if Kurdish nationalism were the only legitimate or even natural political option for a Kurdish person. A Kurd who does not declare unconditional allegiance to Kurdish nationalism, even when it is suicidal to do so, is demarcated as a bastard, a *jash*, etc. In addition to individual Kurds who do not support the Kurdish nationalist platform, the doubly minoritized groups who are perceived as Kurds

---

32 Hereafter, to distinguish this particular use, i.e., Kurd as a reference to the collective, I will italicize the word.

are marginalized or excluded from the identitarian frame of Kurdishness. Thus, by excluding the doubly minoritized perceived Kurds and Kurds who do not support the nationalist platform from the identitarian frame of *Kurd*, Kurdish nationalism unwittingly betrays its oppressive tendency and exclusionary mode of perception.

Kurdish nationalism's claim of the Kurdish homeland, i.e., a sovereign Kurdistan, is not any more legitimate than the Persian nationalist's claim of the Iranian homeland. The anti-Persian-nationalist argument is that there are non-Persian peoples in Iran who deserve equal rights, which is of course valid. But there is nothing in the project of Kurdish nationalism, as expressed by its representatives, ideologues, sympathizers, etc., to indicate that the potential state of Kurdistan would be any less exclusionary than the pan-Persian Iran. The Kurdish nationalist elite has never provided a good reason for why we should assume that an independent Kurdistan state would be more inclusive and diverse than an independent (and secular) Iran or for why the inhabitants of, for instance, a Lori-speaking city, or any city for that matter, should believe that their lives would be better in a Kurdish state. There is nothing in *Kurdayati* that could assure people, whether ethnic Kurds or not, that a state founded on the basis of Kurdishness is inherently better than a state that is founded on Iranianness. To date, Kurdish nationalism has not been able to formulate a nationalist discourse that is not inherently racist. Kurdishness is assumed to be a "race," and Kurdish nationalism self-projects that racism in the name of difference, the right to self-determination, and liberation. It imposes the race identity on vast and varying populations. Those who might disagree with their supposed liberation project are demonized through the deployment of racist terms.

To make things worse, Kurdish nationalist elites, most of whom live in the safety of diaspora, systematically encourage and expect more sacrifices by their fellow Kurds in Iran. These endless sacrifices are romanticized by all available means and the justification lays in the supposed independent Kurdistan state in an unknown future. Kurdish nationalist rhetoric is constructed around *xak* and *xwên*, soil and blood. There are endless references to *xak* and *xwên* in modern Kurdish literature and lyrics, which have contributed to the normalization of a fascistic mentality that is obsessed with individual self-sacrifice as the only notion of heroism and eternal collective self-victimization as the only national/ist narrative.

Like many other nationalist movements whose cycle of development results in fascism, the Kurdish nationalist movement adopts two contradictory images of the collective self. The nation is believed to be indestructible, eternal, and so on, but, at the same time, it is also assumed to be extremely fragile, helpless, and so on. It is treated as a super-historical entity that has countless external, internal, visible, invisible, collective, and individual enemies. It is typically portrayed as a delicate female figure who is at risk of rape by the countless enemies in a cruel and value-less world. Similarly, defending the homeland is supposed to be the highest honor one could wish for, and self-sacrifice is the only way to achieve it. Indeed, death is the shortest if not the only path open for the members of the poor and miserable majority to achieve the patriarchal and patriotic honor or any recognition at all. For Kurdish nationalism, patriotic mobilization first and foremost comes down to motivating the largest possible number of Kurds to sacrifice themselves without ever questioning the purpose, let alone the cause.

The unlikelihood of the actual realization or the feasibility of the nation-state is not a concern for the nationalist elites who seem to strive for something akin to collective suicide as a pathological desire to self-fulfill their worst prophesy about the personified collective called *Kurd*, the nation, as a transcendental victim. They simply refuse to hear any concerns about the actual consequences of the peshmerga armed struggle even though the most evident consequence has been increasing brutalization of the Kurdish population and the militarization of the Kurdistan region. The national liberation project has already undermined its own claim about emancipation and has become retrogressive as an absurdly irrational movement even by the standards of nationalism. According to *Kurdayati*'s value system, only in its loss does the individual Kurdish person's life gain value. One of the ironies I witnessed during the Zhina Mehsa Amini uprising was the semi-religious glorification of death, self-sacrifice. Nearly all these callers for mass sacrifice in Kurdistan were men who live in Europe, North America, and Australia. These enthusiastic male advocates of *Kurdayati* proudly stressed the significance of the Kurdish motto of *Jin, Jiyan, Azadi*, which translates to "Woman, Life, Freedom," but they barely let any women speak, and they seemed to be careless about Kurdish women who would lose their lives every day on the streets and in prisons in Iran. In fact, the call for more sacrifice (for an allegedly free Kurdistan) only got louder across online platforms.

In the case of Iraqi Kurdistan, I have already had that experience, and I am convinced that the Kurdish conflict in Iraq has been one of the most absurd episodes of the 20th century. In the case of Iranian Kurdistan too I have witnessed how chauvinistic, racist, and violent the alleged advocates of political emancipation can be toward their own fellow Iranian Kurdish intellectuals who dare to argue for something other than separation and what in effect would be an ethnic Kurdish state.

Finally, let me share a personal experience that could not be more relevant in terms of its subject matter and political implications. As a side note, I should mention that my mother tongue is Kurdish Sorani, which is the dominant language in the Kurdish political parties in Iran and Iraq. In 2022, I was invited to give a talk to an audience composed of mostly Kurdish intellectuals and activists. Before describing the chauvinistic reaction of the nationalists, I summarize what was and continues to be my position. As also presented in two Kurdish articles

(Ahmed 2022d, 2022e), my argument was and is that it is time to have peshmerga (the Kurdish freedom fighter) retired politically and figuratively because the armed struggle movement has only made things worse for the people it claims to defend. Sociologically, *Kurdayati*'s hero figure, peshmerga, created a terrible role model for the Kurdish youth for generations at the expense of their participation in urban social, political, and intellectual life. In sanctifying the figure of the peshmerga, the movement has unknowingly been glorifying sheer force and martyrdom while at the same time advocating antagonism against all that is urban, intellectual, cosmopolitan, and so on. The sanctification of *xak* (soil) as the sacred notion of home or the mountains as the core element of Kurdishness along with the mystification of death in the name of martyrdom will only perpetuate a death cult. A movement founded on the idea of martyrdom, such as *peshmergayati*, will only further undermine the inherent value of individual lives, especially in the Kurdish area.

Moreover, glorifying the armed struggle will only result in further marginalization of education, urban activism, and civil society while at the same time any presence of militias gives the Islamic Republic, and arguably any future government in Tehran, all the excuses to militarize Kurdistan where most people are already suffering from severe economic disparity and police oppression. Moreover, if not denied the support of the Kurdish elites and the broader Kurdish communities, the peshmerga movement will continue to further the sense of distrust among the larger Iranian demographics, including not only Persians, Azeris, and other groups but also Kurds who perceive themselves as Iranians. Also keep in mind that for a significant portion of the Kurdish-speaking population in Iran it is geographically impossible to be included in any potential Kurdish state, which means even if a Kurdish state is materialized, millions of people will be brutalized and probably forcibly displaced. In addition, Kurds will be denied access to most Iranian cities, universities, and so on. Finally, as my argument goes, the geopolitical likelihood of an independent state in Kurdistan is next to none anyway, which means the armed struggle for independence can only result in unpredictable loss of lives and extreme destruction of life conditions for the Kurdish population, who are supposedly being defended by nationalists using little more than old Kalashnikovs at the hands of miserable working-class youth who have dropped school to join a struggle that has so far, since its initiation in the 1940s, not materialized anything other than death, destruction, and bad poetry.

I have never been able to comprehend how it is possible for any group of people to have such little regard for the lives and wellbeing of the very people they believe they defend. Like all nationalist movements, the Kurdish nationalist movement was a product of educated elites before it became a relatively popular front capable of manufacturing endless mythologies, narratives of victimhood and martyrdom, and, again, terrible poetry.

To my written and vocal presentations about fascism in relation to Kurdish nationalism, one of the constant objections was that the colonized could not be accused of fascism. While I do not know of any good reason for such a proclamation, empirically I have concluded that even in the expression of the objection, signs of fascism can be detected. It seems that most of us come to believe that being oppressed and committing oppression are always exclusive not only on an individual basis or even generational levels, but on racial, ethnic, historical, and metaphysical levels. Somehow, we are made to think, those who experience suffering, and even more so those who speak in their name, are immune to producing or even causing suffering. This issue is at the heart of the problem of fascism, and without addressing it critically, fascism will always be here or just around the corner. If fascism were a virus, I would say, the sense of victimhood, whether justified or not, is more of a potential cause for rather than a prevention against catching fascism.

The most frequent charge I heard was that I did not know enough about Rojhalat, the Kurdish word for the East, which is used also in reference to indicate Eastern Kurdistan, i.e., the Iranian Kurdistan. This charge, to say nothing of the extensive list of nasty comments in writing, was indicative of utter chauvinism among the advocates of *Kurdayati*. I have never been an American citizen or permanent resident, and when I was teaching in universities in the United States, I published extensively on racism in the United States. I faced certain issues in terms of my career and might have lost a number of employment opportunities. Nonetheless, I was never told, at least not to my face and so bluntly, that I did not know enough about the United States because of the fact that I was not from the United States. Yet, these Kurdish nationalist intellectuals and PhD holders had no problem telling one of their fellow Kurds, who happened not to be from Iran, that by virtue of being non-Iranian, he was not eligible to have an informed position on social movements and politics in Iranian Kurdistan. I hope the multiple ironies and utter banality of the nationalist mindset are clear without further explanation.

It is not difficult to point to fascism from without, but we need to comprehend that every fascist movement can be seen as evidence for a fascist environment capable of producing and reproducing fascisms that could swiftly and seamlessly bypass all geopolitical borders, moral norms, and discursive filters. No national or religious group is immune to fascism. The only immunity is the one that must be created through rigorous and continual critique of the unproblematized, celebrated, and sanctified with which an in-group is supposed to identify unconditionally. In MENA, and elsewhere, if there is any hope for leaving this dark age behind, it lays in post-nihilist enterprises that deconstruct and recreate our societal relations and political organizations on the basis of negating the existing forms of oppression. When actual—that is, existing—human beings are protected against exploitative attempts that deny them personhood, humanity will have reached a point at which an inclusive mode of perception could also take shape. Looking back at our age, through a new mode of perception, our world will look utterly absurd, irrational, and entrenched in falsehood. Only when fascism is no longer the dominant form of ideology, will it be easy and considered reasonable to call our age the age of fascism without much theoretical and critical analysis.

5 Re-problematizing Fascism: Lessons for the Bad Left

While debating the issue of fascism in the MENA region in English is extremely frustrating given the already existing Islamophobic and racist stereotypes about Middle Easterners, the anti-fascist struggle in the Middle East will continue regardless of the wrong assumptions of both the right and the left in the West, and those of us who could be part of that struggle through writing ought not to silence ourselves only because some people refuse to unlearn their prejudices. There has always been strong anti-fascist resistance in various forms within the MENA region, but unfortunately the intelligentsia of that region for the most part has been part of the problem. The minority of intellectuals, academics, and artists who choose to stand against fascism in their own countries are often silenced, resulting in the complete absence of anti-fascist critique in the public sphere, except for liberated pockets like Rojava, which has continually been under attack. Given all that, initiating anti-fascist debates in exile is desperately needed if for nothing else then to refute the racist assumption that attributes homogeneity to the MENA societies, whether motivated by antagonistic intentions or not.

Initiating the debate in European and North American exile has of course its own challenges. The most frustrating challenge for those who are fortunate enough to enjoy some freedom of expression by virtue of living in liberal democracies is the lack of appropriate platforms. Due to the Orientalist mindset of the intellectuals and opinion makers, anti-fascist and leftist Middle Easterners, do not fit with the preconceived image of the Middle East as a homogeneous Muslim society. For the Orientalist mode of perception, Muslimhood is a racial identity and race is still a real scientific notion. As a result, in the West, even the left often cannot operate outside the predetermined racist orbit when it comes to MENA.

Ironically, but very commonly, the European and American left more often than not builds alliances with the fatal enemies of their counterparts in the Middle East. Most Middle Eastern leftist forces, activists, and intellectuals, including some of the most fearless feminists, have been caught up in an existential conflict with Islamic authorities and Islamist movements. The norm among white leftists is to endorse those very authorities and movements. This is precisely why even most centers of Middle Eastern studies at American universities are dominated by conservative, nationalist, and Islamist Middle Eastern academics. Of course, another major factor in making such centers represent the oppressive regimes and ideologies in the Middle East is that many of them are funded by Middle Eastern regimes or rich conservative individuals. Consequently, anti-fascists who are exiled from MENA end up being doubly marginalized.

Middle Eastern progressives in exile face the same problem in publication platforms on all levels. When it comes to academic journals, per the custom, the submitted manuscript is sent to reviewers who are deemed expert in the area. Because most experts of the areas of Middle Eastern studies come from privileged backgrounds or are trained or recruited by conservative centers, critical manuscripts that clash with the dominant ideologies have a slim or no chance of receiving semi-objective evaluations. This, in effect, reproduces the censorship to which critical scholarship is subjected under oppressive Middle Eastern regimes.

Outside academia, the situation is arguably bleaker for critical voices who struggle against the forces of fascism in the Middle East. Again, because the left in the West for the most part has not been able or willing to recognize the sociological heterogeneity of the Middle East both socially and politically, those who run left-leaning publications do not tolerate Middle Eastern critical and progressive voices. Card holding Islamists, anti-Marxists, and anti-feminists could easily use left-leaning platforms whereas writers who are in the frontline of anti-fascist intellectual resistance such as Kanan Makiya (Iraqi-American), Maryam Namazie (Iranian-British), and Hamed Abdel-Samad (Egyptian-German) usually are not given a chance to publish their works in those platforms. Of course, more often than not, right-leaning institutions advance their own agenda by adopting such outsiders, but the left has no right blaming such writers for choosing to utilize those platforms. Of course, the left often does exactly that, i.e., accuse Middle Eastern critical voices of what the right is normally accused and often guilty of. Subsequently, the representatives of Middle Eastern forces of fascism end up finding strategic allies in naïve white leftists and liberals while the most progressive anti-fascist voices from the Middle East are left with no choice but use platforms offered by the right in the West.

The same Western liberal and left that fail to imagine the MENA region as anything but *metaculturally* predetermined have failed to conceive left and right outside the totalized religious topography. The fashionable anti-Marxist, culturalist, identitarian, and post-colonialist mentality has contributed immensely to silencing exiles from the MENA region. Even outside the West, this has had fatal consequences for those who compromised with Islamists or nationalists pragmatically on the basis of prioritizing alleged "anti-imperialism," by which it is usually meant anti-Western imperialism alone. To take one example, the Islamic Republic of Iran resisted American imperialism, but the regime has been imperialist from the outset. While the Iranian Marxist intelligentsia and movement at large are too well aware of the fascist nature of Islamism, many Islamist writers and intellectuals exploited the anti-American sentiments of people in Iran and among the Western left-leaning arenas to increase the popularity and the legitimacy of Islamism.

There is a Western liberal/leftist attraction toward those who combine the rhetoric of conventional (Soviet era communist parties line style) anti-American-ism with a selection of post-colonial studies' terminology to spice up what is other-wise typical conservative and imperialist discourses of political Islam. In the Sunni camp, Oxford's Tariq Ramadan is an example of such intellectual ambassadors of Islamism. In the Shia camp Columbia's Hamid Dabashi, the author of *Shi'ism: A Religion of Protest* (2011), has been setting the example for a generation of younger conservative Shia scholars in the West. To dub either of these two figures a "leftist" in Arabic or Persian media would be laughable.

Western academics and intellectuals who normally identify themselves as critical of exclusionary and racist ideologies should, at least, not support the very forces progressives from the MENA region are desperately struggling against. If they want to be sympathetic to the Middle Eastern or North African Other who is demonized by the far right in the West, and if they cannot recognize any progres-sive emancipatory forces in the MENA region, they should be more careful not to take the side of the far right of the MENA region out of pure ignorance. Anti-fascist Middle Easterners and North Africans in exile carry out a struggle against not only various fascist forces in the MENA region but also against racism in the West. It would be helpful if anti-fascist MENA intellectuals did not have to explain what is supposed to be common sensical premises like the fact that in MENA, and every-where else, there is right and left and complicated spectrums of what constitutes relative left versus right-wing politics, ideologies, etc. It would be helpful if more white, self-proclaimed leftists actually adopted a non-Eurocentric mode of percep-tion that did not perceive non-whites merely as helpless homogeneous victims, simply because that is deeply racist despite appearances and has chilling politi-cal consequences. It is not that the culturalist mode of perception entails certain blind spots; rather, it is entirely fictionalizing, oversimplifying, essentializing, and, therefore, fundamentally distortive. Culturalism is incapable of conceiving ongoing social conflicts within non-Western societies, but of course struggles in all societies go on regardless of the degree to which they are recognized elsewhere.

Chapter 6
Fascist Identitarianism, Russophilia, and Russophobia

1 False Dualities in the Neoliberal Epoch

If the post-Soviet chapter in the age of capitalism is neoliberalism, then the proliferation of identitarian modes of perception can be considered as a main aspect of the ideological hegemony of neoliberalism. False duality is, in turn, a defining aspect of the prevalent identitarianism. In the absence of an international/ist egalitarian movement, today even the most direct capitalist and expansionist conflicts over the sources of raw materials and energy are mystified using an *idealist* (as opposed to *materialist*) frame of reference. Thus, fundamentally similar right-wing fronts are portrayed as fundamentally opposing parties with contrasting sets of values. To further distort the reality, the supposed opposing value systems are implicitly, and sometimes explicitly, racialized.

An example of such a false duality is the West versus Russia. The ruling regime in Moscow is superficially depicted as the moral other of the Western bloc. Throughout this conflict, the bourgeois propaganda machine in the West has insinuated that there is an affinity between the left and Putin's regime, often compelling leftist platforms to adopt a defensive discourse thereby repeatedly emphasizing their condemnation of Putin's invasion of Ukraine in the clearest possible words. On the other hand, the self-proclaimed leftists who never get tired of attacking the left to prove their own supposed ability to think autonomously play an effective role as a proxy ideological apparatus of the totalitarian bourgeois system. To these non-Marxist leftists, the left is permanently suspected of having sympathies for authoritarian regimes.

Neither Putin has any sympathy for the left anywhere nor the left could in any way be sympathetic to his anti-communist and racist regime, yet somehow every leftist critique of (capitalist) liberalism is interpreted as a definitive sign of illiberality and, thus, a symptom of authoritarianism. The leaders of the Russian regime are those who literally buried Soviet socialism alive, and they have shown no tolerance for anything remotely communistic. Let us not forget that the Putin regime is the direct successor of the Yeltsin regime, which, along with the broader anti-Soviet Russian nationalist movement was wholeheartedly applauded by the prophets of neoliberalism who, inspired by the likes of Milton Friedman and Francis Fukuyama, declared the beginning of a supposed glorious and eternal reign of capitalist liberalism. Indeed, Putin and the elites that rule the Russian Federation have been

https://doi.org/10.1515/9783111609041-006

not only the fatal enemy of the Russian left but also an ally of various conservative regimes and fascist movements in the world.[33] We should not be deceived by the imposed false duality or compelled to choose a side between two imperialist fronts. One of the outcomes of this ideological imposition is silencing critique. From the perspective of the ruling class in the West, anything short of unconditional approval of NATO's policies is automatically perceived with suspicion, but that should not intimidate the left. The ongoing conflict between NATO and Putin's regime is a capitalist conflict between imperialists.

A post-Putin era could be far worse for most Russians, just as the post-Saddam era has been by far bloodier than the Saddam era for most Iraqis who had already been devastated by both political oppression and the international economic embargo (for more, see Ahmed 2022e). What is clear is that not even Putin's fans believe his regime's propaganda. However, the same thing cannot be asserted about the ways in which the majority of citizens of Western countries perceive their own governments or NATO. There is a common habit of equating NATO's strategic agenda with an imaginary program formed around the political ideals of liberalism.

There is another widely common but less explicit assumption that entails yet another false dichotomy: (civilized) Europeans versus (barbarian) Asians. While Russian aristocratic and bourgeois elites have always considered Russians as Europeans and the unsung gatekeepers of the Christian world, Western European elites systematically othered Russians. Again, both sides operate within the same identitarian mode of perception, which is so fundamentally racist, no amount of political correctness can effectively conceal the centrality of race to its system of interpretation. "Race" may be replaced with less provocative pseudo-concepts such as "culture" or "ethnicity," but at the heart of the ongoing classifications and generalizations race remains both the paradigm and the parameter.

2 Russian Nationalism

The bitterly frustrated Russian nationalists have repeatedly expressed grievances about Westerners' denial of the (racial) Europeanness of the Rus. It should go without saying that Russian nationalists do not have a problem with European white racism or fascist ideologies that adopt the myth of white supremacy per se; rather, what they are upset about is that the Rus are being excluded from

---

33 While Nicholas I was dubbed the "gendarme of Europe" for his role in crushing revolutions in Europe, the label would be even more fitting for Putin given the fact that he has been the final executer of the anti-communist enterprise that was initiated by Gorbachev and inaugurated by Yeltsin.

the (white) family, and their anti-Western rhetoric is primarily a reaction to this "unfair" exclusion. This seems to be the primary sense in which today's Russian nationalism uses the accusatory term of "Russophobia," an otherwise old term indicating different discursive usages in different times. At the forefront of the guilty parties are the liberals because their persistently antagonistic policies suggest an overwhelming tendency to exclude the Rus from the white clan. Until the 2022 invasion of Ukraine, Putin was openly embraced by many conservatives and most far-right parties in Europe and North America. In fact, he served as an inspiring model of a brave white leader who stood up in defense of the threatened West and Christian values and did not shy away from fighting what to conservatives is social and moral decadence. When Western far-right figures pragmatically turned their backs on Putin, the overall sense of martyrdom and betrayal intensified among the Russian nationalists. Only when all doors were shut in his face, did Putin turn eastward, still merely for strategic reasons. Of course, he was dead wrong to assume that the Chinese leadership would receive him unconditionally and with open arms for the sake of his blue eyes.

Historically, there is a deep sense of victimhood, sacrifice, and betrayal that runs through even Russian great literature. Ironically, even some of Lenin's comrades within the Bolshevik leadership habitually distanced themselves from Asianness and preferred to associate with the European canon (to say nothing of Stalin's infatuation with Western leaders and deliberate humiliation of Mao in late 1949 during the latter's visit to Moscow shortly after the triumph of the Communist Revolution in China). The sense of Western betrayal of Russia goes back to the 19th century when the British and French empires repeatedly, and most significantly during the Crimean War of 1853–1856, allied with the Ottomans against Russia. Nonetheless, Russian pan-Slavic nationalists have continued to hang on to their Euro-racist sense of identity. In nationalism, the sense of being betrayed could seamlessly transform into a sense of martyrdom thereby rendering the original nationalist mythology even more metaphysical.

From the perspective of post-Soviet Russian nationalists, if the racial notion of European-ness is taken away from the Russian identity, there is hardly any way to cling to the superiority myth. Therefore, and given the Russian nationalist prolonged frustration with Western Europeans that stretches over two centuries, at least since the reign of Nicholas I to the present, Russian nationalists desperately and urgently had to form a new superiority myth as the nucleus of the identity that would preserve white racism but be independent from Europeanness at the same time.

Interestingly, there is a new turn in Russian nationalism toward so-called Eurasianism or Neo-Eurasianism led by the fascist ideologue Aleksandr Dugin, whose star started to rise with the upswing in Russian nationalism and during the nationalist reign that followed the demise of the Soviet Union. Dugin and his followers advocate for a supposed Russian civilization that is neither European nor Asian. However, the feverish revival of this doctrine is essentially rooted in frustration with the European family and is symptomatic of a neurotic reaction to the European rejection of Russia. If the Russian Army loses the war in Ukraine, it is not unlikely that Putin will fully assume the role of the tragic hero. As someone indoctrinated with idealist nonsense about Russian nationalism and someone who identifies as the embodiment of the Rus's both hope and fate, if he gets a chance, Putin will translate the potential loss of the war into an apocalyptic ending. In the role of the tragic hero, embodying the collective nationalist fate, Putin must have securely and meticulously designed plan A, plan, B, plan C, and so on to leave no chance for his rivals to prevent the apocalyptic ending if and when he is faced with a humiliating loss of the war. In the role of the tragic hero of a nation tragically betrayed by the brothers of blood and faith, Putin will push the button of nuclear annihilation. To Putin, neither a world without the great Russia nor a Russia without him as its great leader is acceptable. If fate has it another way, he will confront that tragic fate in his own way. Putin's way, no doubt, will be nihilistically heroic.

Nihilist heroism is one of the central characteristics of fascist leaders. However, this crisis should not be simply pathologized or reduced to any other sort of abnormality. Putin may be taking bourgeois nihilism to another catastrophic point, but he is not insane. Like many other nationalists, his irrationality is rationalized through a metaphysical frame of reference whereby fate occupies the central region in the system of signification. What makes Putin stand out among all nationalists, whether white or non-white, is a combination of things that must be considered together while keeping in mind Putin's personality. Putin has (1) a racist-imperialist sense of entitlement, (2) a bitter sense of being betrayed by his supposed European siblings, and (3) authority over the use of the largest stockpile of nuclear weapons. In the final analysis, what Putin represents is an immanent global threat within countless crises produced by the capitalist order.

One of the ironies of the racist duality of Europe versus Russia is that the representatives of both camps both distrust and try to use the Turks at the same time. From a Western point of view, while Turkey cannot be perceived as a member of the European family, it is an important military ally to keep Asians at bay. There is more readiness within the EU to welcome a Ukrainian membership, than to accept a Turkish membership, of the Union even though the rulers of the Turkish Republic have been trying to join the European family long before the birth of Ukraine as a nation-state. From the Russian nationalist point of view, Turkey is the only adopted member of NATO and is racially excluded from the actual Western circle of trust. As such, Turkey is an ideal candidate to be used as a Trojan horse. On the other hand, Erdogan is well aware of the racist rules of the international game, and he does not miss any opportunity to exploit the unspoken dualism in the interest of his nationalist and Islamist interests. In this scenario, all sides represent the right. The left is made present fictionally by nationalists, conservatives, fundamentalists, and their apologists only to be blamed for everything that goes wrong. In reality, the crisis is precisely a crisis of the absence of the left.

3 NATO in Today's World

Assuming that the world will survive this era of gentrified violence and universal-ized chauvinism, how will future generations perceive NATO? Would they perceive it the way we perceive the fascist alliance of the late 1930s and early 1940s, when the most exclusionary forces set out to totalize their exercise of power? Hitler's Nazism and Mussolini's Fascism, however, belonged to a rudimentary group of fascist movements that did not have a good chance of endurance mainly because of their self-destructive strategies and the presence of an internationalist movement of anti-fascism.

The absence of a comparable anti-fascist international movement makes the present moment gloomier than the years that led to WWII. However, there is another shift in the reality that renders the contemporary fascist picture almost unrecognizable, and, thus, less problematizable in the public sphere even under liberal democracies, where freedom of expression is constitutionally guaranteed. Most fascist forces, especially in the West, have developed and/or adopted new rhe-torical devices and discursive personas that help them to propagate their undem-ocratic worldview democratically. Such a contradictory frame of reference has become not only possible but also most effectively utilizable under the prevalent system.

The banality of this retrogressive age is a direct result of a global political economy that is shaped primarily through the international hegemony of neoliber-alism and the rise of right-wing nativism and religious fundamentalism at national and local levels. However, the aggressions committed by dominant groups against disempowered social classes, especially in the peripheries, are not perceived as vio-lence while those groups enjoy an ideological hegemony within the broader bour-geois hegemony. NATO is an imperialist alliance par excellence, and its politics of ambiguity can best be exposed in light of a critical analysis of the racist practices and strategies of the bloc as a whole and its state members individually.

If NATO officials had a slightly decent sense of responsibility toward human lives, they would at least admit their utter and shameful failure in Afghanistan after twenty years of occupation. Instead, as the Afghanistan fiasco was still at its peak following the final chaotic "evacuation" of Kabul, the NATO officials and leaders of state members continued to speak the same old language while they were moving more troops to Eastern Europe. NATO's Afghan episode entailed rewarding the Taliban and punishing Afghans, especially the most oppressed groups among them such as women and the Hazaras. Afghanistan and the fate of Afghans, after twenty years of brutalization in the name of fighting the Taliban, were handed to the Taliban in one of the most absurd showdowns in military history. Yet, the Afghan episode was immediately followed by another bizarre chapter of NATO's alleged defense of freedom. This time, the unfortunate receiving side of NATO's gift of freedom and security was the Ukrainians.

For starters, one could easily imagine that had NATO responded positively to the Ukrainian government's repeated pleas to admit Ukraine into the alliance, the Kremlin would not have dared to start the war. Furthermore, even if NATO had explicitly rejected the Ukrainian government's pleas to become a member of NATO, the war might not have taken place since in that case, the Ukrainian officials would not have acted on the basis of false hope. Instead, the NATO heads insisted on the worst of all possible scenarios: complete ambiguity. NATO deliberately created a yellow light situation in Ukraine amounting to maximizing the Kremlin's distrust and minimizing its deterrence, and this meant all options were bad for the Ukrainians.

As if the alliance's disastrous failure in Afghanistan is entirely irrelevant, NATO leaders have continued the same rhetoric shamelessly. Supposedly, the NATO members stood with Ukraine (insofar as that means Ukrainians would do the dying). During the first five months of the war Western governments allocated over €70 billion to the war effort in Ukraine. Then hundreds of billions of dollars followed as the war dragged on.

"The price is worth it," we are told over and over again by a bunch of officials whose own luxuries are part of the costs while Ukrainian victims of the war and victims of the famine caused by the war are considered too insignificant to be included in the "price." Moneywise, $2.3 trillion was the cost of the invasion of Afghanistan, which accomplished absolutely nothing other than destruction, famine, and mass graves. Of course, most of that money went to the manufacturers of weapons and NATO soldiers and contractors as well as the Islamist Afghan warlords who were part of the American-backed government in Kabul. Is there any reason to think that the Ukrainian episode will turn out to be any less scandalous than the Afghan one? Consider the following basic facts:

1. Ukraine is in ruins. Millions of Ukrainians are displaced. Tens of thousands are dead, and many more are injured.
2. While the main objective of the sanctions on the Russian Federation was to dry up the sources of income the government could use to fund its invasion, the exact opposite happened. A year after the start of the war, thanks to the situation created by the sanctions, the price of crude oil, of which Russia exported

more than 10 million barrels a day, doubled, securing a monthly revenue of about $20 billion for the Russian government (Evans 2022).

3. Another objective of the sanctions was, of course, "crippling the Russian economy." Contrary to the predictions of an army of economists, the Russian ruble not only did not suffer a historic fall but in fact gained more value. On July 20, 2022, the ruble against the dollar stood at 1:0.018, while a year prior the ratio was 1:0.014.

The list of absurdities goes on, especially following the NATO summit in Madrid at the end of June 2022. At this summit, it was announced that Sweden and Finland had already made a deal with Turkey, which meant the governments of these two EU member states had given in to the Turkish government's conditions for approving their admission into the NATO club. The details of the agreement were not of much concern for the media. The content of the agreement is typed in what seems to be one of the most scandalous documents to be called a "memorandum" (see NATO 2022). The poor wording of the document (see for instance article 5) makes it read more like the humiliating vows of two frightened children to a bully. The bulk of this embarrassing two-and-a-half-page memorandum comes down to guaranteeing the full compliance of Sweden and Finland with Turkey's ongoing genocide of Kurds in return for Turkey's approval of Swedish and Finish admission into NATO. In effect, the Swedish and Finnish states banned Kurdish prodemocratic activities and agreed to hand in Kurdish exiles to Turkey. These two members of the EU also listed not only the Kurdistan Workers Party (PKK) but also the People's Defense Units (YPG), the sole force on the ground who along with its sister organization Women's Defense Units (YPJ), were able to bring down the Islamic State in Iraq and Syria (ISIS) in the latter's capital city, Raqqa. In short, the memorandum further frees Erdogan's hands to proceed with his plan of the de-Kurdification of Rojava, without any objection from Turkey's Western allies. Erdogan knows European politicians too well to fail to blackmail them during every major crisis. He has been playing on their phobias of immigration for over six years. Now, he invests in the European governments' fear of the Russian boogeyman while at the same time he is busy making other deals with Putin.

About one hundred years ago, on the basis of another agreement between a bunch of European leaders and the Turkish nationalists, the Kemalists, the fate of Kurds was sealed as a colonized people to suffer endless genocidal campaigns. The so-called peace negotiations, which took place in the Lausanne Conference from November 1922 to July 1923, resulted in the *Traité de Lausanne*, signed on July 24, 1923, by all "the parties." However, Arabs, Kurds, and Armenians were not considered to be concerned parties, and, therefore, their representatives had not been invited. In fact, there is no mention of Arabs, Kurds, and Armenians in the document. Basically, the European inventers of nationalist and colonialist genocides rewarded the perpetrators of the Armenian genocide, the Kemalists, who were represented by an army general, and a leading ultranationalist figure called Ismet Inonu, by giving them a vast part of what is historically Kurdish, Armenian, Yezidi, and Assyrian homelands. The area Kurds call Kurdistan was turned into an international colony divided among the French, the British, and the Turkish military forces. In return, the new nation-state, Turkey, recognized the British and French colonial administrations in Syria and Iraq, allowing them to do whatever they pleased in these formerly Ottoman-ruled lands. In effect, this region in Asia, or what is now designated as part of "the Middle East," was divided among the colonial forces as hunting grounds and its disempowered population as nothing more than cattle completely at the mercy of the occupying armies.

Today, more than 40 million Kurds are deprived of all political rights and are subjected to systematic exploitation. Kurds in Turkey have suffered countless forms of colonial oppression from genocidal campaigns, including the genocide of the Yezidi Kurds, who were targeted along with the Armenians, and the genocide of the Zaza Kurds in 1937. The genocidal campaigns against Kurds have expanded to threaten the equivalent of Austria in terms of both territory and population. As of now, parts of the Kurdish-majority regions not only in Turkey but also in Syria and Iraq are shelled on daily bases by the Turkish army and its proxy groups who are composed of jihadis from various parts of the world. The Yezidi survivors of the 2014 genocide have not had a chance to rebuild Sinjar due to the continual Turkish bombardment (Holmes et al. 2021), often by American manufactured F16 fighters. Meanwhile, in the fall of 2021, when Yezidi (Williams 2022) and other Iraqi and Syrian refugees were trying to enter the EU from the Belarusian border (Amnesty International 2021; Lucente 2021), the Polish government, with the blessing of the other members of the EU, heavily militarized and closely policed its border to ensure that the refugees would not have a chance of entering the EU. An unknown number of Yezidi survivors died in the forests on the border between Belarus and Poland from cold and hunger.

In the post-Soviet era, the triumph of neoliberalism was supposed to bring peace and prosperity to the world. Thirty-three years after the fall of the Berlin Wall, how peaceful and prosperous is the world under the rule of neoliberalism?
1. There are more border walls than ever, with the vast majority of them built during the neoliberal era (Vallet 2022). Most of these walls are built specifically to prevent those affected the most by poverty and violence from moving to safer places.
2. The ecological crisis is worse than ever and is only intensifying in complexity and enlarging in scope. There are continual signs of a planetary catastrophe already taking place. Thanks to the prevalent nihilism in the post-Soviet era,

the catastrophe is moralized at best and metaphysicalized at worst (Ahmed 2020).
3. According to UN estimates, "almost 3.1 billion people could not afford a healthy diet in 2020" and "two in three children are not fed the minimum diverse diet they need," and the situation has already worsened significantly over the last two years (WHO 2022; ReliefWeb 2022).

Now let us take a quick look at some of the crises in the creation of which NATO state members have played direct roles:
1. Islamist movements, which had been empowered against communist movements from Indonesia to Afghanistan and beyond, have become a deadly threat to all, especially defenseless and stateless peoples in Asia and Africa, including the Middle East and North Africa. If in the 1980s jihadist groups were armed and funded by the West, today such groups get their support from the Islamist empire Turkey has become, which in turn continues to enjoy the privileges of NATO and the unconditional support of the United States.
2. Populations of several countries, including Iraq, Syria, Sudan, and Venezuela, have been subjected to famine through the imposition of premeditated economic embargos—not to mention the continuation of similar embargos on the populations of North Korea and Cuba.
3. The Iranian regime is closer than ever to producing nuclear weapons while the international regime has done a terrific job impoverishing the Iranian population, thereby weakening the prospects of popular movements of dissent.
4. The world lives under the threat of nuclear destruction as a result of the conflict between the Russian Federation and NATO.

Today, the largest military alliance of democratically elected governments repeatedly and shamelessly brings about destruction, violence, and famines. Considering its endless aggressions and imperialist sense of entitlement, NATO is today's equivalent of the Pact of Steel between Hitler and Mussolini. Both the United States and Turkey, two main state members of NATO, have been involved in endless military aggressions and typically violate the sovereignty of other countries. Presently, Turkey has large occupying forces in both Iraq and Syria. The American officials continue an aggressive propaganda campaign to portray China as a global threat, by which they mean a threat to the absolutist hegemony of Western governments and corporations in the world. American official discourses had already been disseminating Sinophobia, and if the Russian Army had not invaded Ukraine, American foreign policy could have become even more aggressive toward China.

The current international regime, which is shaped by imperialist ambitions, racist motivations, and capitalist conflicts, will only bring more misery and destruction for the vast majority of the inhabitants of the planet. One hundred years after the rise of fascism in Europe, the world is not in a better place. In fact, the threat of a nuclear war renders the present situation incomparably more hazardous. However, what was true then remains true today: the existing order must be negated irrevocably. Such a negation takes a worldwide cosmopolitan movement for universal equality and the realization of an entirely different social, political, and economic order.

Chapter 7
Multi-national Fascism and False Dichotomies in International Relations

Once more, atrocities committed against a marginalized population are used to validate the collective punishment of another silenced population. The sanctions on people in Russia have been justified in the name of defending Ukrainians—as if Western governments' record in manipulating economies is spotless and their mandate to defend others' freedoms is utterly unquestionable. This is another war that has forced many people to choose between two wrongs within a false duality. Put plainly, the Russian nationalists and the NATO bloc do not represent two opposing ideological poles. To the contrary, they represent the same species. Both sides are anti-egalitarian, racist, and, of course, above all, capitalist. Nation-states within the capitalist world order clash, and this is neither the first nor the last such clash. By the same token, we should not be lured into committing the nationalist mistake of equating a state and the population who happen to be under the rule of that state. This is a common, but rudimentary, mistake regardless of whether we speak of democracies, autocracies, or so-called theocracies. The ruling groups in Russia and the NATO countries are guilty of many things, one of which is this war. Similarly, the plights of defenseless Ukrainians and oppressed Russians should not be subject to compromises. The question that should become the subject of wide public discussion and motivate internationalist mobilization is the same old-new one: How can we, the oppressed, join forces against the ruling groups, including our elites and our colonizers? Obviously, that entails another question. Namely, how can we, the oppressed of all countries and regions in the world, stop being used in the ruling groups' wars? The fundamental step toward such a goal is to expose the irrationality of the dominant discourses and, thus, ideologies. These nationalist and capitalist discourses are totalitarian in their influence, but exposing their absurdities could also have a universal effect on their global hegemony.

In this war, we can and should be able to take the side of both the Ukrainian and the Russian oppressed. We should be able to recognize that their plights are in many ways similar even though they might be suffering in different ways at this particular moment. Victims should not compare their right to victimhood but rather claim their uncompromisable equality in the face of their rulers, oppressors, and colonizers. Indeed, there are many Russian citizens, like many Ukrainians, who know for a fact that Putin's regime cannot be a force of liberation in any sense whatsoever. There are also many Ukrainians who realize that the NATO states are concerned about neither Ukrainians' lives nor their freedom. We do not know about

https://doi.org/10.1515/9783111609041-007

them because they are silenced. When and where they are allowed to speak up, their voices are drowned in the frenzy created by the established order, the dominant mode of perception, and the armies of opinion makers whose sole concern is to take one of the two sides in the false duality (of Putin's regime versus NATO). Both sides speak the same language, belong to the same anti-egalitarian type of ideology, and use the peoples they claim to protect as disposable war materials. Both sides have been imposing the maximum exploitation of people and the environment. Both sides have been manufacturing, selling, purchasing, and deploying various means of mass murder. Both sides use the victims to create more victims.

This is precisely why a different hegemony must take place, and its pioneers can only be internationalists from all parts of the world, especially those in the margins of all margins. The only meaningful position to take is the side of the silenced whose voice is the voice of reason and, therefore, whose voice must be echoed loudly in the face of the prevalent barbarism represented by the capitalist ruling groups who have brought the world to the edge of yet another abyss. Once more, this barbaric regime of a few capitalists is pushing the world toward total or near-total destruction. The existing order has once more proved to be death driven, absurd, and unsustainable. It must be stopped. All its fronts and blocs must be denounced. As always, there is another option. That option is the negation of the existing irrationality. Out of such a revolutionary negation, a new world can crystallize step by step.

The discriminatory nature of the international regime has been so normalized, that Western politicians do not even bother to clarify the basis on which they assume a policing role in world politics. Even when addressing ordinary people in the West, they do not bother providing any legal or semi-legitimate ground for their actions in the international arena. Instead, all they need to explain is the potential consequences of their policies at home. Western governments have been somewhat careful not to cause direct financial harm to their constituencies (such as a steep rise in energy prices) without providing some sort of justification. For instance, on March 8, 2022, justifying the imposition of further economic sanctions on Russia, Joe Biden said, "Defending freedom is going to cost. It is going to cost us as well in the United States" (cited in Bade et al. 2022). He was addressing Americans, and the cost he had in mind was the cost of, for example, fuel in the US. British and EU leaders have been using a similar discourse regarding the cost of freedom in relation to energy prices. For the rest of the world, including Ukrainians and Russians, such a "cost" has implications that go far beyond commodity prices.

Indeed, when it comes to Putin's invasion of Ukraine, the common Western discursive strategy is war propaganda, openly encouraging Ukrainians to shed their blood without any guarantee of victory, whatever such a promised victory may mean for millions of brutalized Ukrainian children. In the meantime, the Western governments have been pouring weapons into Ukraine (imagine if these governments had been so quick and efficient in transferring Covid-19 vaccines or basic personal protective equipment to impoverished regions). The same discursive machine that poetically glorifies Ukrainian death deliberately imposes more suffering on Russians who have already been suffering at the hand of Putin's regime. It is a discourse that uses the word "Russia" to refer to the country, the state, the government, and the population interchangeably. As for the sanctions, it does not take a genius to realize that they most severely affect the poor, not Putin or the Russian oligarchy and their thugs.

The dominant racist order has imposed a global apartheid regime. This apartheid regime is legitimized in the name of liberal democracy, but it is totalitarian in every sense. Imagine if, in response to the American invasion of Iraq, the Chinese government had organized international sanctions to starve Americans while threatening to punish Europeans for any attempt to ease the effect of the sanctions on Americans. Imagine then if Chinese politicians had told the Chinese people that it is alright to pay a little more for certain commodities because "defending freedom is going to cost. It is going to cost us as well, in China."

The sense of white entitlement has not changed since the colonial era, and as always, the supremacist exercise of power is masked with some meaningless phraseology about freedom and civilization. The dichotomy of Putin versus Western elites is a false one. Ideologically, politically, and historically, they belong to the same thing, which is the anti-egalitarian, racist, and imperialist bourgeoisie that has been responsible for most of the atrocities and destruction since the colonial era. When they committed genocide in Asia, Africa, and the Americas, or when they fought each other, they did so in the name of freedom and civilization. This is a class that has never stopped employing every idea and ideal, including God and freedom, to recruit the miserable and hopeless ones to their campaigns for total hegemony. It is a class that in the course of its unlimited exploitation creates tragic situations for certain populations, only to exploit those very situations to further totalize its hegemony, thereby creating more tragic situations for other populations, and so on. Therefore, especially since the 19th century, the bourgeoisie has never run out of discursive means of moral distortion. While until the 19th century most individual and mass murders were committed in the name of God, since then, most of the murders have been committed in the name of freedom.

The freedom to which the leaders of the US, the EU, and the UK are referring to justify the war with Russia is not any less absurd than the freedom the 2003 invasion of Iraq was supposed to deliver. After all, whose freedom is so gruesome that it comes at the cost of the collective suffering of entire populations? Why is it that this freedom must always involve punishing the most vulnerable, who are the least responsible for whatever it is that supposedly justifies sanctions, whether the invasion of a neighboring country, persecution of political opposition, or potential manufacturing of "weapons of mass destruction"?

1 The International Apartheid Regime and Sanctions

Economic sanctions are typically presented as a means to disempower the ruling regimes in the sanctioned countries, or to pressure the populations of those countries to bring down their respective regimes. And because the ruling groups in the West have appointed themselves as the global moral authority, they believe it is up to them to decide where and when this method—among others—should be applied. Hundreds of opinion makers shamelessly kept repeating the absurd sanctionist argument. They wanted people in the West to believe that punishing 146 million Russians was somehow in the interest of Ukrainians. Opinion and policy makers who justified the imposition of "crippling" economic sanctions seemed to be obsessed with a sadistic desire to inflict endless suffering on millions of already marginalized people.

There is simply no sound reasoning behind the doctrine of sanctions. We have plenty of rational proof and empirical evidence to assert that sanctions have the exact opposite effect of their proclaimed objectives. Namely, they intensify governments' exercise of power, militarize societies, and destroy the prospect of social peace and political freedoms. By destroying conditions of wellbeing, economic sanctions politically disempower the population in question. Any population that lives under the constant threat of poverty will inevitably become more, not less, prone to democratic underdevelopment, institutional corruption, and subjugation by means of violence. This is a global regime of segregation that uses economic sanctions to collectively cut off entire populations from the rest of the world, which can only make those populations more dependent on their ruling groups.

Only the capitalist logic can rationalize human-made famine in the name of freedom. Only in a totalitarian capitalist world can committing mass murder be morally legitimized through a few meaningless phrases and armies of opinion makers. Only in such a world can the lives of hundreds of millions of human beings be rendered completely faceless, nameless, and worthless. These lives are used in the same way weapons are used, that is, purely for militaristic ends.

The assumption that starving a population severely enough and for long enough would force them to rise up and bring down their ruling regime is utterly barbaric in its indiscriminate cruelty. Policies that are based on such an assumption are also strategically irrational. Civilians who are deprived of both basic needs and political freedoms cannot change undemocratic governments. At the bare minimum, democracy itself must be available and well established for civilians to be able to exercise this kind of political power. Moreover, even in a country where democratic institutions and practices are well established, if the majority of the population experience economic hardships, the collapse of democracy, whether through free elections or armed insurrections, is a likely outcome. The imposition of collective isolation, starvation, and brutalization does indeed drastically change political activities within the population in question, but that change certainly will not amount to a move toward peaceful coexistence or the recognition of political freedoms.

Empirically, the senselessness of economic sanctions is equally evident. The first contemporary cases of severe economic sanctions are those imposed on North Korea, which started in 1950, and on Cuba, which started in 1962, and both increased in the following years and decades. Four decades after the fall of the USSR, both systems are still alive and well. Generations of North Koreans have lived and died under conditions that resemble medieval collective starvation, and today the North Korean regime is more powerful than ever. Yet the sanctionists shamelessly continue their policies of the collective punishment of the North Korean population in the name of peace and freedom. According to the normalized ideology of the prevalent international order, starving 26 million people, who happened to be born in North Korea and have already been brutally oppressed, is somehow supposed to serve the cause of democracy and world peace.

Due to endless sanctions, Cubans have been forced to create a self-sufficient economy while constantly fending off American interventions to destabilize the island. Regardless of one's position on Cuban politics, the Cuban case has proven that sanctionism does not have any justification whatsoever, whether politically, ideologically, strategically, or pragmatically. Of course, there are other sanctioned countries, but there is not a single case where the imposition of economic sanctions on a country actually proved effective in terms of what the self-appointed global punishers allegedly wanted to achieve.

A well-known case is the UN sanctions that were imposed on Iraqis for more than a decade. Between August 1990 and February 1991, the American-led coalition destroyed the infrastructure of the entire country, dropping 88,500 tons of bombs on the country in the first six weeks alone (Allen et al. 1991, 147). Yet not only did they leave Saddam Hussein's regime in power, but they also made sure the regime had enough air force at its disposal to crush the anti-government popular uprisings across the country. As if living under Saddam's regime had not been bad enough, Iraqis were now further punished through a strict embargo on everything, including medicine and food. For thirteen long years, from 1990 to 2003, this same international regime imposed a set of sanctions that were described as "a policy that satisfies the definition of genocide" (cited in Pilger

2000, n.p.). Those are the words of none other than the well-known UN official in Iraq from 1996 to 1998, Denis Halliday, who resigned in protest of the sanctions. In 1996, when asked about the rationale of the sanctions and about the death of half a million children that had already been reported, Madeleine Albright's response was unambiguous: "the price is worth it."[34]

The number of direct casualties is in the hundreds of thousands. The fact that there is nothing close to an accurate estimate of the number of victims of the imposed starvation and the two invasions speaks to the worthlessness of those lives from the perspective of the prevalent international order. There is also the uncalculatable damage caused by the sanctions, including the near-total destruction of the education, industry, and agriculture sectors.

Yet, as if the 1990–1991 war and the imposed famine had not been destructive enough, when the sanctions proved ineffective in bringing about a "regime change," in 2003 the country was invaded once more. In the 1991 and 2003 invasions of Iraq, the American forces alone fired more than 11,500 rounds of depleted uranium weapons (Edwards 2014); more than 1,000 sites in Iraq are contaminated as a result, which continues to have devastating health ramifications for the population (Pax 2016).[35] This is part of the neoliberal package of freedom. The cost of the neoliberal gifts was the starvation of the vast majority of the population for more than a decade, hundreds of thousands of deaths, and the destruction of public institutions, and this cost continues to be paid by surviving Iraqis every day.

In the case of Iran, all Iranians have been paying the price of someone's freedom, except nobody knows whose freedom (Ahmed 2021b). While the regime in Tehran has been brutally oppressing Iranians for forty-five years, to Western governments, further intensifying the suffering of the majority of Iranians will somehow hurt the regime in Tehran. Not surprisingly, the most marginalized, impoverished, and silenced have been suffering the most because of the economic sanctions.

Whatever this mysterious freedom may be, it cannot come at the cost of the suffering of impoverished Russians, Cubans, Koreans, Venezuelans, Iranians, Syrians, or any other population. Sanctions that hurt the wellbeing of entire populations are one of the most barbaric forms of inflicting collective suffering. The Russian-Ukrainian conflict does not change anything about this basic truth. No amount of suffering inflicted on Russians will make any Ukrainian freer, and vice versa.

---

34 This was from an interview she gave to *60 Minutes*, "Punishing Saddam," that aired on May 12, 1996. A clip of her making this statement in the interview can be viewed here: https://www.youtube.com/watch?v=4iFYaeoE3n4.

35 According to a report, more than 286,000 kgs of depleted uranium was used in the country (Zwijnenburg 2013, 15).

2 The Neoliberal Version of Freedom in the Post-Soviet World

Not long ago we were told that communism was the last obstacle to the triumph of democratic liberalism crowned by the sanctity of the free market. Welcome to the post-Soviet world where nationalism has been spreading like a virus, and its fascist variations are gaining more power by the day. Every nationalist group has its own myths and territorial claims, and different nationalist myths and claims inevitably collide with each other. Nationalists fail to see people as concrete human beings. To them, the world is composed of entities called "nations." The nation is the shadow of the people. The nation is personified precisely in order to de-personify the actual human beings it supposedly embodies; it fictionally includes all in order to actually exclude everyone.

The ruling groups have adopted a mindset that disturbingly resembles the racist/nationalist language of WWI, which reached its fascist phase during the interwar period. On one side, there is Euro-nationalism/racism that is quite similar in its discourses and sentiments to those adopted by the nationalists during the first half of the 20th century. Of course, most European elites have made cosmetic adjustments to their exclusionary discourses, replacing race talk with culture talk, and "traits" with "values," etc. (Ahmed 2021a). On the opposing side, there is a despotic regime led by Putin who, like many Russian nationalists, wants to revive the Russian imperialist hegemony that was terminated by the Bolshevik Revolution of 1917.

One of Putin's heroes is General Anton Denikin, the fanatic anti-Bolshevik commander of the White Army in southern Russia from 1918 to 1920. Denikin was a sworn enemy of the Bolsheviks and a fervent opponent of Ukrainians' right to self-determination. Putin's speech before his invasion of Ukraine is quite comparable to Nicholas II's declaration of war in 1914 in terms of the appeal to Russophile tendencies ("Imperial Manifesto" 1914). In fact, Putin barely hides his Tzarist inclinations, and practically, he seems to be attempting to establish a tripartite Russian nation—of Russians, Belarusians, and Ukrainians (or Great Russians, White Russians, and Little Russians, in the Russophile terminology of the 19th century).[36] He is especially influenced by Ivan Ilyin, a Russian anti-communist, nationalist, and fascist philosopher who died in Nazi Germany in 1938. In terms of political economy, the Russian nationalists want a capitalist Russian empire as prescribed by neoliberals such as Anatoly Chubais.[37]

---

36 For more on this, see, for instance, Plokhy 2018.
37 Chubais reportedly left his position as Putin's adviser in late March 2022, but he had been among Putin's supporters since the early days of the latter's rise to power at the end of the 1990s.

Gorbachev brought the USSR to its ultimate death, and the media in the West turned him into an adorable figure for that. Yeltsin went further than his former boss and threw the Soviet project into its grave; he quickly became the new anti-communist hero in Western media. Then, it was Putin's turn to go even further to the right than his former boss, Yeltsin. If Yeltsin was admired by Western liberals, Putin's admirers were further to the right. The trajectory during the first post-Soviet decade steeply moved toward the far right. During the second decade of the post-Soviet era, Putin's star among Russian nationalists and Western fascists started to rise. Until very recently the far right in the West admired Putin for his conservative values and vulgar exhibition of power. Indeed, Putin was well on his way to becoming an inspiration for more and more Western fascist leaders whose followers longed for a father figure, the leader who is invincible but at the same time feels the ordinary people's grievances and speaks like them.

3 NATO, the EU, and Racial Demarcations

There is a famous Chekhovian rule according to which every item on the stage must be used at some point in the play. This has become known as "Chekhov's gun." The common interpretation of this principle is that if there is a gun in act one, you can anticipate what will happen in a later act.[38] In the first chapter of the post-Soviet era, NATO not only persisted but also kept expanding. Of course, the pretext is that the new members demanded membership in the pact. However, NATO neither admitted Ukraine nor explicitly rejected its request. NATO's ambiguous policies and politics suggest that NATO members wanted to fight a war against Russia in Ukraine using Ukrainians. Unfortunately for Ukrainians, Zelenskyy and his allies have accepted the sacrifice of Ukrainians in an imperialist clash between the two parties. Western governments explicitly declare that they will not provide protection for Ukraine, but at the same time, they exploit the hopeless situation of the Ukrainians by playing the pan-European card. NATO might have been able to prevent the war if it had either accepted or rejected the Ukrainian government's repeated membership requests.

What is certain is that no population will become freer, no matter the cost they are asked to pay in order to be admitted into an imperialist camp. On the con-

---

38 This principle is interpreted and used in many different ways. Plokhy refers to it in relation to the threat of nuclear weapons in the beginning of his book, *The Last Empire* (2015, 5). In this book, Plokhy shows that there were many reasons behind the collapse of the USSR, but it was not an American accomplishment, as American politicians claimed immediately after the regime in Moscow crumbled.

trary, all these imperialist forces, including Putin's Russia, NATO, Erdogan's Turkey, and Khamenei's Iran, only generate unfreedom and suffering for those who have already been marginalized. Incidentally, in the name of protecting Syrians, all these parties, in various degrees and forms, have been engaged in the Syrian bloodbath. There has not been a shortage of weapons and fighters, yet Al-Assad is still in power, and the Syrian society and individual is more damaged than ever. The Syrian case is indicative of the irrational violence at the heart of the existing order. Of course, there are other cases of damaged societies and lives in the neoliberal world, where every form of mass murder can be normalized after a while, and where the most privileged are entitled to ask the most marginalized to sacrifice the most. In the neoliberal world, the more we are asked to pay for freedom, the less free we become. Capitalism in all its phases, including the neoliberal one, has never failed to demarcate new regions to pay the ultimate cost. Every time, the doomed population ends up being further slaughtered at the hands of the capitalist class's own creatures, the sung heroes of anti-communism, the likes of Yeltsin, Putin, and other nationalists, conservatives, and fundamentalist thugs.

Recall the liberation scenario faced by Afghans that turned Afghanistan into the first locus of jihad in the world. The jihadis were handsomely funded and armed by the governments of Pakistan, the Gulf countries, and the US in the 1980s in the name of liberation. Since the day the jihadis took power, Afghans have been paying the price for a freedom they have never tasted. In 2001, freedom, as prescribed by the White House, had an added cost. Now the jihadis were the problem. Yesterday's "freedom fighters" were suddenly labeled terrorists. Suddenly, white elites started caring about Afghan women, as if in the 1980s, when the jihadis were fully supported, there had been no women in Afghanistan.

Still, the relabeling of the mujahideen and the repricing of the imaginary commodity, freedom, could have been a fortunate turn of events for Afghans, but alas it was just an indication of another long and deadly chapter of occupation.[39] After twenty years of humiliating occupation, the liberators made a hasty deal with none other than the Taliban and handed them back Afghanistan and its people. Shortly after, as Americans were being lectured about the cost of freedom, the Taliban rulers, Qatar's foreign minister, and an American delegation were enjoying Turkish baklava at a special reunion in Antalya (Associated Press 2022).

---

39 The Concurrent Senate Resolution number 74 in 1984 stated, "the freedom fighters of Afghanistan have withstood the might of the Soviet Army for over four years and gained the admiration of free men and women the world over with their courageous sacrifice, bravery, and determination," adding that "it would be indefensible to provide the freedom fighters with only enough aid to fight and die, but not enough to advance their cause of freedom" (US Congress Committee on Foreign Affairs 1985, 352).

Such is the freedom obtained from buying and selling peoples, countries, and dignities in capitalism's neoliberal world.

Today, it is the Ukrainians' and the Russians' turn to be demarcated, to enter the deadly phase of neoliberalism, where the promised freedom might cost millions of lives, and the resulting unfreedom might cost even more. This is another war the victims are forced to fight and forced to lose. While Putin, just like Erdogan, follows a regressive path to revive yet another long-dead empire, the opposing bloc follows its own traditional measures whereby blood becomes just another cost calculated into the price of raw materials and energy.

This time around, however, the EU and American leaders are prepared to pay some of the cost because Putin committed a different kind of crime, which is not killing civilians per se, something he had already been doing for a long time. In fact, NATO's Turkey under Erdogan has been doing the same thing for a long time. Here is where European capitalist elites expose their deep racist prejudices: it was only when Putin committed the crime against Europeans that he became a war criminal. Keep in mind Ukrainians have never been quite included as members of the European family even though they have not been quite othered as the Rus. To the European tribalist mindset, Turkey is a fence to insulate the European clan from Arabs and Asians. It seems Ukraine's new role is to be another gatekeeper to keep the Rus, Europe's unwanted children, at a safe distance from the clan. However, the European leadership clearly considers Ukrainians more admittable, than Turks, into the Euroclan, which is something Erdogan was sensitive enough to sense and insensitive enough to comment on (TRT 2022). Also, notice how Turkey has been a long-time member of NATO but the European states have resisted admitting the country into the EU. On the other hand, there is not much European resistance against admitting Ukrainians into the EU while NATO membership has not been an option for Ukraine.

Only when he started murdering Ukrainians did Putin become a war criminal for Western elites. Of course, it still took these elites some time to take such a sharp stance, which is not surprising given that Ukrainians have not been considered fully European. Let us face it, what brought the European curse on the Nazis was not mass murder, of which every colonial power—including Spanish, Portuguese, English, French, Dutch, Belgian, Italian, and Turkish colonialism—had been guilty of for a long time. Even Hitler's violation of the territorial integrity of other European states was tolerated. And the ultimate red line was certainly not the genocide of European Jews, which Hitler planned and started executing while he was still considered a legitimate member of the European family. Rather, what brought the Western elites' eternal condemnation upon Hitler without any hope for redemption, as Aimé Césaire argued, was the killing of white Christian Europeans using means that were only meant to be used against non-Europeans. The following passage by Césaire is worth quoting:

> Yes, it would be worthwhile to study clinically, in detail, the steps taken by Hitler and Hitler-ism and to reveal to the very distinguished, very humanistic, very Christian bourgeois of the twentieth century that without his being aware of it, he has a Hitler inside him, that Hitler inhabits him, that Hitler is his demon, that if he rails against him, he is being inconsistent and that, at bottom, what he cannot forgive Hitler for is not crime in itself, the crime against man, it is not the humiliation of man as such, it is the crime against the white man, the humiliation of the white man, and the fact that he applied to Europe colonialist procedures which until then had been reserved exclusively for the Arabs of Algeria, the coolies of India, and the blacks of Africa. (2001, 3)

Putin, like Erdogan, could have gone on bombing cities and killing defenseless civil-ians as long as the victims had not been white Christians. The Ukrainian crisis is the continuation of many similar crises, some of which NATO has had a direct role in creating. The Yezidis, who were starved under the embargo like other Iraqis, suffered a genocide at the hands of Islamists, who have been openly supported by Turkey, a major NATO member. In fact, Al-Baghdadi, the leader of ISIS until he was killed in an American raid in October 2019, turned out to be housed and cared for in a territory that is under the direct control of Turkey and its Islamist proxy groups right at the Turkish border with Syria. His successor, Al-Quraishi, was also living in the same area when he was killed in February 2022, also in an American raid. It is therefore reasonable to assume that NATO members have been well aware of the Turkish state's ties with ISIS and similar groups in Syria.

Dmitry Galkovsky and Aleksandr Dugin may have mastered racism and nation-alism, but they missed the crucial point regarding European nationalism's criteria for blood kinship. Those who liken Putin to Hitler make a good point, albeit uncon-sciously: like Hitler, Putin dared to kill and force the migration of white Christians. This is also the same reason Putin lost his European and American far-right allies. This is not Putin's first war, but it might be his last because he breached the sacred code of white tribalism. That said, Western sympathy, if it can be called that, for Ukrainians is both temporary and limited. Only after they started to be killed in large numbers did privileged Westerners consider them European, but still not European enough to deserve living in peace, rather, just European enough to die for the privileged Europe. Today, Ukrainians are asked to pay the highest price for a freedom in Europe only they cannot enjoy.

Conveniently, Zelenskyy does not miss a chance to further market Ukrainian blood as purely European, and thus as deserving a higher price tag. His soldiers, too, have learned to speak of defending Europe and European values while Ukrain-ians are being sieged by enough weapons to eradicate Ukraine's inhabitants many times over. In the meantime, the tribalists in the EU were convinced that when the cold season passed, they would partake in the sacrifice by cutting down on Russian natural gas. Until then, from their point of view, all Ukrainians need to do is die. After all, membership in the European club, like freedom, has a price tag. Those who have full membership, those whose white clanship is not questionable, pay the regular fee, but those who are not fully admitted must pay with their (or others') lives.

Ultimately, it is the majority of the silenced Russians and brutalized Ukrainians who are pushed into war and poverty while, as in all other imperialist wars, the elites continue to glorify a disaster and endless death of the miserable in the name of freedom and dignity, both of which, to them, mean consolidating more power and accumulating more capital. In this imperialist war, the silenced majority of Russians and Ukrainians will inevitably lose simply because they are being used as the cheapest war materials by Russian nationalist elites, whose conception of a great Russia is not concerned with actual human beings, and by Western elites who proudly push Ukrainians to die for a free Ukraine that is already transforming into a mass graveyard.

Yet, we should ask what this gloomy moment that is caused by capitalism's savagery could bring about. Millions of Russians, Ukrainians, and others who are suffering because of the war and its impact on their livelihoods will reflect on this savagery; they must be asking questions to which the ruling groups have no answers, as Lenin would say (more on this below). Like the anti-war internationalists who opposed WWI, today's anti-war internationalists should be the voice of silent reason and the rational hope, only this time they should be better prepared.

4 Despair and the Coming Revolution

When WWI started, socialists were adamantly against it. In 1915, Eugene Debs, the popular American socialist leader, stated, "When I say I am opposed to war I mean ruling class war, for the ruling class is the only class that makes war. It matters not to me whether this war be offensive or defensive, or what other lying excuse may be invented for it, I am opposed to it, and I would be shot for treason before I would enter such a war." Then he added, "I have no country to fight for; my country is the earth; and I am a citizen of the world" (Debs 1939, 4). On February 8, 1916, in a speech addressing anti-war socialist delegations in Berne, strongly agreeing with Eugene Debs, Lenin said:

> *Neither Russia, nor Germany, nor any other Great Power has the right to claim that it is waging a "war of defence"*; all the Great Powers are waging an imperialist, capitalist war, a predatory war, a war for the oppression of small and foreign nations, a war for the sake of the profits

of the capitalists, who are coining golden profits amounting to billions out of the appalling sufferings of the masses, out of the blood of the proletariat. (2005, italics in original)

He argued that the millions of oppressed and brutalized "are pondering over the real cause of the war, are becoming more determined and are acquiring a clearer revolutionary understanding" (2005). Lenin insisted, "we must not, and we have no reason whatever, to view the future with despair," asserting that "the European War will be followed by the proletarian revolution against capitalism" (2005). In a piece originally published in 1918, he makes a similar point:

Because capitalism has concentrated the earth's wealth in the hands of a few states and divided the world up to the last little bit. Any further division, any further enrichment could take place only at the expense of others, as the enrichment of one state at the expense of another. The issue could only be settled by force and, accordingly, war between the world marauders became inevitable. (1965)

Socialists, including American and Russian internationalists, opposed WWII as well. Trotsky (1939) thought Western democracies both feared and admired Hitler, and he warned that if the fascists are not stopped, they will take over more regions. Anticipating the war, Trotsky added, "It will be the war of slave-owners who cover themselves with various masks: 'democracy,' 'civilization,' on the one hand, 'race,' 'honor,' on the other. Only the overthrow of all slave-owners can once and for all put an end to war and open an epoch of true civilization" (1939, 3).

Fascism, Trotsky argued, "does not come at all 'from without.' In Italy and Germany fascism conquered without foreign intervention" (1939, 3). Like both Lenin and Rosa Luxemburg in 1918 (Lenin 1965; Luxemburg 2004, 364), in 1939 Trotsky insisted that the only possible way to stop the disastrous capitalist wars was a socialist revolution (1939, 3). Much of what was said by these socialists about imperialist and fascist wars in the first half of the 20th century remains true today. Also, whether a revolution is already taking shape or not, as Lenin said, "revolution can never be forecast; it cannot be foretold; it comes of itself" (1965).

Each failed revolution is a foundational step toward the ultimate liberation of human society. Revolutions fail in the short run, but they will inevitably be victorious in terms of the long march toward cosmopolitan emancipation. The cosmopolitan project will continue reviving, each time leaping progressively toward its emancipatory end. As long as inequality exists, there will be revolutions. The more severe the inequality, the more powerful the coming socialist revolution will be. The impoverished may not know what capitalists know about monopolies, but they understand something capitalists cannot grasp. Namely, they understand that certain truths are never outdated or ignorable. These truths concern life itself in its most tangible and real sense. In fact, they live these concrete truths. It is the privileged who need to grasp such truths, including the fact that food, shelter, peace, and dignity are essential needs of all human beings, and those who are deprived of these needs will continue to pursue new revolutions. This truth will never become outdated. And it is a communist premise.

The communism of bourgeois bohemians fell out of fashion everywhere, and communism as such fell out of fashion for bourgeois intellectuals. However, as long as there are people who are deprived of food, shelter, peace, and dignified life, the communist question will continue to haunt capitalist elites. As long as capitalism remains prevalent, communism will continue to be present in multiple revolutionary forms. Every project that aims to challenge capitalism's monopoly on life and negate capitalist hegemonic ideologies of regression is a communist project. The truth of communism, like all basic truths, is simple: when large numbers of people are deprived of their basic needs, large revolutions will take place.

No amount of virtual entertainment, idealist education, subservient spiritualism, rationalized superstitions, sanctified deprivations, mystified subjugations, or celebrated symbolisms will change this basic truth. The revolution is as certain as it was a hundred years ago. In fact, over the centuries, the revolution against enslavement has only become more powerful. Capitalism has proven more boldly than ever that it is a force for destructive irrationality and sadistic destruction. While every communist in the world has been told that communism does not work because it is utopian, what is truly illusional and bizarre is the belief that capitalism is actually working. Merely counting the ecological disasters caused by capitalism should suffice to make this point. By the hour, capitalism is failing and fails those who once believed in its promised land. By the hour, the little fascists that were planted inside those believers are coming out, betraying the real face of the prophets of the post-Soviet world. They actively plan and call for cross-continental wars and collective starvation.

Today's world rulers deploy nuclear weapons on every continent, bomb cities and pour weapons into the destroyed regions, and impose collective starvation on entire populations. This has been the case since the 1950s. The Koreas, Vietnam, Colombia, Afghanistan, Iraq, Libya, Syria, Yemen, Ethiopia, Venezuela, and Ukraine are some of the examples of what liberty amounts to in the capitalist world's imperialist order. Rejecting every morality, religion, nationalism, and patriotism that justifies these massive crimes of violence, communist movements plead guilty to inciting peace forcefully and unapologetically.

Chapter 8
The Colonialist Roots of Fascism: Culturalism as Fascist Mode of Perception

In the final chapter, I bring the problematization of fascism and the critique of fascism studies together. That critique of fascism studies focuses on the allocation of the area to the field of history and the critique of history programs as susceptible of attributing excessive, if not absolute, truth value to the past at the expense of the events of the present. I argue for rescuing the study of history from idealism, which continues to enjoy hegemony over the general mode of perception and in the institutions of knowledge production. It is ironic that historians, like researchers in other fields of study, often render history irrelevant precisely by metaphysicalizing the idea of the origin while, at the same time, fictionalizing the social reality by subjecting it to or simply considering it a product of sanctified ideas.

At the heart of fascism, there is always homogenization. At the heart of homogenization, there are essentializing modes of perception such as racism in its various forms including culturalism. In order for us to negate fascism, we need to better grasp the social history and the present social reality of domination. The dominant names. Those who have the power to name are in control of the industry of values. There can be no negation of fascism without the critique of domination and the dominant social regime that produces, manages, and exploits social antagonism. To negate fascism, we need a philosophy of critique capable of problematizing the sociohistorical conditions that perpetuate fascism and a critical theory of fascism that can diagnose contemporary variations of fascism. Let us revisit the 1880s to better grasp the emergence of what can and should be called fascism. From there, we will make our way back to the present-day reiterations of fascism.

1 From the Fascism of History to the History of Fascism

Revisiting the 19th Century

In 1885, in what has become known as the Berlin Conference, the representatives of European states ratified a treaty about Africa, according to which the European powers took it upon themselves to "watch over the preservation of the native tribes, and to care for the improvement of the conditions of their moral and material well-being, and to help in suppressing slavery, and especially the slave trade" (General Act of the Berlin Conference 1885, article 6), but above all, they asserted

https://doi.org/10.1515/9783111609041-008

their commitment to "the development of civilization" in Africa (article 10). Even the sentimentalist facade that is the language of the document is utterly denigrating and racist, not unlike the contemporary discursive masks of imperialist enterprises. The European powers simply divided about 90 percent of the African continent and its inhabitants among themselves for unlimited exploitation.

In 1884—that is, five years before Hitler was born—German forces already colonized part of West Africa, the present-day Namibia, which they called Deutsch-Südwestafrika, the German South West Africa! Thus, the German Empire started committing what the British Empire had been committing and would continue to do so for a long time. Between 1904 and 1907, the German Army committed systematic genocide of the Herero and Namaqua people. This stage in German history is often designated in terms of industrialization as opposed to imperialization, colonization, and racist expansionism. In fact, from the imperialist perspective of the newly unified Germany, in order to catch up with the British and French empires in terms of industrialization and modernization, this colonialist expedition would be considered a modest step. Germany was not the only new imperial force to follow in the steps of the British and French empires.

In 1880, Belgium colonized Congo, enslaving its population, and, within three decades, mass murdering up to ten million people. With the defeat of Germany at the end of WWI, Belgium was also rewarded Rwanda-Burundi, which had been colonized by Germany since the end of the 19th century. Before and after WWII, the British and the French were the main colonial powers in Africa while Spaniards, Portuguese, Belgians, and Italians also shared in the spoils of the continent. As the colonial subjugation of Africans at the hands of the European states continued after WWII, somehow fascism was not deemed proper to describe them. In fact, even Salazar, the fascist ruler of Portugal from 1932 to 1968, and Franco, the fascist ruler of Spain from 1939 to 1975, were members of the Western club. Their regimes would sometimes be called authoritarians or, occasionally, dictatorships, but the anti-communist camp made sure the term fascism was quickly discarded as something belonging to the past. For the Western bloc, the real evil was communism, so fascists, including Salazar and Franco, were deemed faithful members of the anti-communist camp that was defending "the free world!" Meanwhile, after Stalin's death in 1953, the Soviet Union revived part of the Leninist anti-imperialist and anti-colonial strategy, especially in the African context of liberation movements.

As the age of European colonialism was officially coming to its end in the late 1950s and the early 1960s, the former colonial powers empowered fascist leaders and forces from the colonies to continue protecting Western economic interests and to suppress the international communist movement that had inspired liberation movements across the world. Islamism's strong entrance to the stage took place precisely as part of this post-colonial and anti-communist geopolitical strategy. In the mid-1960s, with the direct support of the United States, Islamists mass murdered up to two million Indonesians in a widespread anti-communist crusade. Islamism was empowered in Pakistan and Bangladesh as well for the same purpose (of fighting off communism). In the 1980s, a wave of Islamist fascism was encouraged, funded, and armed, to fight in Afghanistan. However, this time around the Islamist movement was even more devastating in terms of the financial, militaristic, and logistical resources that were put at its disposal. The anti-communist jihad movement became cross-national, recruiting fighters from all parts of the world while mainstream American politicians and journalists referred to the jihadis as "freedom fighters." Once more, the target was communism.

In fact, the emergence of Islamism, as a contemporary movement of political Islam, is directly associated with the anti-communist campaign immediately following the October Revolution in Russia. The communists were popular in Egypt, Sudan, Yemen, Palestine, Lebanon, Syria, and Iraq, and communist parties were the only parties that reflected the diversity of the population in each country, with Arabs, Kurds, Armenians, Greeks, Muslims, Jews, Christians, and others working together on extraordinary progressive, democratic, and egalitarian platforms. Even by the admission of a conservative historian such as Walter Laqueur, on the eve of the October Revolution, relative to the general populations, there were more Bolsheviks in Egypt than in Russia (1956, 277).

The British colonial administration enticed Islamic religious figures to galvanize popular opposition against the communists. On August 18, 1919, the Grand Mufti of Egypt and the rector of al-Azhar, issued a religious decree denouncing communism as the enemy of religion and God (Yaseen 2011, 17). Conveniently, the British distributed the decree wherever they could in Egypt and beyond. Despite that, the communist movement would increase its popularity in Sudan, Somalia, Ethiopia, Iran, Palestine, Lebanon, Yemen, Syria, and Iraq. In Iraq, for instance, the Iraqi Communist Party (ICP) had more members than all the other parties combined. Most Iraqi Jewish students, Kurdish students, feminists, and other minorities and progressives in Baghdad supported the ICP (see Franzén 2011; Farough-Sluglett and Sluglett 2001, 63). Of the seven million Iraqi, about a million were communists. Then, when the Baath Party came to power through a coup, the massacres began. In the first nine months, the nationalists killed over half a million perceived communists and raped around 100,000 women and girls (Al-Sawt Al-Shuia'ai 1964, 6).

From Nationalism to Fascism

The Frankensteinian monster that is the typical regime in so many parts of the world is not just a creature of colonialism but also a product of anti-colonialist and post-colonial revolutions that went catastrophically wrong, not due to strategic mistakes here and there or betrayals of this and that clique, but rather because the revolutions lacked the negativity essential for any movement capable of resisting oppression as such. Even by coincidence, those revolutions could not have resulted in the realization of democratic systems.

There is no aspect of oppression that the nationalists in the post-colonial states in MENA did not repeat, sometimes even more severely than the way in which it had been committed by the European colonizers. Even the concept of anti-racism, anti-colonialism, or anti-imperialism was too narrow an aim to include all forms of racist, colonialist, and imperialist oppression, let alone class and gender oppression. In some countries, as soon as European colonialism officially ended, the status of millions of people in the newly formed states changed from brothers and sisters in arms to minorities with suspicious agendas or potential collaborators with imperialism. In almost every newly formed state, racist hierarchy, colonialist violence, imperialist hegemony, and class exploitation persisted; merely the faces and identities of the dominant groups changed. Gradually, communism was replaced with national socialism, especially in Egypt, Syria, and Iraq. In Turkey, right from the beginning of the establishment of the republic, a master race identity was enshrined in the identity of the state, subjecting non-Turks to physical genocide. About a century after the Armenian genocide and the mass deportation of Greeks from their homeland, genocidal policies are still enacted against Kurds. In Iran, as if the Shah's Aryanism had not been brutal enough, the Islamists who came to power in 1979 created a regime of segregation with both religious and racist rotating doors for protecting racist purity and nationalist sameness while spitting out the outcast, including Arabs, Kurds, Balochs, Bahais, etc. What started as anti-colonial and anti-imperialist struggles became full-fledged fascism across the region from the Indian Subcontinent to North Africa.

A mindset that conceives entire societies (or even a single society) through a singular term of signification, such as the religious, cultural, or national is a direct embodiment of racism. For instance, identifying the populations of the Near East, or even one part of that region, such as, say, Iran, as "Muslims" is indicative of a racist mentality. Also, it is due to such racist limitations that the dominant frame of reference imposes one-dimensionality and homogeneity on Asians and Africans. It is as if it were impossible for an Asian or an African society to produce political and ideological pluralities, which is why an expression such as "Islamic fascism" or "Iranian fascism" is used and interpreted as a description of Muslims or Iranians in their assumed collectivity. Compare this with the ways in which, say, "Christian fascism" or "German fascism" is used! In this case, because, in the dominant epistemic regime of reference, plurality is already taken for granted, the expression "Christian fascism" is used and interpreted to signify a particular group or ideology within an infinite number of other actual and potential Christian groups and perspectives. Similarly, the use of the expression "German fascism" in no way implies that all Germans were or are fascists thanks to the implicit premise regarding the ideological and political multitude and plurality among Germans. In fact, an expression such as "German fascism" or "white fascism" does not even necessitate a footnote to clarify an ambiguity simply because there is no perceived ambiguity to speak of in the first place. On the other hand, to go back to the racist mentality that denies Asians and Africans multitude and plurality, the use of terms such as Islamic, Iranian, Turkish, Arab, Indian, etc. would inevitably be read to signify a collective as a homogeneous entity composed of identical members/units, so any of these terms would be descriptive of whatever comes after it holistically and essentially.

Culturalism as a Fascist Tool for Homogenization on Continental and Regional Bases

Old fashion racists had no problem deploying the pseudo-scientific concept of "race" to advance their discriminatory practices from slavery and colonialism to lynching and mass murder. Although it is still not uncommon for "race" to be used in the biological sense to assume racial taxonomies, it was bound to be discredited scientifically. After Europe itself was subjected to the horrors of the race project at the hands of European fascists, "race" lost a great deal of its scientific legitimacy and moral appeal, but racism had been too deeply rooted in the dominant ideology and too central to the nationalist mode of perception to be discarded so swiftly. In fact, the elites who control the means of knowledge production wasted no time to rescue racism by constructing a new language of universal discrimination, a language that functions on more nuanced ideological levels.

The new language of the old mentality has developed a defense mechanism that can be described as democratic camouflaging. It not only advances a world order premised on the naturality of racist domination but also does so precisely in the name of plurality. If anything, this language of neoliberal globalization advocates plurality. The vital question is: *plurality of what?* Even in the old-fashioned fascist world, plurality was not denied; in fact, fascist worldviews are premised on the essential plurality of race. Today's fashionable term of "diversity" is, for the most part, another cosmetic operation of the dominant discourse precisely in order not to change the core racist doctrine of the dominant order. The diversity that is widely celebrated in the neoliberal era is not that of political subjects. To the contrary, it is an oppressive form of collectivization and essentialization as in the name of democratic tolerance it imposes racist taxonomical and typological labels on people. Today's ethos of diversity is even more totalitarian than the old one.

The plurality of "race" has simply been replaced with that of "culture." Thanks to culturalism, exclusion through inclusion has become the new, and arguably more effective, tool for dehumanizing populations of entire continents and depoliticizing their realities.

Under the hegemony of the false paradigm of culture, culturalists perceive the non-white Other as either a victim or an aggressor. This mentality lies at the core of culturalism, which has been a dominant form of new-racism since the defeat of Italian (old) Fascism and German Nazism, when "race" was widely discredited as a pseudo-scientific notion. Culturalism is the practice of othering whereby non-whites are essentialized and reduced to similar units whose collective world is fundamentally determined by their belief systems and mythologies. It is a mentality that perceives non-whites as members of homogeneous communities defined and conceived through the collective cultures into which they are, supposedly, born and within which they die. The peoples of the MENA region, for example, are commonly perceived as a collective whole whose world is defined by Islam.

Any movement or individual that contradicts that Muslim image is not only disturbing, but almost non-cognizable to the culturalist mentality. This is precisely why Islamism receives much more recognition than those militant feminist movements in the region that have been struggling against male chauvinism for decades. These secular feminist movements simply do not fit into the anthropologized image of the MENA woman, and so they are routinely dismissed. The purportedly Muslim Other who is progressive by universal standards is as unattractive to the culturalist as an intellectual woman is to a misogynist. The Other is expected to act in accordance with the predetermined collective culture ascribed to her by the culturalist.

Put differently, the culturalist in the West has already taken a moralist position. The culturalist left's position is sympathy and the culturalist right's position is enmity toward the othered Other. The West's Muslim Other to the culturalist leftist is the ultimate victim and to the culturalist right the ultimate threat. When confronted with acts of the Other that are sexist, colonial, genocidal, fascistic, etc., the culturalist left seems to find itself paralyzed by confusion and to the culturalist right that merely confirms their belief about the Other. Western culturalists, whether from the left or the right, cannot conceive of left and right in societies perceived to be Muslim. Non-white societies are perceived as essentially homogeneous and one-dimensional.

Culturalists (in the West) could not have any conception of imperialism within MENA societies simply because they assume that only the West can be imperialist. Societal complexities, class antagonism, political or social polarizations of left and right, and militant progressive movements are simply inconceivable when it comes to the culturalist's perception of those who are perceived as the West's Other. Ultimately, both the culturalist left and right in the West adopt the same reductionist new-racist view of the Muslim Other: both sides, sometimes openly and other times implicitly, generalize Islamism as the actual political representation of all Muslim majority societies. The difference is in their reactions to the perceived Other. Whereas the left generally excuses and sometimes even sympathizes with Islamism as an extension of its tolerance for perceived Muslims, the right demonizes entire societies due to its rejection of Islamism. Still, both sides share the culturalist intellectual deficiency, according to which Islam, Muslimhood, and Islamism are attributed to entire societies as "their culture."

To the culturalist, a non-white person essentially lacks personhood and individuality; she or he is merely a representative of a collective identity. This translates to an inability to see non-Western societies as being composed of individuals capable of autonomous thinking. Liberal multiculturalism and the insincere respect for the Other that is built into it only makes the tendency to culturalize the Other worse because in such superficially "respectful" circumstances, real conversations cannot take place.[40] If a white person makes a sexist or fascist statement, it is because she or he is sexist or fascist. However, if a similar statement is made by a non-white person, it is because of her or his culture, and multiculturalism requires that one respects and tolerates the Other's strange views, however problematic they may be. Obviously, any meaningful respect would require taking the other as an individual seriously insofar as an individual, regardless of background, is capable of acting as a political actor. By sympathizing with the simplistic culturalized image of the Other, the left sometimes ends up aligning with fascist forces, thereby undermining its leftist revolutionary movements.

The culturalist view has been functioning in the interest of fascist forces in Africa and Asia, including the MENA region, for some time. Islamists in particular have exploited the simplicity of this mentality. Under the false assumption that all Enlightenment values are European, and that non-Europeans have their own distinct collective views that are equally legitimate *for them*, the Islamist is (falsely) excused for his or her irrationality on the grounds of respecting the Other's "way of life." The traditional left in the West has (mostly unknowingly) been betraying the left in the MENA region for decades. Egyptian, Iranian, and Turkish leftists are extremely critical of Islamism, and in the Kurdish case, there has been an ongoing existential struggle between liberation movements and the Islamist camps in the region. However, the naïve Western leftist often takes Islamist movements such as the Muslim Brotherhood and Hezbollah to be revolutionary Middle Eastern equivalents of the radical left in the West.

---

40 For more on the racist dimensions of multiculturalism, see Lentin and Titley 2011.

Because the Other can only be either a victim or an aggressor in the culturalist mindset, it is very challenging for the culturalist to see what is taking place in Rojava and Bakûr as anything but another nativist or nationalist movement demanding limited political freedoms and cultural rights. This is despite the fact that the Roja-va-Bakûr revolution dropped the goal of establishing an independent Kurdish state a long time ago, and adopted an inclusive anti-nationalist platform that is without parallel in the region. The Rojava revolution is not any more Kurdish than the Paris Commune was French. Also, there is more internationalism and communism in the Rojava revolution than the Paris Commune. Somehow, the traditional left seems to have fallen prey to what it wants to struggle against, namely imperialist dom-ination. This could explain the traditional left's inability to conceive international revolutionary movements that take place in the margins.

It is obviously even more challenging to convince a culturalist that the Rojava revolution is in fact the kind of revolution that all progressives in the world can and should learn from. This is especially the case when such arguments are put forward by non-white scholars, who are inevitably suspected of being nativists as a matter of course. To the culturalist mentality, the Other can only be the object of sympathy and pity, at best.

Due to the scholastic habit of homogenizing the peoples of the region as the Other of the European colonizer, Orientalist tendencies and distortions persist even within post-colonial studies. This Other, whether demonized or romanticized, crim-inalized or victimized, does not refer to real, concrete, human beings anywhere. Rather, it is a false signifier indicative of the reductionist mentality that dismisses even the most obvious material conditions precisely in order to mythologize everything that is political, historical, and sociological. Culturalism, as a new form of idealist mystification but with the same old racist objectives, is the common way through which the homogenization of the Other is committed nowadays.

2 Negating the Fascist Mode of Perception

Racist and culturalist accounts that have been essentializing Asians and Africans as the non-free Other of the European by Enlightenment philosophers across the board, from Montesquieu and Kant to John Stewart Mill and Hegel,[41] need to be refuted. Even during its best periods, liberalism's political philosophy, including its radical republicanism, failed to recognize equality beyond parts of Europe. The bourgeois project of the Enlightenment simultaneously universalized tribalism and tribalized

---

[41] For more on this, see Emmanuel Chukwudi Eze's *Race and the Enlightenment* (2001).

universalism. It universalized tribalism by imposing a racist structure on the world and tribalized universalism by denying the humanity of those who lived outside the boundaries of the white man's world and its racial strata of privilege. The European racist elites then, like the European racist elites today, simply projected their own nativism on Asians and Africans. The two republics that claimed universal liberty and equality continued to commit enslavement. The dominant Eurocentric narrative, as the economic anthropologist Jason Hickel argues (2018), made most of us internalize capitalist developmentalism, which in turn implies the myth of Euro-superiority on the basis that Europe and Europeanized parts of the world are historically ahead of the rest of the world. Ideologically, this distorted image of history is mainly framed through selective assertions and omissions. Systematic omissions of facts, events, and narratives that contradict the dominant account have complimented acts of commission on the material domains that brutally imposed a global regime of labor division, normalized total domination, concentrated the means of unlimited subjugation, and universalized a system of unlimited control.

Before the British aggressions in the 19th century, the Chinese enjoyed higher life conditions, more advanced public education (for males and females), and a greater and more diverse economy than the Brits, the French, and other Europeans. Before the British and French subjugation of Asian labor and resources, about two-thirds of the world economy were coordinated by China and India (Hickel 2018, 67). Because of British colonialism, India's contribution to the world economy shrank from 27% to a mere 3% (Hickel 2018, 67), and within fifty years, by 1921, the average life expectancy of Indians fell by 20% (Hickel 2018, 93). The policies that were imposed on China through sheer savagery resulted in a steep fall of the Chinese contribution to the world economy from 35% to only 7% (Hickel 2018, 92). Noticeably, the Europeans stood out globally for their advancement in technologies of violence, which were used to irreversibly destroy African civilizations, empires, economies, societies, and social ecologies. In fact, technologies of violence, along with politics of total and unlimited domination, were the distinguishing aspect of the European ruling groups' approach to what would today be called international relations. The European domination of the world was actualized precisely through the pathological obsession with sheer violence. Even more ironically, precisely because of this deeply uncivilized aspect of European hegemony, the racist white bourgeoisie have ended up claiming human civilization as such while assuming an undisputed entitlement to the unlimited exercise of power. In today's "international apartheid regime," the ruling groups in the West continue to essentialize, denigrate, and often even punish entire populations by imposing poverty, famine, and underdevelopment. Such international economic sanctions have devastated entire societies, including the North Korean, Cuban, Iraqi, Sudanese, Iranian, Syrian, and Venezuelan societies.

Whether in China, India, the Americas, or Africa, the Europeans' key advantage was the means of subjugation. If in the Middle Ages the Arabs and Mongols expanded their respective rule by virtue of conquering vast territories using militaristic strategies, from the 16th century onward Europeans, including the Spanish, Portuguese, French, British, and Dutch, adopted the method of coercive subjugation as the primary means of domination. The Islamic invasions too might have produced certain advancements in a number of arenas, but it is absurd to dismiss, whether intentionally or unintentionally, their destruction of entire canons and horizons of possibility. The American (before European colonialism), Asian and African societies were simply too civilized to prioritize the endless subjugation of others everywhere or to prioritize the war industry. While European ruling elites in the realms of knowledge production perceived the African Other as a subject of criminology, it is precisely the European ruling groups' behavior and tendency to prioritize technologies of violence and politics of domination that deserve criminological investigation. In all cases, it is absurd to consider such a tendency as a part of historical progress even if it results in accomplishing advancement in certain areas of inquiry and industry, as it happened with European capitalism.

In the post-slavery and post-colonial era, more effective means than those of coercive slavery and colonialism have been deployed to maintain the absolute relativism according to which Asia, Africa, the Caribbean, and Latin America must serve as suppliers of energy and labor, guarantors of wealth and goods. Of course, the moral monopoly can only follow the track of the material monopoly. Just as the World Bank and International Monetary Fund impose neoliberal policies across the global South in the name of development, mega-capitalists such as Bill Gates, Michael Bloomberg, Jeff Bezos, and Elon Musk lead philanthropism, and thereby dictate the rules and meaning of goodness in the world. Beneath all this neoliberalist world dictatorship, even statements of basic statistics of inequality sound absurd. Today, more than 60 percent of the world population lives in poverty, and about a quarter of those live on less than one dollar a day. The gap between average income per person in the global South versus the global North, as Hickel notices, has tripled since 1960 (2018, 2), or since the dawn of neoliberalism. The average income of a white person in the United States in 2020 was $74,912, which amounts to 147 times Afghanistan's GPD per capita in the same year, 509$. Thanks to the capitalist order, the COVID-19 pandemic became an opportunity to further intensify exploitation. According to Oxfam's May 2022 report, during the first two years of the pandemic, the amount of capital that was collected by billionaires ($453 billion) exceeded the amount in the previous twenty-three years combined. While on average every thirty hours a new exploiter joined the billionaire class, it was expected that one million people would be pushed into extreme poverty every thirty-three hours during 2022. Finally, ten people alone own more than what 3.1 billion people own (Oxfam 2022, 3).

Afghans and Iraqis, who were supposedly liberated, live under the mercy of Islamist militia. They suffered an unknown number of casualties—and those who died in the process of being liberated are not perceived to be deserving even minimal recognition, as a mere number. The liberators blamed Afghans and Iraqis for not defending themselves and for not establishing the rule of law. Today, Afghans and Iraqis who dare to go to the world where liberty is a right as they have been told, realize that Europe had already sold them to another Islamist regime, Erdogan's Turkey, or the Libyan armed groups. Otherwise, they may try their chances between being drowned in the sea and arrival in a continent where millions of voters freely turn to neofascist parties primarily to ensure that non-European refugees do not have a future in Europe. After all, liberal democracy must be protected against those who are unfortunate enough to believe in it. What completes the double irony is that the protection of liberal democracies entails mandating other fascist forces to deal with refugees. Somehow, even when alliances for manufacturing nuclear war technology are formed around what is clearly racist frames, such as the United States-the United Kingdom-Australia 2021 pack, somehow the justification is worded in terms of universality and universal good against the alleged threat, which not surprisingly always comes from the East.

Today's superficially polite liberals and genuinely superficial leftists in the West may tolerate or even adore that Other, but the Other is nonetheless a product of their own Eurocentric mode of perception. The "Muslim" is nothing but a European imaginary creature. No human being in reality can be defined by Muslimness. That same mode of perception once imagined "the Jew" and imposed that essentialist sign on many millions of persons ultimately in order to strip them of their personhood, sociology, history, freewill, and, in one word, humanity. Jewishness, like Arabness, Hinduness, or any other identity, whether proclaimed or perceived—that is, whether subjectively embraced in some sense or objectively imposed through circumstances—is not an essential quality of a person or a society.

Depicting any such identity as if it were a broader category than the subject's humanity is the prime fallacy that characterizes the ideology forms of fascism, including Islamism. Ironically, cultural relativism commits the same fallacy in the name of rejecting absolutism and essentialism. It is no wonder that fundamentalists and neoliberals often share the same mode of perception according to which humanity is divided along sectarian, tribalist lines. It is no wonder that in the name of cultural and moral relativism, in the name of rejecting Eurocentrism, the post-communist Western leftist simply reproduces the worldview of Islamist fundamentalists. It is no wonder that to some intellectual celebrities in the West, Hezbollah represents progressiveness and anti-imperialism for the Middle East. A mode of perception that unwittingly attributes all that is universal, such as life, liberty, equality, and pursuit of happiness, to the white, while at the same time perceives every non-white society as a homogeneous group whose world is supposedly defined by certain cultural boundaries is by definition tribalist, sectarian, and deeply racist. What I want to emphasize about this mode of perception, which is dominant in the age of neoliberalism and fundamentalism, is not its consequential moral wrongness, because that would be another idealist fallacy and useless appeal to an idealist mentality. Rather, the issue problematized here is the *falsehood* of the dominant mode of perception, that is the falsification of both the epistemology and the metaphysics that have been normalized via hegemonic means of domination.

The culturalist mode of perception, which shares the same false premises of fundamentalism, in effect mummifies sociologies, politics, and histories of the world, thereby metaphysically denying the possibility of an egalitarian world in the future. This is precisely the point; in order for the material inequality of conditions of life not to be abolished, alleged metaphysical inequalities among different demographics are ideologically naturalized. To assume that life, liberty, and the pursuit of happiness are unique to a particular group's "way of life" is to assume that there are other groups who do not value life, liberty, and the pursuit of happiness. Indeed, this is the basis on which Americans for generations have been educated, which has ingrained American exceptionalism in the minds of people from all walks of life. That same assumption implies that others might be attracted to death, enjoy unfreedom, and cherish misery. If generations of Americans and Europeans are so deceived as to think that non-whites might enjoy being mass murdered, enslaved, and made miserable, it is hardly surprising that the lives, liberties, and happiness of Asians, Africans, Caribbeans, and Latin Americans have been so insignificant in various arenas of not only foreign policy and international politics but also knowledge production in the academy and the bourgeois public sphere at large. As mentioned earlier, Césaire rightly observed that Hitler's unforgivable crime was not mass murder per se, something all European colonialists had been committing for a long time, but rather it was employing similar means of mass murder against fellow Europeans (Césaire 2001, 3; also, quoted in Fanon 1994, 166).

We must break free from this fascist mode of perception that has been adopted far beyond the continent of Europe and widely internalized by the raced, cultured, and othered Other in the post-communist, neoliberal, Fukuyaman world. In the East, West, South, and North, we need to break free from this new-age mythology that has imposed a false, idealist, structure on a real world composed of real human beings who are suffering because of real conditions of inequality and dehumanization.

European colonialism succeeded in mapping the world according to its own mode of perception, that is, on racist and religious bases. Moreover, the ruling elites in the colonized populations also built the post-colonial states in accordance with the nationalist mode of perception thereby perpetuating a world of antagonistic and exclusionary nations, realizing Europe's right-wing vision of the contemporary world. Even Fanonian anti-colonial revolutionism was stripped of its internationalist framework by the buffoons of nationalism, who took nationalism to be an end in itself and placed themselves at the top of the new pyramid of power. Edward Said noticed the same problem, of the misreading of Fanon's *The Wretched of the Earth*, observing that, "while nationalism is a necessary spur to revolt against the colonizer, national consciousness must be immediately transformed into what he [Fanon] calls 'social consciousness,' just as soon as the withdrawal of the colonizer has been accomplished" (Said 2003, 378). Said adds:

> Fanon also prophesied the continuing dependency of numerous postcolonial governments and philosophies, all of which preached the sovereignty of the newly independent people of one or another new Third World state and, having failed to make the transition from nationalism to true liberation, were in fact condemned to practice the politics, and the economics, of a new oppression as pernicious as the old one [. . .] In effect this really means that just to be an independent postcolonial Arab, or black, or Indonesian is not a program, nor a process, nor a vision. It is no more than a convenient starting point from which the real work, the hard work, might begin. (2003, 378–379)

The colonized fell into a relationship of mimicry with the colonialists thereby rendering movements of national liberation the continuation of the dreadful shadow of the colonial beast devouring the marginalized and the silenced through means of totalitarian assimilation, at best, or genocidal procedures, at worst. The Pakistani state subjugated the Bangladeshis, and today the Bangladeshi Islamists subjugate perceived non-Muslims and non-Bangladeshis. The Tunisian anti-colonial revolutionary elites immediately othered their own Tunisian comrades whose Jewishness suddenly was considered to be incompatible with the national identity (for example, see Memmi 2013). Iraqi Assyrians, then Jews, and then Kurds were perceived as the enemy of the nation even before the British forces left what had just become Iraq on the political map. Yet, in their long struggle to gain their independence, the political leadership in Iraqi Kurdistan reembraced the former colonialists, mimicked the new colonialists, suppressed the population, and persecuted progressive groups (for more, see Ahmed 2018a).[42]

---

42 Ultimately, the Kurdish nationalist leaders in Iraq used their militias as proxies for any foreign power that needed their services to put pressure on Baghdad. During the Iraq-Iran war, these militias, especially Talabani's fighters, openly and proudly aided the Iranian regime against the Iraqi state, which in turn resulted in Baghdad's treatment of some Kurdish areas and towns, such as Halabja, as enemy territory. Today, Barzani's party, the Kurdistan Democratic Party (PDK), is allied

3 Black Consciousness as Anti-fascism

The pioneering critical theorists of anti-colonialism in Africa and the Caribbean, such as Frantz Fanon, Walter Rodney, and Steve Biko, were acutely aware of nationalism's threat to liberation movements, especially in the post-colonial era. Indeed, they all prioritized universalism in the struggle. To Fanon and Rodney, Marxism provided a robust theoretical framework for universalism. They remained true to the Marxian materialist tools of critical analysis and at the same time focused on the implications of the ideological hegemony of European racism that had set the world on the path of tribalism and sectarianism. This is precisely why they did not commit the typical fallacy of departmentalizing race relations and class relations. More than that, they refused to be forced into a place determined by Eurocentrism, a place defined negatively in relation to whiteness. Instead, they relocated whiteness according to an African revolutionary epistemology, which, at the same time, is meant to serve as a genuine universal theory of knowledge. That is also to say, they relocated the center for universal liberation to the margins.

To Steve Biko, black consciousness was revolutionary consciousness, a consciousness that is emancipatory for not only subjugated blacks but also the privileged whose social position had situated them in an oppressive system of racism. In Biko's critical philosophy, blackness is opened up not only to break free from the

---

with the Turkish government against the Kurdish liberation movements in Turkey and Syria while Talabani's party, the Patriotic Union of Kurdistan (PUK), continues to work within the parameters of the Iranian regime's sphere of influence. Even in Baghdad, Talabani's party is allied with the Islamist forces that are supported by Tehran while Barzani's party is a member of a rival coalition led by less fanatic Shia parties. In short, Kurdish nationalism in Iraq has only brought more suffering to Iraqi Kurds when it was in opposition. Since it has been ruling parts of the Kurdish-majority areas, it has proved itself to be just another oppressive force by far worse than the Baathists when it comes to corruption (for examples, see Rubin 2018, and Wille 2020). Also, in terms of the environment, social security, and the rule of law, Iraqi Kurdistan is worse off under the rule of peshmerga, a term and a figure that remains highly cherished among Iranian Kurds, who have had their own oppositional armed groups, or peshmerga, throughout the last eighty years.

Just like the rest of the region and beyond, in Iran, there was a time when the presence of a strong, confident, and popular Marxist movement stood in direct opposition to Persian chauvinism and in the interest of establishing an egalitarian, inclusive, and pluralist political space. In fact, the Kurdish-majority city of Sinne is still called by some people the Red Sinne, indicating its functioning as the hub of the communist movement in Kurdistan, where communists from various parts of Iran also took refuge. Some Persian-speaking Iranian communists who joined the guerrilla movement even became fluent in Kurdish, which is otherwise almost unheard of given the utter dominance of the Persian language and the endless privileges associated with Persian identity. Also, the Azerbaijani and Kurdish leftists have a long history of solidarity and collaboration, the roots of which go back to the 1940s.

Euro-racist imposition but also to become an intellectual sphere with maximum inclusivity and emancipatory potentiality. That is to say, in direct contrast to the European racialization of politics, Biko and his comrades tried to politicize the notion of race and racial relations of power. While the European bourgeois elites essentialized skin color to create and naturalize human hierarchy, the revolution-ary critical theorists of black consciousness reversed blackness to signify a political doctrine for universal equality. Accordingly, I argue that blackness is a revolution-ary aspect to which we all need to aspire. In this sense, the revolutionary subject today should be described as both black and proletarian; and just as members of the bourgeoisie could rebel against their class and join the proletarian cause, members of the racially privileged, whatever their perceived identity may be, could claim political blackness by unlearning what the racist institutions and regimes of knowledge production had made them internalize. Blackness, therefore, should be redefined as both a social condition of marginalization and a philosophical acquisi-tion of epistemological privilege for gaining revolutionary awareness. Like Marx's definition of the proletariat, blackness can be defined in terms of both negativity and its power to negate, both factual sociohistorical circumstances that have real-ized untruth, irrationality, unfreedom, and exploitation and potential revolution-ary power capable of realizing truth, reason, freedom, and equality. In the con-temporary world, just as every form of class exploitation is simultaneously racist regardless of the perceived class position of the exploited and the exploiters, every racist form of oppression is simultaneously capitalist regardless of the perceived racial identities of the oppressors and the oppressed. From the post-nihilist phil-osophical point of view, therefore, there is no controversy in asserting that every position of social privilege, including both bourgeois and racial positions, should be perceived as a shameful intellectual deficit only redeemable through standing with the struggling marginalized and working toward an emancipatory project that aims to negate all socially and historically constructed inequalities. Blacks have been ashamed for too long, and black revolutionaries have already sacrificed more than enough for emancipation; it is time for blackness to become a source of revo-lutionary pride, something all those who are not perceived as black should aspire to become, both philosophically and practically, both socially and politically. Whites who complain about the unfairness of the alleged burden of the so-called "white guilt" might never be able to emancipate their modes of perception from socially determined epistemological underprivilege. At the moment, this problem should not be of too much pedagogical concern for the revolutionary critical theory. Many among those who in one way or another benefit from the enduring conditions of inequality will always appeal to the dominant moral regime, which is of course the values of the dominant structured within a system of domination. There will always be those who on the one hand deny racism but on the other hand claim that they are victims of racist discrimination. To them, the oppressed do not have the right to any expression that may allude to the truth. The moment the victim of racism speaks up, s/he is accused of thinking in terms of race. Have not we all heard of and from the poor white middle-aged man who complains about being discriminated against only because he happened to be white even though he, allegedly, had always been against racism and despite the fact that his best friend or spouse is black, etc.? Ultimately, there is nothing surprising in this kind of scenario because speaking about underprivilege is normally perceived as a threat to the otherwise normalized and unspoken-of regime of privileges.

The denialist (and often aggressive) reaction of many members of the privileged comes from what could be described as a socially developed class instinct for self-preservation or a privilege-defense mechanism. This explains why for conservatives the most natural and rational thing to do is to conserve the existing social norms and mourn what has already been lost to what they perceive is decadence, politically, morally, spiritually, etc. These self-victimizing masses who cannot tolerate the idea of a world without social privileges will inevitably either die off by the time revolutionary movements make a substantial change in the world or unlearn their belief systems after those revolutionary changes will occur to social relations. Either way, the material transformation that takes place will be far more influential than what can be accomplished through political correctness, which unfortunately has become both a strategy for hiding racism by liberal-leaning folks and a target of attacks by fascist-leaning folks. The binary logic of so-called cancel culture and so-called political correctness is another false duality created with a public sphere that is neither public in the democratic sense of reasoning nor relevant in the philosophical sense of politics. Once the relations of privilege are negated, nobody will have reason to feel threatened by egalitarian projects, nor will such projects have to be defined in terms of the proletarian class and blackness.

To Memmi, the bitter experiences of double marginalization, at the hands of both European and Arab racists, were empirical proof of the failure of national liberation movements across MENA. Memmi was (un)fortunate enough to live long enough to witness both the anti-colonial revolutions and the gloomy era that followed the false independence, sovereignty as perceived and practiced by MENA nation-states. However, what Memmi missed is that nation-statism was bound to fail as an emancipatory entity.

Admittedly, nationalism could be emancipatory but only within limited historical contexts and limited geographic and demographic boundaries. Indeed, nationalism frequently played emancipatory roles in various contexts of modernization (including democratization, industrialization, and secularization) and anti-colonialism. However, at best, only during such struggles could it inspire certain political reformations, but the moment it achieves its goal, an independent nation-state, there is no philosophy of emancipation to speak of. Inevitably, nationalism becomes a chauvinistic mode of perception and an exclusionary belief system tantamount to tribalism. Therefore, what brings catastrophe to a nationalist project is not divergence from some supposed original project; rather, nationalism's very maturity is the catastrophe.

Nationalist enterprises in their European birthplaces had already been catastrophic, and it is absurd to believe that it could have been otherwise when mimicked and experimented in Africa, Asia, or Latin America. While nationalism in several cases established democratic structures of governance inwardly, scholars often tend to underestimate or altogether dismiss what those very nation-states committed against the excluded and the non-Europeans. Whether in the case of French, English, German, Dutch, Italian, or Spanish nationalism, chauvinism has always been a defining feature, as the communists, starting with Marx, have observed. Unlike nationalism, communism was philosophically conceived and politically conducted as an anti-exclusionary, anti-oppressive, and, thus, necessarily revolutionary movement. While Stalinism is habitually brought up as the ultimate and damning case against the communist claim to democracy and internationalism, what many enthusiastic revisionist historians often dismiss is the communists' struggle against Stalinist regimes. In short, communism was a dream that could become a nightmare, but nationalism left to its own devices is a nightmare in the making.

That said, communists from Marx to Lenin were among the strongest supporters of national liberation movements not only in Europe but also in Asia, Africa, and the Americas. To Marx, class antagonism takes the form of national liberation for the colonized. As Losurdo (2016) shows with astonishing details and paramount textual and historiographical evidence, whenever and wherever nationalism is an emancipatory movement of resistance against domination, a liberation movement against foreign and imperial rule, Marxism fully endorses it. Class domination is indistinguishable from colonialist, racist, and nationalist oppression, so class struggle also must entail anti-colonial, anti-racist, and anti-nationalist domination.

When class struggle, anti-colonial resistance, national liberation, or anti-racism is abstracted in separation of the rest, the outcome is disastrous, turning all against all in every conceivable way. The post-colonial era did not turn nightmarish overnight. Furthermore, the nightmare that has been actualized was certainly not inevitable or predetermined. Rather, it began to take shape at the same time as the universalist and emancipatory force within anti-colonialism started to lose ground. That was the force Fanon and Rodney so adamantly supported in everything they uttered and practiced. Again, the fact that such a force existed and was popular, it means it is possible. It means Asia and Africa, the Caribbean, and Latin America, are not the metaphysically doomed geographies that are imagined according to racist maps and mapped according to racist ideologies.

Chapter 9
Negations: Perpetual Critique and Emancipatory Praxis

There is nothing more definitive of the 20th century than fascism and anti-fascism. This proposition is accurate when anti-fascism is primarily understood to be communism. The only reason anti-fascism is not understood to be communism primarily is that history is written by the dominant. To say history is written by the dominant is to say the dominant's ideology has been internalized by almost everyone. In other words, the distortions are ingrained in the dominant mode of perception. Nonetheless, it is possible to uncover some of the distortions, unlearn some of the falsehood, and problematize fascism accordingly, which is this book's goal.

Before and after WWII, in the West and East, various nationalist, religious, and liberal states and forces within alliances and separately fought against communists. For just over six years some liberal states were forced to fight Nazism, whereas for over sixty years they fought communism. In fact, the anti-communist machine continues to operate globally. What happened after both WWI and WWII involved imperial rearrangements in terms of the redistribution of colonies. While in Africa and West Asia the concerned imperial powers were Europeans, in East Asia, Hirohito's Japan was a challenging imperial player. After WWII, Japan was out, and the United States was in as the most powerful member of the imperialist club. The US imperialist enterprise now stretched from the Americas across both the Pacific and the Atlantic.

When fascism started threatening liberalism in Europe during the interwar period, the bourgeois liberal elites continued to live in denial until it was too late. Even then, many of them simply blamed Stalin's infamous pact with Hitler for the overwhelming expansion of the Third Reich over vast parts of Europe. After the war, both East and West Germany undertook processes of de-Nazification. In the United States and much of Western Europe, however, there was nothing that even remotely could be called de-fascistification. If anything, with Hitler out of the way, fascists, including Franco and Salazar, became valued members in the anti-communist camp led by the US, the UK, and France. In the meantime, the USSR was quickly ejected from the alliance that had been formed during WWII to defeat Hitler. In 1938, while Stalin was still hoping to form an alliance with Britain and France to stop the rise of fascism, the leaders of these two countries instead joined a pact with Hitler and Mussolini signing the Munich Agreement.

Before and after the war, Stalin desperately tried to form an alliance with Britain, France, and the United States. The blockade on the anti-fascist camp in

https://doi.org/10.1515/9783111609041-009

Spain between 1936 and 1939 and then the capitulation of most of the European states to Hitler were supposedly less detrimental than the Hitler-Stalin Pact of 1939, which lasted two years. Be that as it may, while Stalin was actively wiping out the Bolsheviks who had survived the war against the White Army and the war against Nazism, Western governments were mobilizing against an alleged communist conspiracy led by the USSR. Stalin kept proclaiming communism for propaganda purposes (to legitimize his regime in the name of the communist movement), and Western governments kept labeling Stalin's regime as communist for their own propaganda purposes (to delegitimize the communist movement).

Both Stalin and the West stood against the Maoist revolution in China. Just as the West was blockading the Chinese people to starve them as a punishment for liberating themselves from Japanese imperialism, Hirohito (1901–1989), the emperor of Japan, was welcomed into the anti-communist pact as if the hundreds of thousands of civilians who were burned alive in Hiroshima, Nagasaki, and Tokyo by the American war machine were to be blamed for Hirohito's earlier decision to attack Pearl Harbor. The two empires settled their accounts, so now it was time to join forces to ensure the subordination of the colonized peoples in Asia. The Chinese and the Vietnamese communists refused that arrangement, and the response by the alleged defenders of democracy was the indiscriminate starvation of the Chinese and the murder of millions of Vietnamese.

Despite Stalin's ultimate destruction of the Bolshevik project of internationalism, liberation movements were emerging one after another across Asia and Africa. From the 1950s, Maoism and the Cuban revolution gave anti-colonial and anti-imperialist movements a decisive push, so the European colonial powers were forced to retreat in most parts of Africa and Asia. The American ruling class invented neo-imperialism, which would later be called globalization. This model of imperialism was founded on economic monopoly, the strategic use of military force, and ideological hegemony. The ideological strategy for hegemony focused on anti-communist propaganda. At the same time, the American state and its allies in North America, Latin America, Europe, Asia, and Eurasia engaged in a crusade against communist movements across the world. Dubbing the supposedly global bloc of communist powers as "the evil empire" was just an ideological sign of the length the neo-imperial camp had been ready to go to to fight communists everywhere. This was the beginning of a golden age for fascism in all its forms, whether religious including Catholic and Islamist variations, or purely racist nationalism. Indeed, while the Portuguese Estado Novo, Spanish Flange, Turkish Kemalism, and pan-Arab Baathism were supported unconditionally to wipe out communists, Islamism was also being courted as another anti-communist crusader.

In Indonesia, Pakistan, Afghanistan, and the Arab kingdoms, Islamism, supported generously by the United States and Britain, proved itself as an uncompromising anti-communist force. With the collapse of the "evil empire," the neo-imperialist/neoliberal camp started to be agitated by its Frankensteinian fascist monsters in the Arab world, including Saddam Hussein's Iraq. In the meantime, Shia Islamism had created its own empire in Iran, and Sunni Islamism was on the rise from Sudan to Afghanistan. Today, the Sunni Islamist empire is led by Turkey. The regions from Pakistan and Afghanistan to Syria, Yemen, Somalia, and Sudan live their season in hell perpetuated by Islamists. The other peripheries of the capitalist world system, including India and much of Africa and Latin America, continue to suffer from devastating economic crises while the ruling groups in every nation-state try to utilize all material and ideological means to keep things under control as millions are on the move, to escape the hell of poverty, droughts, and violence, toward the centers of the capitalist system.

In most of the centers of the capitalist world system, meanwhile, fascism is either on the rise or already ruling. Wherever communism was uprooted, fascism in one way or another rules. Even in what once were called liberation movements, with a few exceptions, the post-Marxist era has been predominantly fascistic. In the 20th century fascism emerged because of and within the crises of capitalism. Today, the crises of capitalism are in many ways more severe, and the ensuing destruction is more encompassing societally, geographically, politically, and ecologically. Samir Amin was right to argue that this wave of capitalist crises entails the rise of another wave of fascism (2017, chap. 3). Today fascist forces in the United States, Italy, France, Austria, Holland, and the Scandinavian states are increasingly emboldened. As mentioned in Chapter 1 of this book, despite all this, most elites, including academics and journalists, seem to be more concerned about the employment of the term fascism than the rise of fascist forces or whatever you want to call them. It is more accurate to say fascism has already been ruling, but what we are witnessing is the rise of forms of fascism that are too similar to the interwar period models.

Liberal elites in the future might portray these times, as fascism has not completely taken over, as a golden age. They will not mention that things were already bad for the marginalized. How could they if they share the same mode of perception as those to their right when it comes to the extreme centralization of economic power? Bourgeois elites since the 1880s have been morally too confident to allow for any skepticism to creep into their managerial minds and missionary hearts. As Adorno notes, "the nineteenth century came up against the limit of bourgeois society, which could not fulfill its own reason, its own ideals of freedom, justice, and humane immediacy, without running the risk of its order being abolished" (2005a, 154).

Whenever the choices come down to communism and fascism as the only two main options, liberal bourgeois elites go for fascism without hesitation. When things get out of control and the catastrophes are universalized by fascists, there is a chapter of universal terror after which the unspoken alliance between fascists, liberals, and social democrats are quickly forgotten, paving the way for a rebirth of liberalism's self-portrayal as a progressive force. Thinking along these lines, Adorno writes, "for countless people life was not at all bad under fascism. Terror's sharp edge was aimed only at a few and relatively well defined groups" (2005a, 95). Then he adds, "Fascism essentially cannot be derived from subjective dispositions. The economic order, and to a great extent also the economic organization modeled upon it, now as then renders the majority of people dependent upon conditions beyond their control and thus maintains them in a state of political immaturity" (2005a, 98).

In the United States, the Democratic Party's poor decisions are not mere strategic mistakes; rather, they speak to the elites' interests, fears, and anxieties. Even a small concession to the working class, which is what supporting Bernie Sanders would have amounted to, is out of the question for the Democratic Party. Their stance was bound to give the Trumpist movement an ideal opportunity to increase its tactics and velocity, rendering an overwhelming fascist takeover inevitable. But, from the point of view of class analysis, neither the trajectory nor the enabling denialism is surprising. If there is a historical pattern, it is precisely this. The conditions of fascism have persisted, and fascism has only advanced its political strategies and methods of popular appeal. By giving voice to some of the most widespread racist assumptions, it has secured a comeback, once more, as an honest platform inspired by a bond of brotherhood. In the meantime, liberal elites made the hollowness of their belief in their ideals evident. Just like in the 19th century, the bourgeoisie had to either abolish itself for the sake of its ideals or invent a new mythology.

1 The Problem of Idealism: When Fascism Studies Obscures Fascism

Somehow the field of fascism studies has become increasingly confined within the discipline of history. If this assessment is accurate, inducing its implications is not difficult. Assigning a topic to any particular field of study within the humanities and social sciences is neither neutral nor arbitrary. In fact, the disciplinary distribution and departmentalization of scholarship are inseparable from ideological hegemony and social domination. For instance, the very designation of an area called Middle East and North Africa studies is reflective of neo-orientalism. The endless emphasis on cultural studies is an embodiment and perpetuation of homogenization of the white man's racialized other, which has its roots in the early days of anthropology. By the same token, the implicit allocation of fascism studies to the field of history entails certain politics of knowledge production.

More to the point, by mandating history departments to oversee fascism studies, the academic establishment has already institutionalized an ideological prejudice according to which researching fascism primarily and by default concerns the study of the past. This unspoken resolution, which effectively unproblematized fascism, was made in order to undermine the communist struggle against fascism, as part of a much larger campaign to portray communism as the only existing threat to democracy. Franco was still around, and in fact treated very well by the Western bloc when fascism studies were sidelined. In reality, fascism studies actively contributed to the process of the de-problematization of fascism.

From the 1920s to the 1960s, much of the important scholarship about fascism was conducted by Marxists, but later fascism studies were rendered obsolete when it was institutionalized and practically allocated to liberal and conservative historians to be taken to the epistemic museum where death certificates are systematically issued for living groups, movements, places, and so on. The strategy is twofold: first, experts issue a death certificate for fascism as something from the past; the general framework of the scholarship is premised on the assumption that fascism is no longer around. Fascists change their appearances and utterances in order not to change as fascists. While carefully camouflaging itself to blend into the new environment, the fascist performance also preserves enough signs to be recognized by followers and sympathizers of old fascism.

By no means are historians' accounts of fascism homogeneous,[43] but there seems to be a common disciplinary problem of past-centrism (not to be confused with historicism or historical determinism). Past-centrists perceive events in their contemporary age through the lenses of historical events as represented or imagined by historians. Within the dominant regime of knowledge production, the perceived past becomes an epistemological fetish with unlimited and eternal metaphysical value. Thus, the present is always and only a subject for potential analogy and disanalogy. Most conservatives try to find dissimilarities. The non-orthodox who are nonetheless past-centrists try to find similarities. The core of the dispute comes down to determining essential conditions or traits that would suffice for designating today's phenomena as other editions of yesterday's phenomena.

Astonishingly, fascism studies may be only second to religious studies in terms of the severe submission to past-centrism. Note in fascism studies, as well as in religious studies, even unorthodox scholars are fundamentally orthodox because they do not challenge the premises and conventions of the area as a sub-field. That is to say, unless the assumed metaphysical value of the "origin" is disregarded, and,

---

43 There are significant differences between the respective perspectives of (from right to center-left) Ernst Nolte, Stanley Payne, Roger Griffin, and Robert O. Paxton.

further, unless the myth of the origin is rejected, all approaches within the field of study will remain inherently orthodox, conservative, and conventional.

Measuring the significance and insignificance of the present by the standard value of a historical moment or event in the past is a cognitive habit that exceeds certain disciplines of scholarship. As Foucault hints, the belief regarding the purity of the origin has roots in religious traditions (1984, 79), which can be explained in terms of Freudian psychoanalysis whereby the unconscious, where the primordial is deposited, is decisive in the psychic economy. Still, such a critique of fascism and fascism studies would be gravely lacking without realizing the prominence of the material conditions within which illusion, falsehood, myth, and irrationality are produced. The same relations of domination that produce fascism also produce knowledge and determine the status of knowledge authority.

The hegemony of power entails, among other things, the authority to name. To name is also to define. Sometimes, to define something is to relegate it to the dead past only to ensure its persistence in the future under the extra protection of camouflaging, whereby the entity implements strategic changes precisely in order to guarantee its persistence in a new environment. Those who control the means of naming are affiliated with those who control the means of production. The class affiliation may be more determining than the proclaimed affinities. Those who work in the apparatuses of the production and distribution of definitions have unquestionable fidelity to the prevalent order. Their skills of neutralization of the worldviews of the dominant are gained effortlessly precisely because the dominant worldviews are continually naturalized and re-naturalized. Therefore, those who control the means of knowledge production are objectively situated to confine objectivity to the parameters of class interest.

The mode of knowledge production under capitalism is capitalist. This prevalent mode of perception and production entails the hegemony of idealism. That is to say, precisely in order to naturalize and perpetuate its domination within the realm of the material conditions, capitalism imposes, naturalizes, and perpetuates a completely non-materialist—that is, idealist—worldview premising sanctified ideas and ideals. For every social force to be dominant it must take attention away from the processes and principles of the domination—that is, hegemonize the mode of perception. Social domination is not sustainable without ideological hegemony. Ideological hegemony implies that the dominated unconsciously identify with the social roles assigned to them within the system of domination. Idealism is both the ideological mechanism and system according to which utter falsehood, i.e., illusion, is internalized and totalized. The domination of capitalism entails idealism as the hegemonic frame of reference in the world. It is through this hegemony that an otherwise unsustainable social reality of violence, unfreedom, and exploitation is naturalized and perpetuated. The idealist hegemony entails an idealist mode of perception and knowledge production. Within that hegemony, naming is essential in terms of both the perception of reality and the production of truth. The power to name is also power over time and space and vice versa.

The ideological formation in the capitalist mode of production could be liberalism, but ultimately, the ideological formation is inseparable from the impositions of the relations of production, which are also the relations of power. Disagreements, arguments, and debates among past-centrists fixate on the historical origin or mother event and the comparability or incomparability of the present moment or event. The present is assumed to be a reproduction of the past or something even more inauthentic. Thus, for instance, in the case of Trump's rise to power, historians who specialize in the history of fascism kept focusing on the same methodological question, namely, whether there is enough resemblance between the movement Trump represents and the interwar fascism in Europe. Naturally, some were affirmative, and many more insisted that the analogy was false. Ultimately, both the yeas and nays were rooted in past-centrism. Roger Griffin, Matthew Feldman, and Stanley Payne did not consider Trumpism as fascism. Others had to wait to see more of Trump's acts and confirm the similarities between those acts and the acts of Hitler and/or Mussolini. For instance, Robert O. Paxton was in the nay camp until January 6, 2021 attack on Capitol Hill, which made him switch to the yea camp (2021). Ruth Ben-Chiat similarly ran comparisons to point out the similarities between Trump's rhetoric and the rhetoric of Italian Fascism and German Nazism. Even after producing a list of the similarities, Ben-Chiat seems to favor the term "authoritarian" for Trump (2023). Others outside the field of history, such as Shane Burley (2017), David Neiwert (2017), and Jason Stanley (2018), rang the alarm about the rise of fascism in the United States, but they too based their arguments on comparative methods with the implicit premise being if there are sufficient analogies between a movement and the European interwar fascism, then that movement is fascist.

The comparative approach is not always problematic, but it is not always necessary either. Denoting movements such as those represented by the Republican Party under Trump's leadership, the French National Rally, the Brothers of Italy, Hungary's Fidesz, and the Freedom Party of Austria (FPÖ) as fascist movements may be valid even if the deployed method to reach the conclusion is a historical-comparative one. These movements embody ideological *forms* that could and should be classified as fascism. They are not second, third, fourth, or tenth editions of interwar fascism but rather the continuation of forces that existed long before Mussolini. Adorno put it very well, stating, "the past will have been worked through only when the causes of what happened then have been eliminated. Only because the causes continue to exist does the captivating spell of the past remain to this day unbroken" (2005a, 103). If anything, today's movements are more, not less, fascist than those from the 1920s, 1930s, and 1940s. This means today's movements have significantly evolved their political strategies, ideological discourses, liberal immunities, postmodern resilience, and scholarly politics or, in short, adaptability and adoptability.

Today's popular fascist movements are popular precisely because they do not look like the models of interwar fascism. Many fascist forces change in order to stay fascist. Fascist groups that have not changed cannot realistically hope to have any popular appeal. This happens across the board. Imagine if liberals did not change over the last century or so. Today, it is inconceivable for American politicians to act like their 1900s–1940s predecessors. To give a tangible example of how much liberal discourse has changed, consider the following statements from a speech by Theodor Roosevelt, the Republican president from 1901 to 1909, delivered in the same year he was awarded the Nobel Peace Prize:

> A great many white men are lynched, but the crime is peculiarly frequent in respect to black men. The greatest existing cause of lynching is the perpetration, especially by black men, of the hideous crime of rape—the most abominable in all the category of crimes, even worse than murder. Mobs frequently avenge the commission of this crime by themselves torturing to death the man committing it; thus avenging in bestial fashion a bestial deed, and reducing themselves to a level with the criminal. (Roosevelt 1906)

Ironically, these words are supposed to be critical of the barbaric violence that had been (and would continue to be) committed against African Americans. In 1918, the Democrats in the Senate blocked an anti-lynching bill proposed by a Republican member from Missouri. Franklin Roosevelt, the Democratic president whose term in the White House coincided with Hitler's reign, refused to support another anti-lynching bill. The apologia that is widely presented on Franklin Roosevelt's behalf is that he could not support the bill for fear of antagonizing white supporters from the South. Often apologists, albeit unwittingly, provide more insight into the grotesqueness of the situation in question. Today, an American president would come across as radically different from Theodor Roosevelt or Franklin Roosevelt, but nobody infers from this fact that liberalism ceased to exist. On the contrary, it is taken for granted that liberal strategies and discourse must have undergone change in order to remain effective as a political force.

Also, I should underline that I do not want to suggest in any way that there is a fundamental and categorical distinction, let alone antagonism, between liberalism and fascism. Both liberalism and fascism are ideological forms that stem from capitalist relations of production. In fact, more often than not, capitalist liberalism is the environment that makes the emergence and growth of fascism possible. This is one of the central themes that the Frankfurt School critical theorists kept emphasizing in their works.

In Adorno's words: "that fascism lives on, that the oft-invoked working through of the past has to this day been unsuccessful and has degenerated into its own caricature, an empty and cold forgetting, is due to the fact that the objective conditions of society that engendered fascism continue to exist" (2005a, 98). As noted, "for countless people it seemed that the coldness of social alienation had been done away with thanks to the warmth of togetherness, no matter how manipulated and contrived; the *völkisch* community of the unfree and the unequal was a lie and at the same time also the fulfillment of an old, indeed long familiar, evil bourgeois dream." As cited earlier, in Chapter 2, Adorno states, "even Hitler's *va banque* gamble was not as irrational as it seemed to average liberal thought at the time or as its failure seems to historical hindsight today" (2005a, 95).

Not surprisingly, Adorno came under a lot of fire from the intelligentsia as if his critics sensed that his assessment had the power to cut through the meticulously woven veils of epistemic and ideological reformation. Today, as in the 1950s, Adorno's critique is more relevant than the textbook-like compare-and-contrast exercises that supposedly inform us whether we should be concerned, whether what we are faced with is fascism, whether democracy is in safe hands etc. Adorno made enemies for himself because he considered the endurance of fascism "*within* democracy to be potentially more menacing than the survival of fascist tendencies *against* democracy" (2005a, 90, emphasis in original). Detecting the launching of a long-term campaign to derail future analyses and problematization of fascism, Horkheimer too contended, "whoever is not willing to talk about capitalism should also keep quiet about fascism" (2005, 226).

The political economy of knowledge production will continue to create the illusion that institutionalized scholarship stands outside and above history, that knowledge authorities are on the side of democracy against authoritarianism in the arena of politics. No anti-fascist movement will be effective if it does not recognize the totalitarian regime that exercises power in myriads of ways in all arenas, spheres, and spaces of social and individual life. The struggle then is to negate that totalitarian regime.

2 The Way Forward: Negation

Having the 20th century's experiences of revolution behind us, we have every reason to be skeptical about not only reformism but also revolutionism. This is not to justify conservatism, but precisely to expose the conservatism that is hidden in the very structures and reference frames of many revolutions and, thus, invalidate such revolutionary projects in favor of revolutionizing revolution in terms of both conception and praxis. Revolutionaries who lack a wholistic philosophy as a negative scheme capable of conceiving and problematizing regimes of oppression in their multidimensional complexities will certainly be unable to challenge, let alone negate, the totalitarian sociopolitical order that sustains inequality and unfreedom. The destruction of lives, hopes, youths, and revolutionary energy are the only certain outcome of a revolution that is meant to target one social or political problem in its reductionist, that is falsely abstracted, form assuming it to be the root of all social and political problems. More often than not, the new regime that takes shape during the chaos is something more monstrous than the fallen one. The age of the revolutions in the style of the October Revolution may be over anyway, but that makes a critical theory of revolution even more desperately needed to negate oppression in its totality.

A revolution that is motivated by hope for the imminent establishment of just order is arguably more problematic than a reformist platform that operates as an accomplice in the established order. In the final analysis of things, revolution cannot realize emancipatory progress if it is not motivated by hopelessness as opposed to hope, by the negation of *what is* as opposed to a positive prefiguration of *what ought to be*, by the rejection of existing suffering as opposed to sacrifice for assumed prosperity in the future.

The French-Romanian thinker Emile Cioran, in one of his aphorisms, states, "only optimists commit suicide, the optimists who can no longer be [. . .] optimists. The others, having no reason to live, why should they have any to die?" (2012, 87). When applied to revolutions, this hypothesis may be even truer. Optimistic revolutions that promise a swift and drastic transition to a promised land quickly commit suicide qua a progressive and an emancipatory force. In such revolutions, revolutionaries end up killing or being killed, if not both. Some of them also may go into exile and die quietly or prepare for the next state of emergency to "straighten things up."

The negation of the existing violent reality that is framed by exclusionary politics is imperative for creating a new horizon of possibilities. To negate the existing falsehood and the reality of suffering, we must not remain ignorant of ignorance. Untruth, like unfreedom and inequality, is at the heart of the reality in the most materialist sense of the word. In order for us to be able to negate this reality neither heroism nor good intentions without a philosophical system of total negation will do. At their roots, the crises are neither moral (corrupt politicians who must be replaced by moral ones, etc.) nor cultural (the assumption that some societies are just not fit for democracy, etc.). Rather, these are crises of the real, the actual, the true, and the rational. In order for the reality to be changed drastically, the dominant regimes of untruth, unfreedom, and inequality must be negated. Such a revolutionary project necessitates a robust negative philosophy. In all cases, however, we must comprehend the social and historical aspects of the existing reality and the magnitude of its crises. For anything to be negated adequately, it must be comprehended in its complexity as both a product and production. It is precisely the scope of the hopelessness in the existing reality that determines the scope of material change that is needed. Oppression cannot be ended on the basis of false hope, flirtation with the ruling ideologies, bourgeois nihilism, or bohemian resignation. Rather, the realization of a rational, post-nihilist, post-nationalist, post-religious society based on the participation of free and equal subjects necessitates the courage to face the existing hopelessness, and the revolutionary will to negate the reality.

A reformist is someone who claims that the existing order can be fixed without a radical change in the social relations of power and privilege. In effect, pseudo-progressive opinion makers, educators, humanitarianists, and politicians play an indispensable role in the normalization and perpetuation of oppressive systems of exploitation. Half-Marxist and non-Marxist self-proclaimed progressives often hold circumstances, protecting the dominant order from collapsing, while fascist forces recruit, regroup, and prepare for a future charge to take over the state. Marxism is ultimately a negative theory for social change and a critical method of negation. However, party politics and the Stalinist doctrine of "socialism in one state," in the name of Marxism, produced a positivistic mode of interpretation aiming at a positive political agenda and the domination of state politics.

An emancipatory epistemology must be negative in both its philosophical orientation and it conceptual procedures because the existing social reality is structured around and through normalized relations of domination. It also follows that critique is an inseparable aspect of social emancipation. Therefore, the essential framework of the struggle to progressively change the world is defined by negativity; the only way for the new to be born is the negation of the old, to rephrase Gramsci's observation that "the old is dying and the new cannot be born." One of the mystifying sources of illusion is the spatial idealism that prioritizes social spaces over social practices, i.e., the assumption that new spaces come into being from nothing. This illusion seems to be rooted in the long centuries of the theological hegemony of the production of knowledge. In western parts of Asia, the regions around the Mediterranean Sea, and most of Europe, for centuries God was the absolute source of existence and truth, which has made the birth of the human as a politically active and historically autonomous social agent a painful and prolonged process in the West, in this case including MENA. Every revolutionary period of social movements has been followed by severe fallbacks into regressive reactions often bringing about violence and destruction on catastrophic levels.

The antipode of spatial idealism is spatial materialism, just as the antipode of traditional historicism is historical materialism, but this should not be taken as a separation between the spatiality and the historicality of the social reality, as some contemporary thinkers seem to assume. Social space is both a product and a production.[44] It is produced through the dialectical entirety of social relations, and, at the same time, it conditions the continuation of the social regime of power and privilege. As such it is always already grounded in the actual social relations of material production and power relations. Therefore, there cannot be any new social space except through a social rapture—that is, a socially imposed historical discontinuity. Discontinuity does not imply a new beginning; rather, it means a near-total, even if momentary, negation of *what is*, thereby rendering *the new, as transformation*, inevitable. What is perceived as spatially new is merely the condition for, as opposed to the actual, historical discontinuity.

There is no such thing as "space" in itself, without the social. Also, as Lefebvre argues, it is misleading to refer to the space of this and the space of that (1991, 5). There is a unity and continuity of space. What is fragmental is our experience of space, and what is abstract is our false conception of space. Any possibility of a revolutionary transformation of space requires a unitary and dialectical comprehension of both the dominant mode of spatial production and the production of suffering within the produced space.

3 Final Remarks

Ultimately, fascism is a manifestation of a social regime that is inherently exclusionary and violent. The totalitarian regime of capitalism, whereby capital is the absolute source of power, has thingified all that is human rendering homeliness, or being at home as a mode of spatiality, unattainable. There have never been so many people living at the mercy of such a small number of people. The concentration of power is so excessive and defused that deploying terminologies such as tyranny, despotism, and authoritarianism would be misleading. The complexity and magnitude of the systematic exercise of oppressive power is beyond the grasp of political science, which is indeed political but certainly not a science. The barbarism of our age, within a highly opaque frame of total domination, has reached unmatched levels.

Fascism is never merely an ideological problem. To comprehend the problem, critical analyses of the social conditions that produce fascism are essential. Also, to negate fascism, a post-nihilist philosophy and collaborative praxis to negate the dominant order are needed (Ahmed 2022a). This book is a contribution to that end and from that perspective. Ending a book like this on a hopeful note is considered

---

44 For more on this see Lefebvre 1991; Ahmed 2019b; Bahozde 2024.

appropriate, but it is crucially important to emphasize that it is precisely the scope and depth of the hopeless reality that we need to grasp, which requires a lot of courage. Only if we are able to comprehend the magnitude of the hopelessness that is entailed in the existing disastrous order, will we be able to meaningfully think of creating conditions for real, as opposed to false, hope. Still, there is no guarantee whatsoever that any such thing will ever happen. Hope is not metaphysically determined. Rather, metaphysics itself is a product of hopelessness desperately denied. Things might only get worse for a long time to come. The difficulty of imagining such a future is completely irrelevant to the possibility of such a future. Violence does not fix itself, and there is nothing more characteristic of the essence of the prevalent order than violence. Violence only makes its environment more violent, which in turn only produces more violence. This is exactly the problem with fascism as a nativist yet quickly spreading movement crossing local, regional, and continental boundaries.

Everything suggests that more misery will be imposed on larger numbers of people. Atrocities that would have been hardly imaginable a couple of years ago are already daily news now. What might become daily news within a year, two, or ten, may very well be unimaginable today. A book on the problem of fascism may be expected to offer or at least touch upon or the very least hint at solutions. Morally, that makes sense, but regardless of the moral pressure, "solutions" should not be included if they are not induced from the critical analysis and the philosophical framework within which the book advances. Otherwise, any supposed solutions would be misleading.

That said, there is a hopeful proposition we could justifiably induce from the dialectical framework and the critical philosophy of history. Namely, since there has been a moment at which human emancipation objectively, universally, and historically has been conceived within an egalitarian and inclusive philosophy, and since that philosophy, even if for one short moment in human history, gave rise to a worldwide movement of emancipation, we can assert, both empirically and rationally, that it could happen again and again until it will be the revolutionary event capable of negating and therefore transforming the historical and spatial conditions of unfreedom. In the late 19th century and the first half of the 20th century, despite the catastrophic rise of fascism in all its racist, colonialist, and imperialist manifestations, and in contrast to all the gloominess and barbarities that were imposed on the world, a moment of universal hope for human emancipation was created whereby the end of not only fascism but also all the barbarisms of the pre-human history was in sight. Just as capitalism was globalizing utter violence, the largest and most internationalist revolutionary movement in world history was created targeting all the devices and products of social and political domination. The movement was called communism.

Those who control the regimes of ideological and material production have created a global myth according to which communism is dead. The myth comes with countless other myths and mythologies, some of which utilize theology while others are simply formed around neo-tribalist formations of exclusionary identities. Fascism is a term to designate this class or form of ideologies and movements. Today, fascism can be detected everywhere. Nonetheless, this fascist reality is founded on falsehood, irrationality, and violence. Therefore, when a new international and internationalist movement emerges, the fall of the existing false order could be more abrupt than what anyone currently could imagine.

The facts that support the prospects of the rational, cosmopolitan, and egalitarian camp have infinite historical power once they are perceived within a philosophy of negation and realized within a movement of liberation. Arguably, the most important fact in this context is that as long as inequality is imposed in a social reality, there is a potential social force to negate the imposed order in favor of realizing a new social reality conditioned around equality.

Let us now figure the broader expression of this factual statement. The oppressive system may be totalitarian enough to impose a hopeless reality of limitless social subordination and submission, but by doing so that system negatively and inevitably will necessitate a force against the false reality. Falsehood may be at the heart of a reality, but such a reality is not indefinitely sustainable. A reality that is based on extreme falsehood, e.g., extreme exploitation and oppression, ultimately, at some point, explodes under the pressure of the contradictions it continually and increasingly creates within the same social world. The destruction of the existing oppressive order is just a matter of time. The crucial question is whether a social movement can be formed in order to turn the crisis or the collapse into a progressive event, a moment to negatively contain the forthcoming explosions and convert their destructive force into progress forward toward the end of the pre-human history, which is a history of irrationality, mythology, violence, and tribalism, toward the beginning of the human history or what once people, following Marx, called communism. Today, the collapse of capitalism is even more probable, but the rise of fascism is also stronger precisely in order to protect the regime of domination. Fascism takes various shapes and forms, but they all intensify and count on internal homogenization and external othering. Fascism capitalizes on capitalist crises in order to prevent the possibility of social change toward a more rational world.

Fascism is nihilistic. Anti-fascism must be post-nihilistic. Fascism adapts its shape according to each locality. Anti-fascism, therefore, cannot take place if it is not unapologetically communistic in its perspective and strategy. Fascism exploits hopelessness and produces false hope while realizing more misery for everyone. Anti-fascism can only start by negating false hope. Anti-fascism must have the courage to reject superstitions and tribalism starting from the nearest to the farthest, which entails unlearning culturalism. Fascism is a power cult, and as such it invests in popular ignorance. Global anti-fascism must search for its revolutionary models in the margins that have created successful anti-fascist movements through rigorous re-education, that is, negative or post-nihilist pedagogy. A post-nihilist pedagogy entails unlearning metaphysicalized falsehood and undoing the bourgeois episteme. Anti-fascism amounts to militant campaigns against the cults of power that have been sanctified in various institutions of class including family, religion, and the state.

References

Abdulrahman, Shaban. 2014. "دور النظام العربي في تمكين الصهيونية." [The Arab Regime's Role in Empowering Zionism]. *Aljazeera*, July 31. https://www.aljazeera.net/knowledgegate/opinions/2014/7/31/دور-النظام-العربي-في-تمكين-الصهيونية.

Adorno, Theodor W. 2001. "Freudian Theory and the Pattern of Fascist Propaganda." In *The Culture Industry: Selected Essays on Mass Culture*, edited by J. M. Bernstein, 132–157. London: Routledge.

Adorno, Theodor W. 2004. "Antisemitism and Fascist Propaganda." In *Stars Down to Earth and Other Essays on the Irrational in Culture*, edited by Stephen Crook, 218–232. London: Routledge.

Adorno, Theodor W. 2005a. *Critical Models: Interventions and Catchwords*. Translated by Henry W. Pickford. New York: Columbia University Press.

Adorno, Theodor W. 2005b. *Minima Moralia: Reflections on a Damaged Life*. London: Verso.

Ahmed, Saladdin. 2011. "Return of Revolutions." *Critical Legal Thinking*, April 12. https://criticallegalthinking.com/2011/04/12/return-of-revolutions/.

Ahmed, Saladdin. 2014a. "10 Things You Must Know About Kurds from the 'Other Syria.'" *Your Middle East*, May 12. http://www.yourmiddleeast.com/opinion/10-things-you-must-know-about-kurds-from-the-other-syria_23527.

Ahmed, Saladdin. 2014b. "YPG and PKK Forces: The Unsung Heroes of the War Against the Islamic State." *The New Middle East*, August 11. http://new-middle-east.blogspot.ca/2014/08/ypg-and-pkk-forcesthe-unsung-heroes-of.html.

Ahmed, Saladdin. 2015. "Culture as 'Ways of Life' or a Mask of Racism? Culturalisation and the Decline of Universalist Views." *Critical Race and Whiteness Studies* 11 (1): 1–17. https://philarchive.org/rec/AHMCAW.

Ahmed, Saladdin. 2017. "Faşizm Hayatta ve İyi!" [Fascism is Alive and Well!]. *Demokratik Modernite* 21: 29–32. https://demokratikmodernite.org/fasizm-hayatta-ve-iyi/.

Ahmed, Saladdin. 2018a. "Panopticism and Totalitarian Space." *Theory in Action* 11 (1): 1–16.

Ahmed, Saladdin. 2018b. "The Inauthenticity of the Left in the Kurdish Liberation Movement in Iraqi Kurdistan." *Critique: Journal of Socialist Theory* 46 (1): 65–76.

Ahmed, Saladdin. 2019a. "The Left's Culturalism and Rojava." *Contours Journal* 9: 1–20.

Ahmed, Saladdin. 2019b. *Totalitarian Space and the Destruction of Aura*. Albany, NY: SUNY Press.

Ahmed, Saladdin. 2020. "The Ecological Crisis, Apocalypticism, and the Internalization of Unfreedom." *World Review of Political Economy* 11 (1) (Spring): 115–140.

Ahmed, Saladdin. 2021a. "Why 'Islamo-Leftism' Is Just Another Conspiracy Theory." *International Journal of Socialist Renewal LINKS*, March 5. http://links.org.au/islamo-leftism-conspiracy-theory.

Ahmed, Saladdin. 2021b. "Universal Discrimination and the Democratic Camouflaging of Culturalism." *International Journal of Socialist Renewal LINKS*, March 27. http://links.org.au/universal-discrimination-democratic-camouflaging-culturalism.

Ahmed, Saladdin. 2022a. *Revolutionary Hope after Nihilism: Marginalized Voices and Dissent*. London: Bloomsbury Academic.

Ahmed, Saladdin. 2022b. "Mahsa-Amini: An Event in a Marginalized Space." *TELOSscope*, October 3. https://www.telospress.com/mahsa-amini-an-event-in-a-marginalized-space/.

Ahmed, Saladdin. 2022c. "The Cost of Freedom in the Neoliberal World of Blood and Oil." *Marxism and Science* 1 (2): 223–241.

Ahmed, Saladdin. 2022d. "نەژادپەرستیی ناتوانێت کەس رزگار بکات" [Racism Cannot Liberate Anyone]. *Dengekan*, October 29. https://dengekan.info/archives/39241?fbclid=IwAR0WWxJbgv4cBtJAZ_9_HH9BPnnDrik7NBZ9qbP2fiDSLXKeyd8fEjsHMrY.

https://doi.org/10.1515/9783111609041-010

Ahmed, Saladdin. 2022e. "نەخێر نەژادپەرستیی ناتوانێت كەس رزگار بكات و مەرگخوزازیش شایستەی كەواندنه" [No, Racism Cannot Liberate Anyone and Thanatophilia Should Be Denounced] *Dengekan*, November 15. https://dengekan.info/archives/39392.

Ahmed, Saladdin. 2023a. *Critical Theory from the Margins: Horizons of Possibility in the Age of Extremism.* Albany, NY: SUNY Press.

Ahmed, Saladdin. 2023b. "Fascism as an Ideological Form: A Critical Theory." *Critical Sociology* 49 (4–5): 669–687. https://journals.sagepub.com/doi/epub/10.1177/08969205221109869.

Ahmed, Saladdin. 2023c. "'Jerusalem Flood' and Erdogan's Caliphate Project: The Islamist Reconquista as a Doomsday for Palestinians." *Eurasia Review*, November 5. https://www. eurasiareview.com/05112023-jerusalem-flood-and-erdogans-caliphate-project-the-islamist-re conquista-as-a-doomsday-for-palestinians-analysis/.

Ahmed, Salah. 2008. "ناكۆكییەكانی دوو دانیشتن" [The Disputes of Two Debates]. Sulailamiya. Iraq: Ranj.

Al-Arzusi. n.d. بعث الامة العربية ورسالتها الى العالم [Resurrection of the Arab Nation and Its World Mission]. Damascus: Al-Taraqi Press.

Al-labwani, Kamal. 2019. "الربیع الصهیونی فی دول الممانعة." [The Zionist Spring in the Axis of Resistance]. *The Levant*, November 22. https://thelevantnews.com/2019/11/الربیع-الصهیونی-فی-دول-الممانعة/.

Al-Sawt Al-Shuia'ai. 1964. المنحرفون من الحرس القومی [The Deviants from the National Guard]. https://u. pcloud.link/publink/show?code=XZSzi97ZeQL7li7JT7SCRGpF06IPPkNpgzxy.

Ali, Tariq. 2022. *Winston Churchill: His Times, His Crimes.* London: Verso Books.

Allardyce, Gilbert. 1979. "What Fascism Is Not: Thoughts on the Deflation of a Concept." *The American Historical Review* 84 (2): 367–388. https://doi.org/10.2307/1855138.

Allen, Thomas B., F. Clifton Berry, and Norman Polmar. 1991. *War in the Gulf: From the Invasion of Kuwait to the Day of Victory and Beyond.* Atlanta, GA: Turner Publishing.

Alsaid, Ibrahim. 2018. "یمتلكون أكبر شركاته.. كیف سیطر الیهود على سوق الإباحیة؟" [They Own the Largest Companies: How Did the Jews Control the Porn Market?]. *Aljazeera*, July 18. https://www. aljazeera.net/midan/intellect/sociology/2018/7/18/.

Amin, Samir. 2017. *October 1917 Revolution: A Century Later.* Wakefield, Quebec: Daraja Press.

Amnesty International. 2017. *Blood-Soaked Secrets.* London: Amnesty International. https://www. amnesty.org/en/latest/campaigns/2018/10/blood-soaked-secrets/.

Amnesty International. 2020. "Turkey: Imprisoned Journalists, Human Rights Defenders and Others, Now at Risk of Covid-19, Must Be Urgently Released." Amnesty International, March 30. https:// www.amnesty.org/en/latest/news/2020/03/turkey-imprisoned-journalists-human-rights-de fenders-and-others-now-at-risk-of-covid-19-must-be-urgently-released/.

Amnesty International. 2021. "Belarus/EU: New Evidence of Brutal Violence from Belarusian Forces Against Asylum-Seekers and Migrants Facing Pushbacks from the EU." Amnesty International, December 20. https://www.amnesty.org/en/latest/news/2021/12/ belarus-eu-new-evidence-of-brutal-violence-from-belarusian-forces-against-asylum-seekers- and-migrants-facing-pushbacks-from-the-eu/.

Arendt, Hannah. 1979. *The Origins of Totalitarianism.* San Diego: Harcourt Brace & Company.

Arendt, Hannah. 1994. *Essays in Understanding 1930–1954: Formation, Exile, and Totalitarianism.* Edited by Jerome Kohn. New York: Schocken Books.

Asgharzadeh, Alireza. 2007. *Iran and the Challenge of Diversity: Islamic Fundamentalism, Aryanist Racism, and Democratic Struggles.* London: Palgrave Macmillan.

Associated Press. 2022. "Qatar Hosts Taliban-US Meeting on Sidelines of Turkey Summit." *KTSP.com*, March 11. https://apnews.com/general-news-1d0513927a72f9ca8117d26a292f3fb3

Ayers, Alison J. 2024. "'The Fire This Time': The Long Crisis of Neoliberal Capitalist Accumulation and Spectre of Neofascism." *Critical Sociology* 50 (3): 413–435. https://doi.org/10.1177/08969205231195229.

Bade, Rachel, Eli Okun, and Garrett Ross. 2022. "POLITICO Playbook PM: Biden's Warning to Americans: 'It's Going to Cost Us As Well.'" *Politico*, March 8. https://www.politico.com/newsletters/playbook-pm/2022/03/08/bidens-warning-to-americans-its-going-to-cost-us-as-well-00015188.

Bahozde, Saladdin Ahmed. 2024. *The Death of Home: Aura and Space in the Age of Digitalization*. Berlin: De Gruyter.

Bahozde, Saladdin. 2025. *Fascism in the Middle East: Nationalism, Islamism, and Imagining Other Futures*. London: Routledge.

Ben-Chiat, Ruth. 2023. "Trump's 'Vermin' Speech Echoes Fascist Rhetoric." *Lucid*, November 13. https://lucid.substack.com/p/trump-really-doesnt-want-you-to-call.

Benjamin, Walter. 2004. "Goethe's Elective Affinities." In *Selected Writings*, vol. 1, *1913–1926*, edited by M. Bullock and Michael W. Jennings, translated by Stanley Corngold, 297–360. Cambridge, MA: Harvard University Press.

Benjamin, Walter. 2006. "On the Concept of History." In *Selected Writings*, vol. 4, *1938–1940*, edited by Howard Eiland and Michael W. Jennings, translated by Harry Zohn, 389–400. Cambridge, MA: Harvard University Press.

Bozarslan, Hamit. 2014. "Kemalism, Westernization and Anti-liberalism." In *Turkey Beyond Nationalism: Towards Post-Nationalist Identities*, edited by Hans-Lukas Kieser, 28–36. London: I. B. Tauris.

Burley, Shane. 2017. *Fascism Today: What It Is and How to End It*. Chicago: AK Press.

Césaire, Aimé. 2001. *Discourse on Colonialism*. Translated by Joan Pinkham. New York: Monthly Review Press.

Churchwell, Sarah. 2018. *Behold, America: The Entangled History of America First*. New York: Basic Books.

Churchwell, Sarah. 2020. "American Fascism: It Has Happened Here." *New York Review of Books*, June 22. https://www.nybooks.com/daily/2020/06/22/american-fascism-it-has-happened-here/.

Çiçek, Cuma. 2017. *The Kurds of Turkey: National, Religious and Economic Identities*. London: I. B. Tauris.

Cioran, E. M. 2012. *All Gall Is Divided*. Translated by Richard Howard. New York: Arcade Publishing.

Cox, Ronald W. 2019. "In Defense of Revolutionary Socialism: The Implications of Bhaskar Sunkara's 'The Socialist Manifesto.'" *Class, Race and Corporate Power* 7 (2). https://www.jstor.org/stable/48645449.

Cox, Ronald W. 2021. "Capitalism and Neo-Fascism." *Class, Race and Corporate Power* 9 (1). https://www.jstor.org/stable/48644432.

Dabashi, Hamid. 2011. *Shi'ism: A Religion of Protest*. Cambridge, MA: Harvard University Press.

Debs, Eugene V. 1939. "In What War Shall I Take Up Arms and Fight." *Socialist Appeal*, April 4. https://www.marxists.org/history/etol/newspape/themilitant/socialist-appeal-1939/v3n21-apr-04-1939.pdf.

Del Boca, Angelo, and Mario Giovana. 1970. *Fascism Today: A World Survey*. Translated by R. H. Boothroyd. London: Heinemann.

Eagleton, Terry. 1976. "What Is Fascism?" *New Blackfriars* 57 (670): 100–106. http://www.jstor.org/stable/43246521.

Eco, Umberto. 1995. "Ur-Fascism." *The New York Review of Books*, June 22. https://sites.evergreen.edu/politicalshakespeares/wp-content/uploads/sites/226/2015/12/Eco-urfascism.pdf.

Edwards, Rob. 2014. "US Fired Depleted Uranium at Civilian Areas in 2003 Iraq War, Report Finds." *The Guardian*, US ed., June 19. https://www.theguardian.com/world/2014/jun/19/us-depleted-uranium-weapons-civilian-areas-iraq.

Elaph. 2024. ""المئات" و "العشرات" و "العديد" وسط تغيب لدقة"." [Lack of Accuracy from Several to Tens to Hundreds]. *Elaph*, March 2. https://elaph.com/Web/News/2024/03/1530693.html.

Esposito, Roberto. 2008. "Totalitarianism or Biopolitics? Concerning a Philosophical Interpretation of the Twentieth Century," translated by Timothy Campbell. *Critical Inquiry* 34 (4): 633–644.

Evans, Brian. 2022. "Russia Is Earning $20 Billion Per Month in Oil Sales as Higher Crude Prices Lift Export Revenue 50%, Says IEA." *Business Insider*, May 12. https://markets.businessinsider.com/news/commodities/russian-oil-sales-20-billion-month-export-revenue-jumps-iea-2022-5.

Eze, Emmanuel Chukwudi. 2001. *Race and the Enlightenment: A Reader*. Oxford: Blackwell.

Fanon, Frantz. 1994. *Toward the African Revolution: Political Essays*. Translated by Haakon Chevalier. New York: Grove Press.

Farough-Sluglett, Marion, and Peter Sluglett. 2001. *Iraq Since 1958: From Revolution to Dictatorship*. London: I. B. Tauris.

Fitzhugh, George. 2011. *Cannibals, All! Or Slaves Without Masters*. Project Gutenberg. https://www.gutenberg.org/files/35481/35481-h/35481-h.htm.

Foucault, Michel. 1984. "Nietzsche, Genealogy, History." In *The Foucault Reader*, edited by Paul Rabinow, 76–100. New York: Pantheon Books.

Franzén, Johan. 2011. *Red Star over Iraq: Iraqi Communism Before Saddam*. New York: Columbia University Press.

Freud, Sigmund. 2010. *The Interpretation of Dreams*. Translated by James Strachey. New York: Basic Books.

Friedrich, Carl J., and Zbigniew K. Brzezinski. 1956. *Totalitarian Dictatorship and Autocracy*. Cambridge, MA: Harvard University Press.

Fromm, Erich. 1965. *Escape from Freedom*. New York: Avon Books.

Fukuyama, Francis. 1992. *The End of History and the Last Man*. London: Penguin.

Gandesha, Samir. 2020a. "A Composite of King Kong and a Suburban Barber: Adorno's Freudian Theory and the Pattern of Fascist Propaganda." In *Spectres of Fascism: Historical, Theoretical and International Perspectives*, edited by Samir Gandesha, 120–141. London: Pluto Press.

Gandesha, Samir. 2020b. "Introduction." In *Spectres of Fascism: Historical, Theoretical and International Perspectives*, edited by Samir Gandesha, 1–26. London: Pluto Press.

General Act of the Berlin Conference on West Africa. 1885. February 26. https://loveman.sdsu.edu/docs/1885GeneralActBerlinConference.pdf.

Gentile, Giovanni. 1995. "Fascism as a Total Conception of Life." In *Fascism*, edited by Roger Griffin, 53. Oxford: Oxford University Press.

Gentile, Giovanni. 2002. *Origins and Doctrine of Fascism: With Selections from Other Works*. Translated by A. James Gregor. Piscataway, NJ: Transaction Publishers.

Gramsci, Antonio. 1978. "Elemental Forces." In *Selections from Political Writings (1921–1926)*, edited and translated by Quintin Hoare, 38–40. London: Lawrence & Wishart.

Gregor, A. James. 1974. "Fascism and Modernization: Some Addenda." *World Politics* 26 (3): 370–384. https://doi.org/10.2307/2009935.

Gregor, A. James. 2006. *The Search for Neofascism: The Use and Abuse of Social Sciences*. Cambridge: Cambridge University Press.

Griffin, Roger. 1991. *The Nature of Fascism*. London: Routledge.

Griffin, Roger. 2018. *Fascism*. Cambridge: Polity Press.

Hamdi, Samir. 2013. "مثالًا ومصر تونس :المضادة الثورة صناعة"." [Manufacturing Counter-revolution: Tunisia and Egypt as Examples]. *Noon Post*, September 7. https://www.noonpost.com/442/.

Hanioglu, M. Sükrü. 2011. *Atatürk: An Intellectual Biography*. Princeton, NJ: Princeton University Press.

Hanioglu, M. Sükrü. 2014. "Turkism and the Young Turks, 1889–1908." In *Turkey Beyond Nationalism: Towards Post-Nationalist Identities*, edited by Hans-Lukas Kieser, 3–19. London: I. B. Tauris.

Hernández, Miguel. 2019. *The Ku Klux Klan and Freemasonry in 1920s America: Fighting Fraternities*. London: Routledge.

Hickel, Jason. 2018. *The Divide: A Brief Guide to Global Inequality and Its Solutions*. New York: Random House.

Hobsbawm, Eric. 1996. *The Age of Extremes: The Short Twentieth Century 1914–1991*. New York: Vintage Books.

Holmes, Amy Austin, Diween Hawezy, and Brett Cohen. 2021. "Five Years of Airstrikes: Turkish Aggression and International Silence in Sinjar, 2017–2021." International Center for the Study of Violent Extremism, August 2. https://www.icsve.org/five-years-of-airstrikes-turkish-aggression-and-international-silence-in-sinjar-2017-2021/.

Horkheimer, Max. 2005. "The Jews and Europe." In *The Frankfurt School on Religion: Key Writings by the Major Thinkers*, edited by Eduardo Mendieta, 225–242. London: Routledge.

Horkheimer, Max, and Theodor Adorno. 2002. "Elements of Anti-Semitism." In *Dialectic of Enlightenment: Philosophical Fragments*, edited by Gunzelin Schmid Noerr, translated by Edmund Jephcott, 137–172. Stanford, CA: Stanford University Press.

HRW. 2021. "Erdoğan's Onslaught on Rights and Democracy Targets Women, Kurds, LGBT People, Democratic Safeguards." Human Rights Watch, March 24. https://www.hrw.org/news/2021/03/24/turkey-erdogans-onslaught-rights-and-democracy.

Ihring, Stefan. 2014. *Attatürk in the Nazi Imagination*. Cambridge, MA: The Belknap Press of Harvard University.

"Imperial Manifesto." 1914. Collection Nr. 19 of Laws and Decrees of All-Empire Significance with Respect to Finland. July 24 (August 6). https://histdoc.net/history/germany1914.html.

Jefferson, Thomas. 1787. *Notes on the State of Virginia*. Philadelphia: Richard and Hall. https://docsouth.unc.edu/southlit/jefferson/jefferson.html.

Kallis, Aristotle A. 2003. "'Fascism', 'Para-Fascism' and 'Fascistization': On the Similarities of Three Conceptual Categories." *European History Quarterly* 33 (2): 219–249. https://doi.org/10.1177/02656914030332004.

Kermani, Mirza Aghakhan. n.d. میرزا آقاخان کرمانی: پدر فلسفه‌ی تاریخ ایران. [Mirza Agha Khan Kermani: The Philosophical Father of Iranian History]. Edited by Bahram Roshan Zamir. n.p.: n.p.

Khomeini, Ayatollah Mosavi. 1985. *The Little Green Book: Selected Fatawah and Saying of the Ayatollah Mosavi Khomeini*. Translated by Harold Salemson. New York: Bantam Books.

Knapp, Michael, and Joost Jongerden. 2014. "Communal Democracy: The Social Contract and Confederalism in Rojava." *Comparative Islamic Studies* 10: 87–109. https://doi.org/10.1558/cis.29642.

Köves, Margit. 1997. "Lukács and Fascism." *Social Scientist* 25 (7–8): 27–38. https://doi.org/10.2307/3517602.

Köves, Margit. 2004. "Fascism in the Age of Global Capitalism." *Social Scientist* 32 (9–10): 36–71. https://doi.org/10.2307/3518207.

Landa, Ishay. 2018. *Fascism and the Masses: The Revolt Against the Last Humans, 1848–1945*. London: Routledge.

Laqueur, Walter. 1956. *Communism and Nationalism in the Middle East*. New York: Praeger.

Lefebvre, Henri. 1991. *The Production of Space*. Translated by Donald Nicholson-Smith. Malden, MA: Blackwell.

Lenin, V. I. 1965. "Speech in Polytechnical Museum, August 23, 1918." In *Lenin's Collected Works*, vol. 28. Translated and edited by Jim Riordan, 78–83. Moscow: Progress Publishers. https://www.marxists.org/archive/lenin/works/1918/aug/23a.htm.

Lenin, V. I. 2005. "Speech Delivered at an International Meeting in Berne, February 8, 1916." Marxist Internet Archive. https://www.marxists.org/archive/lenin/works/1916/feb/08.htm#fwV22E030.

Lentin, Alana, and Gavan Titley. 2011. *The Crises of Multiculturalism: Racism in a Neoliberal Age*. London: Zed Books.

Levin, Mark R. 2021. *American Marxism*. New York: Threshold Editions.

Losurdo, Domenico. 2015. *War and Revolution: Rethinking the 20th Century*. Translated by Gregory Elliott. London: Verso.

Losurdo, Domenico. 2016. *Class Struggle: A Political and Philosophical History*. New York: Palgrave Macmillan.

Löwenthal, Leo. 1989. *Critical Theory and Frankfurt Theorists: Lectures–Correspondence–Conversations*. New Brunswick, NJ: Transaction Publishers.

Löwenthal, Leo, and Norbert Guterman. 2021. *Prophets of Deceit*. London: Verso.

Lucente, Adam. 2021. "Thousands of Iraqi, Syrian Refugees Shiver at Belarus-Poland Border." *Al-Monitor*, November 12. https://www.al-monitor.com/originals/2021/11/thousands-iraqi-syrian-refugees-shiver-belarus-poland-border.

Luke, Timothy W. 2021. *Screens of Power: Ideology, Domination, and Resistance in Informational Society*. Candor, NY: Telos Press.

Luke, Timothy W. 2022. *The Travails of Trumpification*. Candor, NY: Telos Press.

Luxemburg, Rosa. 2004. *The Rosa Luxemburg Reader*. Edited by Peter Hudis and Kevin B. Anderson. New York: Monthly Review Press.

MacLean, Nancy. 1995. *Behind the Mask of Chivalry: The Making of the Second Ku*. Oxford: Oxford University Press.

Madison, James H. 2020. *The Ku Klux Klan in the Heartland*. Bloomington: Indiana University Press.

Martinot, Steve. 2008. "The Question of Fascism in the United States." *Socialism and Democracy* 22 (2): 17–44.

Marx, Karl. 2010a. "Introduction to Contribution to Critique of Hegel's Philosophy of Right." In *Marx and Engels, Collected Works*, vol. 3, translated by Clemens Dutt, 175–187. London: Lawrence & Wishart.

Marx, Karl. 2010b. *Marx and Engels, Collected Works*, vol. 37. London: Lawrence & Wishart.

Matin-Asgari, Afshin. 2018. *Both Eastern and Western: An Intellectual History of Iranian Modernity*. Cambridge: Cambridge University Press.

Memmi, Albert. 2013. *The Pillar of Salt*. Lexington, MA: Plunkett Lake Press.

Middle East Eye Staff. 2017. "'Disgusting': Iraqi Paper Depicts Kurdistan as Woman Facing Rape." *Middle East Eye*, September 29. https://www.middleeasteye.net/news/disgusting-iraqi-paper-depicts-kurdistan-woman-facing-rape.

NATO. 2022. "Trilateral Memorandum." North Atlantic Treaty Organization. https://www.nato.int/nato_static_fl2014/assets/pdf/2022/6/pdf/220628-trilat-memo.pdf.

Neiwert, David. 2017. *Alt-America: The Rise of the Radical Right in the Age of Trump*. London: Verso.

Ngai, Mae M. 1999. "The Architecture of Race in American Immigration Law: A Reexamination of the Immigration Act of 1924." *The Journal of American History* 86 (1): 67–92. https://doi.org/10.2307/2567407.

Nolte, Ernst. 1965. *Three Faces of Fascism: Action Française, Italian Fascism, National Socialism*. Translated by Leila Vennewitz. New York: The New American Library.

Nolte, Ernst. 1979. "What Fascism Is Not: Thoughts on the Deflation of a Concept: Comment Author." *The American Historical Review* 84 (2): 389–394.

Öcalan, Abdullah. 2013. *Liberating Life: Woman's Revolution*. Cologne: International Initiative Edition. https://www.freeocalan.org/wp-content/uploads/2014/06/liberating-Lifefinal.pdf.

Öcalan, Abdullah. 2017. *The Political Thought of Abdullah Öcalan: Kurdistan, Women's Revolution and Democratic Confederalism.* Translated by Havin Güneşer. London: Pluto Press.

Oxfam. 2022. "Profiting from Pain: Oxfam Media Briefing." Oxfam International, May 23. shorturl. at/mwzCD.

Pax. 2016. "US Broke Its Own Rules Firing Depleted Uranium in Iraq." PAX, October 6. https:// paxforpeace.nl/news/overview/us-broke-its-own-rules-firing-depleted-uranium-in-iraq.

Paxton, Robert. 1998. "The Five Stages of Fascism." *The Journal of Modern History* 70 (1): 1–23. https:// doi.org/10.1086/235001.

Paxton, Robert. 2004. *The Anatomy of Fascism.* New York: Alfred A. Knopf.

Paxton, Robert. 2021. "I've Hesitated to Call Donald Trump a Fascist. Until Now." *Newsweek,* January 11. https://www.newsweek.com/robert-paxton-trump-fascist-1560652.

Pegram, Thomas R. 2011. *One Hundred Percent American: The Rebirth and Decline of the Ku Klux Klan in the 1920s.* Chicago: Ivan R. Dee.

Pilger, John. 2000. "Squeezed to Death." *The Guardian,* US ed., March 3. https://www.theguardian. com/theguardian/2000/mar/04/weekend7.weekend9.

Plokhy, Serhii. 2015. *The Last Empire: The Final Days of the Soviet Union.* New York: Basic Books.

Plokhy, Serhii. 2018. *Lost Kingdom: A History of Russian Nationalism from Ivan the Great to Vladimir Putin.* London: Penguin Books.

Polanyi, Karl. 2001. *The Great Transformation: The Political and Economic Origins of Our Time.* Boston: Beacon Press.

Prashad, Vijay. 2014. *The Poorer Nations: A Possible History of the Global South.* London: Verso.

Reich, Wilhelm. 1970. *The Mass Psychology of Fascism.* Edited by Mary Higgins and Chester M. Raphael. New York: Farrar, Straus, and Giroux.

ReliefWeb. 2022. "The State of Food Security and Nutrition in the World 2022: Repurposing Food and Agricultural Policies to Make Healthy Diets More Affordable [EN/AR/RU/ZH]." Reliefweb, July 6. https://reliefweb.int/report/world/state-food-security-and-nutrition-world-2022-repurpos-ing-food-and-agricultural-policies-make-healthy-diets-more-affordable-enarruzh.

Roosevelt, Theodor. 1906. "Annual Message of the President." Office of Historian. https://history. state.gov/historicaldocuments/frus1906p1/annual.

Rubin, Michael. 2018. "The Continuing Problem of KRG Corruption." In *Routledge Handbook on the Kurds,* edited by Martin Gunter, 329–340. London: Routledge. https://doi. org/10.4324/9781315627427.

Said, Edward. 2003. *Reflections on Exile and Other Essays.* Cambridge, MA: Harvard University Press.

Soleimani, Kamal, and Davoud Osmanzadeh. 2021. "Textualising the Ethno-religious Sovereign, History, Ethnicity and Nationalism in the Perso-Islamic Textbooks." *Nations & Nationalism,* March 1. doi:10.1111/nana.12705.

Srinivasan, Bhu. 2017. *Americana: A 400-Year History of American Capitalism.* New York: Penguin.

Stanley, Jason. 2018. *How Fascism Works: The Politics of Us and Them.* New York: Random House.

Steiner, H. Arthur. 1935. "Fascism in America?" *The American Political Science Review* 29 (5): 821–830. https://doi.org/10.2307/1947225.

Tax, Meredith. 2016. *A Road Unforeseen: Women Fight the Islamic State.* New York: Bellevue Literary Press.

Ter-Matevosyan, Vahram. 2015. "Turkish Experience with Totalitarianism and Fascism: Tracing the Intellectual Origins." *Iran and the Caucasus* 19 (4): 387–401.

Thomas, Marilyn, Jack Horton, and Benedict Garman. 2024. "بي بي سي تتحقق من مزاعم إسرائيل بقتل ١٠ آلاف مقاتل من حماس" [BBC Checks Israel's Claim to Have Killed 10,000 Hamas Fighters]. *BBC Arabic,* March 1. https://www.bbc.com/arabic/articles/c2jxll10zy3o.

Tibi, Bassam. 1997. *Arab Nationalism: Between Islam and the Nation-State*. New York: St. Martin's Press.

Traverso, Enzo. 2019. *The New Faces of Fascism: Populism and the Far Right*. Translated by David Broder. London: Verso.

Trotsky, Leon. 1939. "Only Revolution Can Put an End to War." *Socialist Appeal*, April 4. https://www.marxists.org/history/etol/newspape/themilitant/socialist-appeal-1939/v3n21-apr-04-1939.pdf.

TRT. 2022. "Erdogan to EU: 'Treat Türkiye Like Ukraine' for Bloc's Membership." *TRTWorld*, March 1. https://www.trtworld.com/turkey/erdogan-to-eu-treat-türkiye-like-ukraine-for-bloc-s-membership-55195.

Turner, Henry Ashby. 1972. "Fascism and Modernization." *World Politics* 24 (4): 547–564. https://doi.org/10.2307/2010456.

US Congress Committee on Foreign Affairs. 1985. *Survey of Activities: 98th Congress*. Washington, DC: US Government Printing Office.

UTV. 2020. "الأنفال وحلبجة وعلي حسن المجيد | شهادات خاصة مع د. حميد عبد الله". [Al-Anfal, Halabja, and Ali Hassan Al-Majid | Special Testimonies with Dr. Hamid Abdulla]. August 21. https://www.youtube.com/watch?v=XuqfmNMpbdg.

Vallet, Élisabeth. 2022. "The World Is Witnessing a Rapid Proliferation of Border Walls." Migration Policy Institute, March 2. https://www.migrationpolicy.org/article/rapid-proliferation-number-border-walls.

Vaziri, Mostafa. 2013. *Iran as Imagined Nation*. 2nd ed. Piscataway, NJ: Gorgias Press.

Whitman, James Q. 2017. *Hitler's American Model: The United States and the Making of Nazi Race Law*. Princeton, NJ: Princeton University Press.

WHO. 2022. "UN Report: Global Hunger Numbers Rose to as Many as 828 Million in 2021." World Health Organization, July 6. https://www.who.int/news/item/06-07-2022-un-report—global-hunger-numbers-rose-to-as-many-as-828-million-in-2021.

Wille, Belkis. 2020. "The KRG Needs to Listen to Critics, Not Arrest Them." Human Rights Watch, June 15. https://www.hrw.org/news/2020/06/15/krg-needs-listen-critics-not-arrest-them.

Williams, Jessie. 2022. "Between Belarus and Poland, Yazidi Refugees Found Only Cold and Hunger – Then 'Came Back to Nothing' in Iraq." *The Globe and Mail*, January 13. https://www.theglobeandmail.com/world/article-between-belarus-and-poland-yazidi-refugees-found-only-cold-and-hunger/.

Yaseen, Abdulkadir. 2011. الحركة الشيوعية المصرية: الجذور- القسمات - المال (١٩٢١-١٩٦٥) [The Egyptian Communist Movement: The Roots, the Divisions, the Finance (1921–1965)]. Cairo: The Egyptian Public Institution for Books.

Zia-Ebrahimi, Reza. 2011. "Self-Orientalization and Dislocation: The Uses and Abuses of the 'Aryan' Discourse in Iran." *Iranian Studies* 44 (4): 445–472. http://www.jstor.org/stable/23033306.

Zinn, Howard. 2015. *A People's History of the United States*. New York: Harper Collins.

Žižek, Slavoj. 2008. *Violence: Six Sideways Reflections*. New York: Picador.

Zwijnenburg, Wim. 2013. "In a State of Uncertainty: Impact and Implications of the Use of Depleted Uranium in Iraq." IKV Pax Christi. www.ikvpaxchristi.nl/media/files/in-a-state-of-uncertainty.pdf.

Index

Note: Page numbers followed by "n" refer to notes.

https://doi.org/10.1515/9783111609041-011